OTHER BOOKS BY DEKE SHARON

A Cappella Arranging (with Dylan Bell)
A Cappella (with Brody McDonald and Ben Spalding)
The Heart of Vocal Harmony
A Cappella Warmups for Pop and Jazz Choirs (with JD Frizzell)

Songbooks
Contemporary A Cappella Songbook: Volume One (SATB)
Contemporary A Cappella Songbook: Volume Two (SATB)
I Feel Good—Contemporary A Cappella Songbook: Volume Three (SATB)
A CASA Christmas (SATB)
Good Ol' A Cappella (TTBB)
Sh-Boom (TTBB)
A Cappella Jazz Classics (SATB)
A Cappella Jazz Standards (SATB)
A Cappella Jazz Broadway (SATB)
Natural Woman (SSAA)
Girls Just Wanna Have Fun (SSAA)
Respect (SSAA)
Shout (SATB)
Love Songs A Cappella (SATB)
Deck The Hall (SAB)
Songs For All Occasions (SATB)
plus hundreds of published octavos

SO YOU WANT TO SING A CAPPELLA

So You Want to Sing

Guides for Performers and Professionals

A Project of the National Association of Teachers of Singing

So You Want to Sing: Guides for Performers and Professionals is a series of works devoted to providing a complete survey of what it means to sing within a particular genre. Each contribution functions as a touchstone work not only for professional singers but also for students and teachers of singing. Titles in the series offer a common set of topics so readers can navigate easily the various genres addressed in each volume. This series is produced under the direction of the National Association of Teachers of Singing, the leading professional organization devoted to the science and art of singing.

So You Want to Sing Music Theater: A Guide for Professionals, by Karen S. Hall, 2013

So You Want to Sing Rock 'n' Roll: A Guide for Professionals, by Matthew Edwards, 2014

So You Want to Sing Jazz: A Guide for Professionals, by Jan Shapiro, 2015

So You Want to Sing Country: A Guide for Performers, by Kelly K. Garner, 2016

So You Want to Sing Gospel: A Guide for Performers, by Trineice Robinson-Martin, 2016

So You Want to Sing Sacred Music: A Guide for Performers, edited by Matthew Hoch, 2017

So You Want to Sing Folk Music: A Guide for Performers, by Valerie Mindel, 2017

So You Want to Sing Barbershop: A Guide for Performers, by Diane M. Clarke & Billy J. Biffle, 2017

So You Want to Sing A Cappella: A Guide for Performers, by Deke Sharon, 2018

SO YOU WANT TO SING A CAPPELLA

A Guide for Performers

Deke Sharon

Allen Henderson
Executive Editor, NATS

Matthew Hoch
Series Editor

A Project of the National Association of
Teachers of Singing

ROWMAN & LITTLEFIELD
Lanham • Boulder • New York • London

Published by Rowman & Littlefield
A wholly owned subsidiary of
The Rowman & Littlefield Publishing Group, Inc.
4501 Forbes Boulevard, Suite 200, Lanham, Maryland 20706
www.rowman.com

Unit A, Whitacre Mews, 26-34 Stannary Street, London SE11 4AB

All chapter-opening illustrations were created by Matthew Robertson.

British Library Cataloguing in Publication Information Available

Library of Congress Cataloging-in-Publication Data
Names: Sharon, Deke, author.
Title: So you want to sing a cappella : a guide for performers / Deke Sharon.
Description: Lanham : Rowman & Littlefield, [2018] | Series: So you want
    to sing | "A Project of the National Association of Teachers of Singing." |
    Includes bibliographical references and index.
Identifiers: LCCN 2017028707 (print) | LCCN 2017030520 (ebook) | ISBN
    9781538105887 (electronic) | ISBN 9781538105870 (pbk. : alk. paper)
Subjects: LCSH: Singing—Instruction and study. | Vocal groups.
Classification: LCC MT820 (ebook) | LCC MT820 .S536 2018 (print) | DDC
    783/.043—dc23
LC record available at https://lccn.loc.gov/2017028707

Printed in the United States of America

CONTENTS

Series Editor's Foreword   ix

Foreword   xi

Acknowledgments   xv

Introduction   xvii

Online Supplement Note   xix

WHO   THE STYLES AND GROUPS THAT SET THE STAGE FOR CONTEMPORARY A CAPPELLA

1 Precontemporary A Cappella   3

2 Contemporary A Cappella: A Personal History   9

WHAT   THE ORIGINAL AND MOST POWERFUL INSTRUMENT: THE HUMAN VOICE

3 Singing and Voice Science   *Scott McCoy*   37
       Anatomy of an A Cappella Group   *Deke Sharon*   55

4 Vocal Health for the A Cappella Singer   *Wendy LeBorgne*   61
       A Cappella Group Health *Deke Sharon*   81

HOW   CONTEMPORARY A CAPPELLA'S EXTENDED VOCAL TECHNIQUES AND PRACTICES

5 Vocal Techniques and Vocal Instruments   87

6 Vocal Percussion for Everyone   *Kari Francis*   101

7 Blend   127

8 Rehearsal Techniques   133

9 Using Audio Enhancement Technology   *Matthew Edwards*   141

10 A Cappella Audio Tech   *Tony Huerta*   163

WHEN   SING FOR YOUR LIFE: A CAPPELLA ENSEMBLES FOR ALL AGES

11 Scholastic A Cappella   179

12 Professional A Cappella   189

13 Recreational A Cappella   195

WHERE   CAREERS: OPPORTUNITIES FOR FULL- AND PART-TIME EMPLOYMENT IN A CAPPELLA

14 In the Theater   201

15 In the Recording Studio   233

16 In the Rehearsal Room   265

17 Behind the Scenes   283

WHY   THE REASON A CAPPELLA MATTERS

18 Harmony through Harmony   325

19 Conclusion   331

Appendix: List of A Cappella Festivals around the World   333

Further Reading: A Cappella Books and Resources   343

Index   345

About the Author   369

SERIES EDITOR'S FOREWORD

In recent decades, the a cappella phenomenon has exploded. A ubiquitous fixture on college and university campuses across the United States and abroad, a cappella is a distinct, idiosyncratic, and popular genre that is here to stay. For this reason, a book titled *So You Want to Sing A Cappella* was envisioned from the early planning stages of the So You Want to Sing series. But whom could we contract to write such a book? Our go-to authors are usually National Association of Teachers of Singing (NATS) members, and these individuals are often applied singing pedagogues in academia. That really wouldn't work for this title, as most collegiate a cappella groups are not official school of music ensembles. Rather, they are usually student-run organizations composed primarily of nonmusic majors.

Well, we went straight to the top of the profession, and he said yes. Deke Sharon needs no introduction within the a cappella world and beyond. In fact, he is often referred to as the "father of contemporary a cappella." Deke is a multifaceted talent who wears many hats as a producer, director, arranger, composer, and teacher of the genre. He is a professionally trained musician (educated at Tufts and the New England Conservatory) who has devoted his life to promoting and encouraging the art of a cappella. In recent years, he has achieved international recognition for his work as music director and arranger of the three *Pitch Perfect* movies, starring Anna Kendrick and distributed by Universal Studios. Deke was a pleasure to work with throughout this entire process. Most satisfying was the energy and enthusiasm he brings to his art form; the joy he brings to his role as an educator and promoter of all things a cappella is infectious.

What you hold in your hands is Deke Sharon's magnum opus: everything a newcomer to a cappella would want to know and more—a gigantic "brain dump" from the master of the genre. In addition to Deke's content, Kari Francis and Tony Huerta also make a cappella–specific contributions within this volume. Like other books in the So You Want to Sing series, several additional chapters round out this volume: Scott McCoy contributes a chapter on voice production, Wendy LeBorgne discusses aspects of vocal health, and Matthew Edwards addresses the basics of audio enhancement technology.

The collected volumes of the So You Want to Sing series offer a valuable opportunity for performers and teachers of singing to explore new styles and important pedagogies. I am confident that voice specialists, both amateur and professional, will benefit from Deke Sharon's important, one-of-a-kind resource. It has been a privilege to work with him on this project. *So You Want to Sing A Cappella* is an invaluable resource for any performer or teacher interested in exploring this fascinating culture.

Matthew Hoch

FOREWORD

There has never been a more exciting time for a cappella music. With the a cappella group Pentatonix regularly topping the charts and selling out stadiums, singers across the world are asking themselves, "Can we do it too?" The answer is yes. But you don't have to have a number one album and perform at the Grammys to enjoy serious success with a cappella, nor do you have to be a full-time musician to be a part of this incredible genre.

Before the group Straight No Chaser (aka SNC) became a national a cappella powerhouse, we were just one of dozens of successful collegiate groups. We had built a loyal following at Indiana University (IU), where we started in 1996. We were well known among IU alumni and, like many college groups, had a good reputation among a cappella fans. As is the tradition in collegiate a cappella, the original members graduated and passed the reins to other undergrads. The thought of SNC one day selling millions of albums and touring the world under a major record label was simply not on the radar.

Then, along came a little website called YouTube.

In 2007, just for the hell of it, we uploaded a grainy 1998 campus concert video of the original members singing our comical "12 Days of Christmas." That winter, we watched with our jaws on the floor as the video racked up millions of views. Our jaws dropped through the floor again when the CEO of Atlantic Records, Craig Kallman, contacted us about doing a Christmas album. He said he loved what he saw online and believed there was a big opening for a group like ours.

A few months later, the original members of SNC reunited in New York and signed a multiyear deal with Atlantic Records. That was in 2008. We were living in different cities, pursuing different careers. Even with the backing of a major label, we couldn't afford to leave our jobs and sing full-time. We rehearsed and recorded during weekends and vacation. After lots of hard work, our album *Holiday Spirits* debuted late in the fall. By Christmas, the unthinkable happened: we hit number one on iTunes and Amazon! Boom. That was it. We quit our jobs and committed to SNC full-time.

The first years of professional a cappella were tumultuous, to say the least. Money was tight, and we didn't sell many tickets in some cities. But we sang on. And by the fall of 2010, Straight No Chaser was a major touring enterprise. Our follow-up albums did well on the charts. Our PBS specials were seen by millions. Concerts coast to coast started to sell out.

We made it!

I believe our success was the result of a growing demand that had built up over the years for singing that was pure. No magic studio tricks. Just voices, microphones, and showmanship.

Public demand for a cappella was solidified when the hit NBC show *The Sing-Off* showcased dozens of groups to a national audience, and in doing so launched the most successful a cappella group in modern history.

But even if your group isn't the next Pentatonix, it has never been easier to make a cappella a part of your life as a hobby, or even a full-time career. From my days as a sophomore in the late nineties trying to get sorority girls to attend our concerts at the student union to prepping for our performances on *The Today Show* many years later, I'm amazed by how a cappella has exploded. And it's not showing any signs of slowing down.

In this book, Deke Sharon and his coauthors give you many insights into how to create great a cappella and have a great a cappella career. From starting up a group with good vocal technique and musicianship to touring major concert venues, Deke knows more about this business than anyone.

It's a business not only for performers. With arranging, directing, vocal coaching, and recording (to name just a few), there are many a cappella career options on both sides of the microphone. What Deke can't give you is passion for a cappella. You'll need lots of it . . . and some badass arrangements.

Dan Ponce

Dan Ponce is the founder and first music director of Straight No Chaser. He lives in Chicago and is an anchor for WGN-TV.

ACKNOWLEDGMENTS

First of all, I would like to express my deep appreciation and thanks to the incredibly creative and thoughtful chapter authors Matthew Edwards, Kari Francis, Tony Huerta, Wendy LeBorgne, and Scott McCoy. In the timeless words of many a prohibition-era mob mistress, you class up the joint.

Thanks also to my insanely talented brother Matthew Robertson for his lovely drawings throughout the book, all of which are available for sale via his website (alongside his other colorful, imaginative art): http://www.matthewrobertsonart.com.

If it takes a village to raise a child, it takes a small army to proof my writing. Luckily the a cappella community is quite the eager army. Many thanks to Charlie Arthur, Andrea Canny, Stefanie Chase, Betsy Sabatini Coyne, Trist Curless, Ian Duh, John DeFerraro, Cynthia Hansen Ellis, Neil Ghosh, Kerry Kaempf-Wood, John Newell, John Pickering, Rob Redei, and Johanna Vinson.

Many thanks to my lovely family—Katy, Cap, and Mimi—for all your support, hugs, and hilarity.

Finally, thank *you* for purchasing this book and working to spread vocal harmony. You're a part of the a cappella community now, which means you are family and, as such, are welcome to contact me anytime

if you have questions, need advice, and so on. My e-mail is deke@
dekesharon.com, and I can be found on all the major social media platforms (Facebook, Twitter, LinkedIn, etc.). Drop me a line anytime.
Really. I don't mind. It's what I do.

INTRODUCTION

Through most of human history, there was no need for a book titled *So You Want to Sing A Cappella*. A cappella was the first music, and for a very long time the only music, on earth. Like birds, crickets, and whales, we're biologically wired to sing. Our prehistoric ancestors sang long before the invention of other instruments, both to each other and with each other, be it around the fire after a long hunt, to make the work of harvesting or building pass more easily, or to celebrate a harvest and make the long winter nights pass more warmly.

How do we know this? Because the tradition of singing continues to this day around the world, especially in aboriginal tribes. Music is an integral part of their sense of community and connection. The pioneering vocalist Bobby McFerrin once told me a story of his good friend Yo-Yo Ma, the cellist, who went to Africa to learn about music from their culture. On the first day, he approached the chief of the tribe and announced that he'd like to play music for everyone that night at 8:00 p.m. "You want to make music?" replied the chief. "Let's make music now!" "No, I'd like to play my cello for you tonight," said Yo-Yo Ma, to which came the reply, "Fine, let's make music tonight then." But no, Yo-Yo Ma wanted to play and have everyone listen. This made no sense to the chief, and it shouldn't make any sense to us either. Yo-Yo Ma thought he wanted to perform his music, but instead he learned that music is meant to be a shared experience, not just a one-way street.

Music is communication, as natural as speaking, and yet, with all the technological breakthroughs and advancement in human culture, we find ourselves in the year 2017 needing a book about how to perform one of the most basic acts throughout human history: singing. Be it singing alone or singing with others, the experience is deep, powerful, and central to our ability to connect with others, to listen, to create, and to learn that together we're capable of so much more than we are alone.

This book is structured to give you insight into all aspects of singing a cappella throughout your life. Whether you come upon these words while you're in middle school or after you've retired, there will be plenty of information to help you find a group you love, learn to be a better harmony singer, and maximize your experience through productive rehearsals and impactful performances. To that end, I've done my best to include information for singers and educators at all levels. My apologies if anything in this book is too basic. I would rather include more information than less, even if it appears obvious. Some readers may not be familiar with the a cappella community and its practices.

Feel free to jump around, read this book out of order, and refer to sections when they are of interest or applicable to you. You may initially be interested in vocal technique and then later want to consider career options. This book is a bit encyclopedic in scope with no specific through-line, so you shouldn't feel any remorse about jumping around.

If you ever find yourself discouraged or if you're ever overwhelmed, just remember your ancestors who sang every day without books, guides, rules, music theory, conductors, sheet music, arrangements, choreography, judges, stages, or microphones. They just sang. Sang when they worked, sang when they played. Sang alone and with others. Sang when they were happy, sad, angry, or afraid—for others or for themselves. Remember that when you do the same—when you sing, wherever you are and for whatever reason—you are in a small way tipping the scales, bringing the world back into its proper alignment: a place that is full of people singing wherever they go. Then once again, in a tiny corner of the universe hurtling through unimaginable darkness and silence, this spinning orb we're on will resonate with the sound of voices in harmony.

ONLINE SUPPLEMENT NOTE

So *You Want to Sing A Cappella* features an online supplement courtesy of the National Association of Teachers of Singing. Visit the link below to discover additional exercises and examples, as well as links to recordings of the songs referenced in this book.

http://www.nats.org/So_You_Want_To_Sing_Book_Series.html

A musical note symbol ♪ in this book will mark every instance of corresponding online supplement material.

WHO

The Styles and Groups That Set the Stage
for Contemporary A Cappella

I

PRECONTEMPORARY A CAPPELLA

Before the invention of tools, let alone instruments, there were voices, so it's clear that a cappella was the first music, and the only music, for eons. If you've ever sat around a campfire with some friends and just started singing, this is the way music was made through most of human history: informal, unwritten, communal, and aural. Songs weren't owned by anybody; arrangements were simply the result of people's voices intertwining. Some form of drum or percussive instrument likely came along thereafter. Still, vocals were firmly entrenched at the forefront of prehistoric music, where they have remained throughout global culture through to modern times.

The term "a cappella" comes from Italian, meaning "in the style of the chapel." When holding smaller church services in a chapel, there were usually only a handful of singers present providing the music. Over time the expression came to refer to any group of unaccompanied singers. Many styles of music were primarily or entirely a cappella throughout history:

Gregorian chant: Back in the year 1000, monks would sing Roman Catholic masses in perfect unison. Pope Gregory likely didn't invent it, yet we still call it "Gregorian chant" because he took the time to record and organize the thousands of existing plainchants. One very useful invention was Guido D'Arrezzo's five-line staff, which is the basis of our current musical notation. ♪

Traditional Jewish: Jewish rites have been performed in synagogues without instruments since biblical times through the middle ages, relying on a cantor to lead the musical parts of the service. ♪

Native American: Although sometimes accompanied by hand drums and other percussion, the human voice is at the center of Native American music, both religious and secular. ♪

Madrigals: Ranging from two- to eight-part harmony, madrigal songs were usually unaccompanied, and based in storytelling, covering a wide range of topics both sacred and secular, with a harmonic language that explored dissonances that wouldn't again be heard in classical music until the twentieth century. ♪

Renaissance polyphony: At the same time as the rise of the madrigal, composers such as Palestrina, Thomas Tallis, and William Byrd created a new style of complex, interwoven four- and five-part vocal harmonies that laid the groundwork for Western classical music. ♪

Sea shanties: As Europeans took to the seas, a new style of singing and song came to life on the working decks of sailing vessels, reaching a peak during the nineteenth century. ♪

Field holler: As sailors sang to pass time during long days of work, so did slaves and later sharecroppers across the plantations of the Southern United States. In time they were adopted by chain gangs and railroad workers. These were often in call-and-response form and played a role in the birth of spirituals, the blues, and eventually rhythm and blues (R&B). ♪

Classical choral: As classical music grew to include more and more instruments, composers would still return to unaccompanied voices, creating some of the genre's most beautiful works. ♪

Sacred harp: This style is also known as "shape note singing," because the note heads are shaped differently based on the scale (e.g., "fa," the fourth degree of the scale, is in the shape of a triangle, "so" is an oval, and "la" is a square). This Southern US tradition of singing four-part hymns is often sung sitting in a square, so everyone can hear each other. ♪

Sängerfest/Liederfest/Liederkranz: Around 1809, this tradition began in Germany and Switzerland. Over the next hundred years, it became one of the most popular type of singing groups across the European continent. Haydn, Mendelssohn, Schubert, Bruckner, and Wagner wrote several great pieces for men's choirs and women's choirs with these ensembles in mind.

Folk music: Every culture around the world has its own folk music tradition—songs that have stood the test of time and are known by the entire community, even if the author has been forgotten. From lullabies to doing the laundry, these simple, timeless songs are often sung unaccompanied. ♪

Irish/Scottish/Gaelic mouth music: One notable example of a region's folk music comes from the Gaelic tradition in Ireland and Scotland. Both dance music and work songs, the term "mouth music" likely comes from the Gaelic phrase "port-a-beul," which means "tunes from the mouth." ♪

Gospel: Born in African American churches in the Southern United States during slavery, gospel music was originally almost exclusively a cappella, drawing on the call-and-response that was also frequently heard in field hollers and work songs, and built on the tradition and repertoire of Negro spirituals (which were also predominantly a cappella). After emancipation, the style grew and the harmonies became more complex and developed, thanks to groups such as the Fisk Jubilee Singers and the Fairfield Four. ♪

Barbershop: Originally, barbershop quartet singing was an African American tradition, as can be heard in the oldest existing recording (on wax cylinder) of the 1893 Unique Quartet singing "Mama's Black Baby Boy." In 1938 O. C. Cash and Rupert Hall formed the Society for the Preservation and Encouragement of Barber Shop Quartet Singing in America (SPEBSQSA), now known as the Barbershop Harmony Society, to preserve and promote the barbershop musical tradition, which is responsible for keeping this tradition alive and growing. Not wanting to let the gentlemen have all the fun, women later formed Sweet Adelines International and Harmony Incorporated, both devoted to promoting women's barbershop singing. ♪

Mbube: When we think of "The Lion Sleeps Tonight," we think of the classic doo-wop version by the Tokens, or perhaps the movie *The Lion King*, but in fact this song from the 1920s, written and recorded by Solomon Linda, created such a stir in South Africa that it sparked an entire style of a cappella singing, based on and named after this one amazing song. And yes, "Mbube" means "lion" in Zulu. ♪

Isicathamiya: As the South African Zulu a cappella tradition grew and developed, it morphed into this gentler, more carefully harmonious style, whose best-known practitioner is the amazing Ladysmith Black Mambazo. ♪

Taiwan: As is the case in many parts of the globe, Taiwan's aboriginal a cappella tradition has influenced popular music and remains alive in new incarnations, such as the O-Kai Singers who sing the original melodies in the original language but with new harmonies and interpretations. ♪

Klapa: Similarly, Dalmatia's a cappella tradition, Klapa, which means "group of friends," reflects that region's culture. The tradition remains alive today, with annual festivals and new compositions. The group Klapa S Mora represented Croatia in the 2013 Eurovision song contest.

Bulgarian women's choir: The unique, dissonant, haunting straight-tone harmonies of the Bulgarian women's choral tradition found a global audience when popularized by Le Mystere Des Voix Bulgares. ♪

Collegiate a cappella: Although glee-club singing, often a cappella, was very popular at the turn of the century, it was the Whiffenpoofs in 1909 who are credited with starting the collegiate a cappella tradition, breaking off from the glee club as a smaller ensemble. The tradition slowly spread throughout the Ivy League and the East Coast, then expanding rapidly once vocal percussion was introduced (from around two hundred collegiate groups in 1990 to over three thousand today). ♪

Close harmony: As jazz became the popular music across America, vocal groups began to incorporate the more complex chord progressions, resulting in "closer" harmonies so named because the notes were closer together. From the Comedian Harmonists of Germany to the Mills Brothers in the United States, vocal harmony began to incorporate vocal instrumental sounds and idioms as well. ♪

Doo-wop: Although none of the major recordings were a cappella, many of the great groups and songs of the doo-wop era were originally a cappella (before the producers insisted on adding instruments). With its soaring melodies and rhythmic backing vocals built on repetitive patterns and syllables, doo-wop was an important step toward today's contemporary a cappella. ♪

Vocal jazz: As jazz became more complex in the 1960s, and ensembles shrank from swing bands to small combos, vocal harmony groups developed as well, embracing vocal improvisation and even more complex harmonies. In time this tradition found its way into schools as well, resulting in a rich scholastic vocal jazz tradition that continues today. ♪

Contemporary Christian: Several American Protestant groups worship without instruments, including the Amish, Baptists, Mennonites, and the Church of Christ. Whereas more traditional churches tend to also remain musically traditional, the Church of Christ has embraced modern music and modern a cappella, resulting in the style embracing contemporary a cappella idioms with groups such as Acappella and the A Cappella Vocal Band (AVB). ♪

This is by no means a fully comprehensive list of all styles of a cappella throughout time around the globe, but hopefully it has given you a sense of the depth and breadth of a cappella traditions and the influence they've had on music history. A web search on any of them can lead you to a wealth of information that will enrich your life: books, recordings, and performances.

2

CONTEMPORARY A CAPPELLA

A Personal History

Histoy is an inherently imperfect pursuit, with countless biases deeply interwoven into every fact and assertion. As well meaning as every author is, the fact remains that there is no such history as a perfectly comprehensive, unbiased history. Everyone writes from his or her own point of view, and those views change as the world changes. Moreover, I must admit that I'm no historian. I'm a guy who has spent his life surrounded by vocal music, endeavoring to create community and spread harmony. I have a specific perspective that is by its very definition biased and limited in perspective, as I'm on the ground in the middle of it all, actively working to alter, well, history itself.

For this reason, and for the simple fact that there has never before been written a definitive comprehensive history of contemporary a cappella, I have chosen to unabashedly write from my own perspective. This may seem unnecessarily self-aggrandizing at times, as I find myself at the center of the story repeatedly (perhaps by definition), but there is no other way for me to fully share my own perspective clearly and honestly, as a false modesty would likely lead me to leave out details that may now or one day prove useful or important. I beg your indulgence, hope I don't come across as impossibly narcissistic, and leave it to someone in the future to one day create a more traditional third-person history of today's vocal harmony.

The story of contemporary a cappella begins in the 1980s, where as a student I first became aware of, and then obsessed with, an exciting new way to approach popular a cappella.

THE EARLY AND MID-1980s

The term "a cappella" meant nothing to most Americans in the year 1980. If they were familiar with the term, it referred to a classical choir, church music, doo-wop, or perhaps barbershop. Various traditional forms of a cappella (as listed above) could be found, but it was limited to recreational singing, most often in the form of school choirs, local barbershop choruses and quartets (thanks to the Society for the Preservation and Encouragement of Barber Shop Quartet Singing in America [SPEBSQSA], Sweet Adelines International, and Harmony Incorporated), and of course various church choirs.

Professional popular a cappella was almost nonexistent. Sweet Honey in the Rock ♪ was singing their all-female African American politically progressive harmonies out of Washington, D.C. The Persuasions, ♪ first discovered by Frank Zappa, had been performing their post-doo-wop R&B harmonies around the Eastern Seaboard and beyond for a decade. If they happened to be on tour or on *The Tonight Show*, you might catch a glimpse of England's King's Singers ♪ or Swingle Singers, ♪ although both would often perform classical music and sometimes perform with instruments both live and on their albums.

And that was it.

It was into this world that I first became aware of and fell in love with popular a cappella, as a young teenager in San Francisco, California. It was a frustrating love, because it was so very difficult to foster. No organizations existed, no lists of groups could be found, and searching for albums was a lengthy, confusing process—scanning the "vocals" section of the local Tower Records and used record stores in hopes of coming across a gem.

Occasionally a vocal group, such as the Manhattan Transfer, would release an a cappella song, such as "Nightingale Sang in Berkeley Square," ♪ which I learned about because my choral director at San Francisco University High School, Dr. Bruce Lamott, brought in a transcription for us to learn in the Camarata (select chamber chorus). My interest was piqued, and from there I learned about Gene Puerling, the Singers Unlimited, ♪ who sadly didn't tour and only sometimes sang a cappella, and his earlier work with the Hi-Lo's, ♪ for whom a cappella was even less common.

This is why I was overjoyed when I just happened to be living in the birthplace of one of the most important new professional a cappella groups: the Bobs (short for "Best of Breed"). ♪ The year was 1982. I was just starting my freshman year in high school and was introduced to the most experimental, cutting-edge sound that had come to a cappella in years if not decades. They sang unexpected cover songs for an a cappella group, eschewing the obvious already-harmony-laden choices (such as Crosby, Stills & Nash) for groups like the Talking Heads, with dissonant chords and straight tone singing that made them sound almost foreign at times, like a Bulgarian women's choir. Most notably, unlike almost all a cappella groups of the previous decades, they primarily sang their own original music: quirky, timely, and unmistakably unique.

To a young singer such as myself, they were a revelation. They taught me that you could make a career of professional a cappella; you could develop your own sound, sing original music, and pave your own road. When I look back I don't think there was or is a group that has had a more profound effect on me, and perhaps on the history of contemporary a cappella, than the Bobs. Sadly most young singers don't know of them, or assume they were a kind of comedy ensemble (their music is at times funny, but that's not what makes them special). Perhaps like many greats of the past—such as Ray Charles and Tony Bennett—they will in time experience a wave of great respect in which a new generation rediscovers them during their later years.[1]

If the Bobs were one major pillar of my early a cappella inspiration, another was the Nylons, ♪ from Canada. Formed by four actors, their harmonies were initially simple, yet they quickly found themselves pushing beyond simple doo-wop revivalist harmonies, most notably by using a drum machine to give their performances a more modern sensibility. Their album *One Size Fits All* was the standout during this era, bridging the gap between traditional doo-wop tropes and a modern 1980s synth/drum machine pop ethos.

It was around this time that I was cast in my first high school musical theater production: as Ewart Dunlop, lead of the Barbershop Quartet in *The Music Man*. ♪ I was initially frustrated as the director almost decided on *South Pacific* in which I was to play one of the two primary leads (Lt. Cable), but it turned out to be one of the biggest unexpected breaks I would get, as not only did I fall in love with the tight barbershop harmonies but also we decided to keep the quartet going for the rest of the school year—and for the following three years as well. Personnel changed each year, but I remained music director of the quartet throughout. Early on, we sang several songs from the *Barberpole Cat* songbook and dug through existing doo-wop published sheet music, stripping out the piano parts, but it became clear that our repertoire options were limited, so I began to arrange out of necessity. My first arrangement was the Beatles' "When I'm Sixty-Four," and by my senior year we won a Bay Area arts competition with a four-part arrangement

I'd done of "Bohemian Rhapsody," which now seems almost passé but then was quite unexpected and unusual, vocal guitar solo and all.

Perhaps the biggest influence of all on me was when the Tufts Beelzebubs came to San Francisco University High School (SFUHS) and performed for the entire student body. Christòpheren Nomura, now a successful operatic baritone who most recently performed in George Takei's Broadway musical *Allegiance* to rave reviews, was four years ahead of me at SFUHS and brought the group back as part of a West Coast tour. I was stunned. The energy in the room was electric, and even though they mostly weren't well-known pop songs, the audience rapturously listened on the edge of their seats throughout. I had never seen a vocal ensemble like it before; even though these were amateur, scholastic singers, not a single member was disengaged, standing still and singing. They all bobbed and grooved in their double arc as they sang, engaging with each other, the audience, and the music. Each song had its own sound and character. It's like I'd been experiencing choral music primarily in black and white, and I was first seeing Technicolor.

Thankfully, Chris sent back some arrangements from the group, which my group eagerly digested and sang (to the extent we could, with only four parts). I learned to arrange largely by studying the chord voicings and choices made by arrangers that are unknown to the vocal music world but rank as legends to me: Gene Blake, Andy Cranin, and Marty Fernandi. I aspired to have my little quartet bring the energy and power that I'd seen the Beelzebubs wield song after song. I knew it could be done but not how, so much of my high school years were a process of finding out how to capture that magic: trial and error while arranging, directing, and performing.

A cappella during this decade was little more than a casual recreational pursuit for most, which is exactly how the Harmony Sweepstakes were formed. Lisa Murphy, of Marin County's Mayflower Chorus, put together a casual community event to amplify the fun sing-along jam sessions she enjoyed with the group. Little did she know that the event would grow steadily throughout the 1980s and by the 1990s become, for a while, the preeminent launching pad for some of the biggest professional groups of the era, including m-pact, ♪ the Edlos, ♪ the Knudsen Brothers ♪ (now performing in Branson MO as "Six"), North Shore A

Cappella, ♪ SoVoSo, ♪ Toxic Audio, ♪ and Naturally 7. ♪ At the time it was not yet a series of regional competitions with a national final; it was a single event in an outdoor amphitheater during a warm summer night.

Other standout a cappella groups and moments during the mideighties were few. During one of my visits to Tower Records, they were playing a new album by a local artist that made me immediately run to the counter to purchase. Bobby McFerrin's pioneering album *The Voice* hit me like a bolt of lightning, as it did many other vocalists at the time, as it blended jazz, improvisation, and body percussion, utilizing his incredibly precise singing and wide vocal range to apparently sing multiple vocal lines at once. "Blackbird," ♪ the opening track, was often imitated by my peers and me but never duplicated. This album announced to the world that our previous understanding of the limits of the human voice were completely wrong.

If Bobby was the king of solo a cappella vocal technique, the king of foresight into the sound and technique of multitracked contemporary a cappella was undoubtedly Todd Rundgren. His album *A Cappella* ♪ was groundbreaking at the time, using early sampling technology to allow himself to not only sing all the vocals but also create a range of instrumental and percussion parts that he would process and play back on a keyboard. It's all there: drum machines, guitars, synthesizers—all vocal, all a decade before the sound of a cappella caught up with him.

For the general public, the album that introduced the freshest a cappella harmonies was Paul Simon's Grammy-winning *Graceland*, featuring multiple a cappella tracks by South Africa's Ladysmith Black Mambazo. ♪ The harmonies themselves were simple, but the richness of the vocal tone and conviction with which they sang presented some of the most powerful vocal harmony of the 1980s and beyond.

In Europe, the Flying Pickets had a huge hit with a cover of Yaz's "Only You," ♪ which never made it to the United States and yet somehow became a song that a cappella groups, both recreational and collegiate, began performing, if only because there was such a lack of other inspiration and new repertoire ideas always required looking far and wide.

Perhaps the best-known a cappella song from this period wasn't even actually technically a cappella: Billy Joel's "Longest Time," ♪ which featured an instrumental bass anchoring layers of doo-wop flavored harmonies. The song of course has been performed countless times since then a cappella, including by Billy Joel himself in concert, so the confusion is understandable.

THE LATE 1980s

This little a cappella hobby was about to get an upgrade thanks to radio and the Billboard charts. Unbeknownst to everyone, including the groups initially involved, a cappella started hitting the airwaves and didn't stop for a decade. The first a cappella group to have a big radio hit was the Nylons, with their version of the classic rock song "(Na Na Hey Hey) Kiss Him Goodbye," ♪ originally a number one hit in 1969 by Steam, it climbed back to number eleven in its a cappella incarnation in 1987.[2]

It should be noted that many of the greatest doo-wop songs of all time were written and originally performed a cappella by the great vocal groups of the era, but to the last when they were brought in the studio, although producers featured the vocals, they added instruments to support the group sound. There was a community and subculture of doo-wop stretching from the 1950s lasting until some point in the 1990s (thanks in part to the now-defunct United Group Harmony Association, headed by Ronnie Italiano, and a few small independent record labels and radio stations who loved the classic sound), but alas none of it ever made it to the top forty.

Several other a cappella songs made the charts, including Shai's "If I Ever Fall in Love," ♪ "It's Alright" by Huey Lewis and the News, ♪ and All 4 One's "So in Love," ♪; the last was Az Yet's version of "Hard to Say I'm Sorry" with Chicago lead singer Peter Cetera. ♪

However, only one a cappella song in history reached the top of the Billboard charts, and it simultaneously became one of the songs most associated with the 1990s: Bobby McFerrin's playful "Don't Worry, Be Happy." ♪

Another group that deserves great respect for many reasons is Boyz II Men, including the fact that they were the only group to have two different a cappella songs on the Billboard charts during this era ("It's So Hard to Say Goodbye to Yesterday" ♪ and "In the Still of the Nite" ♪).

With rare exception, these songs shared a sound and style that was very reminiscent of the street-corner harmonies popular during the doo-wop era and as a result relied primarily on a soaring lead vocal over block harmonies and finger snaps. They helped to popularize the concept of a cappella, but it was a sound and style that was more nostalgic than forward thinking, a flashback to a generation before. In addition, most of the hits came not from a cappella performers but rather from pop groups that would have a single song or two in which they put down their instruments and sang. To this end, a cappella was more of a dalliance than a commit-ment, with full-time professional groups continuing to push the envelope but not necessarily getting their share of attention or accolades.

The major exception to this was Take 6, ♪ whose members were dar-lings of the music establishment ever since their first album came on the scene. Their albums would sell gold and platinum, even without radio play, perhaps the result of an unusual fan base that spanned from vocal harmony fans to gospel and contemporary Christian listeners. Take 6 often attempted to get a song on the radio, but their dense harmonies, complex chord changes, and laid-back attitude never clicked on the airwaves—but they did with Grammy voters over the years, which is why they have ten wins and twenty-four additional nominations. They have also won ten Dove Awards, a Soul Train Music Award, and were inducted into the Gospel Music Hall of Fame in 2015.

A cappella also began to grow outside the United States. In addition to the Flying Pickets, Montezuma's Revenge ♪ from the Netherlands re-leased their debut album in 1989, which I was somehow lucky enough to pick up in a used CD store in San Francisco around 1989.

At this time, as a cappella first found its way onto the airwaves, I found my way to college, perhaps the first person in history to choose his future alma mater based on its collegiate a cappella group. Tufts Univer-sity has a double-degree program with the New England Conservatory of Music (NEC), so I could study music at a conservatory, get a tradi-tional liberal arts degree alongside it, and sing in a collegiate a cappella group all the while. Getting into two competitive colleges wasn't hard for me, and I was preparing for my Beelzebubs audition for four years, so what could go wrong?

I walked into the audition nervous, excited, and ready to show this legendary group (at least in my mind) what I could do. The audition started with the music director asking me to sing scales to test my vocal range. I already knew my range, so I announced my high note, my low note, and my break, and was spot on when they tested me. Next came a solo, which they liked, followed by some sight singing: Vaughan Williams's "Bushes and Briars," which I felt compelled to let them know wouldn't be a fair test because I knew the song from their album *Score*, but they had me do it anyway. First tenor? Perfect. Second tenor? Perfect. Baritone? Oops—I let them know I got one note wrong in the second half of one measure. I sang a Bb; the proper note was a C. Either would work in the chord.

And so it went, me making sure they knew I knew what I was doing, but I grossly overestimated whom I was singing for. I assumed every member of the Tufts Beelzebubs that I idolized were musical prodigies, with theoretical knowledge to match their superlative performing ability. Little did I realize they were composed almost entirely of guys who like to sing with little knowledge of theory or a cappella. Perhaps one or two of the members of any college a cappella group even today are music majors, but that seemed completely impossible to me at the time. Most college a cappella singers back then couldn't read music, knew not even basic music theory, and were shocked to see this "overzealous" (their words), lanky Californian hang on their every word, talk like a music geek, and generally make them uncomfortable.

I, of course, didn't make the Beelzebubs in this audition and was heartbroken. I spent most of my freshman year studying, making friends, working on my music skills, and preparing for the next audition. I learned of a little-known clause in the Tufts housing contract that allowed freshmen to leave the dorms and live in a specialty house. I convinced a fellow NEC double-degree classmate, Eric Valliere, to room with me at the Arts House, a small arts-focused Victorian on the edge of campus with an eclectic mix of students. He agreed, we had a great time in our new environment, and when the spring rolled around and the end-of-the-year auditions for the Bubs loomed, I convinced him to audition with me, as it would be great to both be in the group at the same time. He reluctantly agreed—and got in the group, whereas I didn't. He went off to spring rehearsal with the group, and I stayed behind wondering if I'd ever get in the group.

When the fall rolled around again, I realized my problem; if I was seen as overzealous, it was time to prove I could be just like all the other guys: too cool for school, or at least for a cappella. I walked in the audition room, and when they asked what solo I'd like to sing, I said, "I don't know, what do you want to hear?" I'd prepared nothing. They said, "How about 'Summertime'?" So I sang a jazzy, swung version, without much care. When it came to every other question I did what they asked but continued my nonchalant demeanor. In the end, with Eric in the room to assuage any fears, I was finally admitted to the group. Little did I know that this story would make it into the nonfiction book *Pitch Perfect* and later be crafted into the story of Benji, the awkward, overeager, wannabe Treblemaker who practices magic and has *Star Wars* posters all over his room. I assure you, I had no *Star Wars* posters and have never done a magic trick. I recall I had a poster of a Renoir painting, and a Monet, for what it's worth.

The group starting singing my arrangements right away, and by the next round of officer elections I was made music director. My experiences in high school were decidedly helpful, but this was the big leagues, at least to me, and there was still much to be learned about peer leadership, performing for diverse audiences, repertoire, and the like, all of which I approached with great enthusiasm and focus. I've said more than once that for college I actually attended Beelzebub University.

One of my desires was to sing music different from all other collegiate a cappella groups. At the time, there was a standard repertoire of about thirty songs, at least some of which every group sang. The songs were and still are all classics, drawn from doo-wop, vocal pop, vocal jazz, and the like (such as the songs mentioned earlier in this chapter), but they were all predictable and more importantly not the songs that college a cappella audiences were listening to in their dorm rooms.

Although I would never have put it in these terms at the time, it was and is clear to me that, above all, collegiate a cappella is an elaborate mating ritual, as is most singing in the animal kingdom. Crickets, birds, whales—most of the time when we hear animals making sound, it's to attract a mate, which is an undercurrent in pretty much all student-run collegiate a cappella as well. Sure, the themes and styles of our music would vary, but if you shut off the sound and took a look at the performers, then and now, the facial expressions and body language pretty uniformly scream, "Look at me! Love me!" Perhaps there is no purer form of human expression than this.

To make the audience, particularly the women in the audience, love us, it was clear to me that if we could be singing a song that was just climbing up the pop charts and making its way onto college radio, we'd be the coolest a cappella group in the country. We'd be like a garage rock band playing the latest hit songs, just with our mouths. Most collegiate groups were lucky if they had someone who arranges in the group, and those people were lucky if they turned out a new song once a semester, whereas I was arranging weekly. I'd pass by Tower Records on my way back from NEC to Tufts, and on Tuesdays the Billboard chart listings would be updated in a big display above the 45s. My dream each week was to anticipate the right song: arrange it Tuesday night, teach it Wednesday and Thursday nights, and perform it Friday and Saturday nights for collegiate audiences on our numerous road trips.[3]

It was in 1989 that I'd just seen *Say Anything* with the epic scene of John Cusack holding the boom box above his head, and I noticed "In Your Eyes" had just started creeping up the pop chart. "What a perfect song to make women fall in love with us," I thought, so I bought the Peter Gabriel album, brought it back to my dorm room, and dove in. However, I couldn't make the arrangement work. The instruments were too densely layered, the texture too rhythmic. Refusing to be deterred, I grabbed a piece of orchestral staff paper and started writing out what I heard, in hopes of translating it into vocal idioms later. Once I had the parts sketched out I started assigning voices and ended up with a seven-part vocal arrangement plus solo line and five additional percussion parts—all of which we had to figure out how to do with our voices, because this was a cappella after all. "Vocal percussion" was the term I used to explain what we'd be doing. There was a shaker, a talking drum (I was in a West African drum ensemble for a year at Tufts, so I knew the basics), a hi-hat, a kick, and a snare; the other vocal parts were almost as obtuse, with several guys singing synthesizer parts in which I had them morphing their vowels (from "aa" to "ah" to "ee" to "oh" and so on) to create a vocal filter sweep effect.

When I brought this into the group, they looked at me with crossed or rolled eyes. "Please, just try it. Give me an hour. I promise it will be worth it." And they were used to my crazy schemes (I once brought in an arrangement that wove together eight songs), so they were patient with me, and it paid off. That weekend we performed at a college up in

Maine, and as soon as the last chord of "In Your Eyes" rang out in the hall I felt I was in a scene at the end of a movie: complete silence for almost too long . . . then a huge wave of screaming as the audience leapt to their feet. For a ballad. In the middle of our set.

It was clear I'd found something, so I took the next year, my final year of college, to figure it out. As much as vocal percussion is the most recognizable element, it was by no means the only one. My goal was to unlock the potential within an a cappella group to create instrumental sounds and textures such that we'd be able to perform the kind of songs and sounds that pervaded college radio: Pink Floyd, Duran Duran, the Who, U2, and so on. Every college group was singing the clearly vocal songs, like Crosby, Stills & Nash's "Southern Cross"; I wanted to sing the clearly nonvocal songs, so we could be different, pioneering, and cool.

We toured the eastern half of the United States, made a CD (*Foster Street*) ♪ that sold over five thousand copies just after our college shows in a three-month period (which was unheard of), and developed a sound, so you can imagine the excitement with which I approached Staag Night, the annual gathering of Bubs old and new (there's a very tight-knit alumni association that stays engaged with the current group). I wanted to show the arrangers who inspired me what I had done, I wanted the general alumni to hear this new sound that was electrifying collegiate audiences, and I'm sure I wanted to show the alums who didn't admit me to the group that I'd proven my worth.

We sang song after song in front of a raging fireplace at the North Andover Country Club, our entire year's repertoire, to applause that diminished after each performance. The rousing homecoming that I'd anticipated was anything but, and it was afterward when a couple of outspoken members of the group, including my idol Andy Cranin, pulled me aside and told me something I'll never forget: "You're ruining the Beelzebubs."

To their ear, the clear four-part harmonies of past iterations of the Bubs were the gold standard, and a twelve-part arrangement was both inscrutable and impossible for older alums to easily sing along with. They hated the instrumental sounds, most of all the vocal percussion (which was referred to as "that spitting"), and thought the modern music (which is now deemed "classic rock") was often tuneless and not well suited to a cappella. In their minds, not only was I failing on all fronts as an arranger and music director, but also I was ruining this beloved group that for over twenty-five years had been a leader in collegiate a cappella. I was stunned.

But I was not deterred. Crestfallen that the alums did not like or appreciate what we were doing, I left the event with a realization that change is difficult and will be met with resistance. Audiences loved our music, and other college groups started copying us, so clearly we were doing something right. I didn't know the future; I didn't know that this sound would become the de facto sound of all collegiate and eventually professional a cappella. I just knew that it felt right, so I and we kept going.

I should note that the nexus of vocal percussion and beatboxing didn't exist in our minds. There is a great deal of overlap now, but in the 1980s beatboxing was largely of the Fat Boys variety "brrrr-huh-stick-a-stick," clearly vocal and attention drawing, whereas vocal percussion was highly imitative, a replica of drum sounds, and meant to fade into the group sound rather than draw attention. It remains the case today that the two are parallel pursuits, with many vocal percussionists largely incapable of delivering a great solo like any beatboxer, whereas many a beatboxer has trouble fading into a group and maintaining a consistent, metronomic beat for three minutes. Just as hip-hop and rock were on very different paths at the time, so were vocal percussion and beatboxing.

THE EARLY 1990s

As the eighties became the nineties and a cappella continued to pepper the airwaves, PBS aired a special as part of their Great Performances series called *Spike and Co. Do It A Cappella.* ♪ Spike Lee and Debbie Allen acted as hosts, creating a little through-line among a cappella performances by Take 6, the Persuasions, Ladysmith Black Mambazo, the Mint Juleps (an all-female sextet from England), and an unknown group from New York City called Rockapella that would soon thereafter become the music for a new PBS kids show called *Where in the World Is Carmen Sandiego?* ♪ cementing their music in the minds and hearts of a generation. It was an unusual show in that it was a onetime experience, never replicated, and a cappella was so infrequent on television at the time.

Rhino Records also released a compilation CD called *Modern A Cappella* in 1992 that featured an odd assortment of tracks:

1. National Anthem—En Vogue
2. I Feel Good—Bobby McFerrin
3. Only You—The Flying Pickets
4. Zombie Jamboree—Rockapella
5. Higher and Higher—The Mint Juleps
6. Caravan of Love—The Housemartins
7. Spread Love—Take 6
8. Unomathemba—Ladysmith Black Mambazo
9. Heaven—Longhouse
10. Silhouettes—The Nylons
11. My Husband Was a Weatherman—The Bobs
12. Papa-Oom-Mow-Mow—The Persuasions
13. Mighty Love—Todd Rundgren
14. Leave It—Yes
15. Walk Like an Egyptian—The Bangles
16. The Hallelujah Chorus—The Roches

This track list is notable if only because a cappella in the public eye is effectively reflected here. There are some of the legitimate a cappella pro groups becoming known by the public (Bobs, Bobby McFerrin, Ladysmith, Nylons, and Rockapella), a couple of British groups with hit a cappella songs in Europe (Flying Pickets and Housemartins), and a few pop artists who had no a cappella hits but were somehow able to produce a track that was either incredibly basic or a studio recording from which the instruments were stripped out (En Vogue, the Bangles, Yes, and the Roches). In all, as an a cappella lover it was both exciting to see this compilation in music stores and frustrating because there were many new groups springing up that were decidedly more a cappella. Sadly, Rhino never made another album, just as PBS never made another special, and this brief mainstream interest in a cappella waned as quickly as it waxed.

It was around this time that I was determined to both create an a cappella community and make a career of a cappella. My sense of community during my last couple of years of college was limited to what I knew—the collegiate a cappella world—and with four years of road trips to other colleges at which most concerts had at least three groups, I'd made friends among many of the host and guest groups, with which I would later cross paths. I wanted to find a way to maintain the friendships and more importantly lay the groundwork for an ongoing community, so I set out to create a newsletter, which I called the *Collegiate A Cappella News* (*CAN*). ♪

I had access to the Beelzebubs mailing list, the best of any collegiate group in the nation, but it wasn't definitive, so I reached out to a non-singing fan of a cappella. Rex Solomon, a recent Brandeis grad who collected and rated a cappella groups and albums in a master spreadsheet, was someone I'd heard about when he contacted the Bubs in the past to buy the group's latest albums. He was a true fan of a cappella, friendly and willing to share, and even offered to print and send the newsletter from his family business (Houston Jewelry), so with the combined database I used my new Mac SE30 computer and the program Pagemaker to create the *CAN*.

The *CAN* featured news (submitted by various groups), letters to the editor (called "Kick the Can"), road trip tales (a great way to share the various stories that were previously oral tradition), directing and touring tips, and the like. After only two editions I was getting letters from fans of a cappella and professional groups asking if I might expand the scope of the newsletter, which I was happy to do (and flattered that there was interest), but I didn't want to change the name *CAN* so I needed a word that meant both modern and yet didn't discriminate as to style (I wanted barbershop, classical, and doo-wop groups to feel welcome alongside pop groups), so I settled on the word "contemporary."

Back in the late eighties I started getting contacted by other a cappella groups that liked my arranging style and asked if I'd arrange for them. I was flattered and gladly did, becoming "The Ultimate A Cappella Arranging Service" (an homage to my mother's business at the time, "The Ultimate Kitchen and Bath," which sold high-end designer kitchen cabinetry such as Poggenpohl alongside fancy Italian hand-painted tiles, bidets, and the like). And after putting a quarter-page ad for this in the *CAN*, my arranging work steadily increased.

Moreover, I knew I wanted to start a professional group upon graduation, and this newsletter was the best place to get the word out to the two hundred or so collegiate groups that existed. As a test run, I'd created a summer quintet with a couple of high school buddies called the Mach 5 (named after Speed Racer's car). We performed at summer festivals, at sporting events, and down in Fisherman's Wharf, and generally tested the waters to see how a new group could get started in the San Francisco Bay Area.

My last year in the Bubs I was scouting during road trips as well, hand selecting the most talented guys in other groups, most notably a Brown Jabberwock named Andrew Chaikin who on his own had developed the most impressively realistic vocal drum kit I and possibly anyone had ever heard (he performs now as "Kid Beyond"). I convinced six other guys to move to San Francisco to start the House Jacks. The early days in the group were fun but confusing, as we endeavored through long rehearsals and over late-night diner meals how to truly become an a cappella rock band, the first a cappella group not only with a designated vocal percussionist but also with believable vocal guitars, original music, and gigs in rock clubs, everything. We wanted to create a new sound and a new image for a cappella. Break the mold.

As soon as I returned to San Francisco I bought a book on forming your own nonprofit, I convinced some of my friends to sit on the board of directors, I filed the paperwork, and the Contemporary A Cappella Society of America was born. Step one was to find inexpensive ways to popularize a cappella and motivate the community, and the easiest, least expensive way to do that right out of the gate was to create the CARAs: the Contemporary A Cappella Recording Awards. Having recently read a history of the Grammys (*Broken Record*), I was frustrated that many Academy voters not only never heard all the recordings in the categories they were voting for but also would vote in blocks for albums on their label, albums by friends, and so forth. Determined to avoid this and give equal recognition to unknown groups, the CARAs were designed to ensure that people voting in each round heard every recording. This wasn't hard in the early days, because the people voting on the CARAs were all in San Francisco, within a short drive. In time this hurdle would be overcome by creating mixed tapes and burned CDs with all nominees, and eventually downloadable tracks online.

As for the categories, I was determined to underscore my vision of a pan-stylistic contemporary a cappella community by rewarding best album and song in barbershop, classical, doo-wop, world, and religious categories as well as pop/rock, R&B, holiday, and the like. So long as there were four albums or songs to judge by different groups, we had a category. As for the collegiate recordings (it would be a while before there were enough high school albums), it made more sense to divide them up into male, female, and mixed categories, and further award best soloist and arranger as well as song and album.

A couple years later, I was approached by Adam Farb, an eager graduate of the Brown Derbies, looking for a way to create a career of a cappella. Around the same time, I realized if the world heard the very best a cappella recordings the way I was—via my own mix tapes—they would fall in love with it, so I suggested we make an annual compilation album with one great track per group. My wife Katy supplied the name—*Best of College A Cappella*—and thus *BOCA* was born. We quickly realized the biggest problem would be distribution: how can we get this in the hands of eager college students and lovers of collegiate a cappella with no way to get it in stores? The answer was to require all groups on the CD to purchase a limited number of copies (fifty) at a very low rate (six dollars each), which would then result in all of them selling it alongside their own CDs at shows. None of them would voluntarily do it most likely, but since they knew all of the other colleges were selling an album with their music on it, they willingly did, and found that the albums sold out quickly. We let them reorder at the same low price, which meant that many groups were making a bigger profit on *BOCA* than on their own discs, and before long *BOCA* was in great demand.

As the Harmony Sweepstakes grew to incorporate several annual regional semifinals around the country, those regions coalesced into having their own a cappella scene. For instance, Denver had groups such as the 17th Avenue Allstars ♪ and the Diners, both of which would perform weekly at a local restaurant/club called Acappella's. If you went to Seattle, you were bound to see the Trenchcoats, ♪ which later changed their name to the Coats in reaction to the Trenchcoat Mafia shootings, a necessity because they did several school shows throughout the year. I brought the Harmony Sweepstakes back to Boston in 1991, producing it with the Beelzebubs and local favorites North Shore A Cappella, which performed at restaurants around the North Shore of Boston. They took the region and went on to win it all. So it went throughout the 1990s: although a few groups toured nationally, most professional groups tended to be regional, well-known and loved in their home cities, but not known beyond.

There was also another tier of professional groups: not on the radio but still touring the nation, particularly colleges, thanks to successful performances at NACA (National Association of Campus Activities) showcases. Groups such as the Blenders, Regency, and the House Jacks had a national following, often visiting the various regional groups above as they knit together long van tours throughout the fall and spring when college was in session.

Other groups, such as Boston's Ball in the House, would find success in this market and augment it with younger scholastic educational shows in elementary and high schools, which instead of a 60 to 120-minute collegiate performance took the form of 30 to 50-minute shows in which performance was interwoven with demonstration of a cappella vocal techniques (especially vocal percussion) and vocal music history. There were also a few groups that had a specific cultural following, such as the Flirtations, ♪ an openly gay quintet fronted by gay activist Michael Callen. They would perform in cities and at gay rights events, and can be seen in the Tom Hanks movie *Philadelphia* (in the party scene).

A former Yale Whiffenpoof and venture capitalist Don Gooding turned his back on big deals and decided to pursue his first love—a cappella—so he started an online mail order catalog: Primarily A Cappella. Throughout the nineties, this was the singular place to find a cappella recordings, and groups would send in twenty CDs at a time, replenishing when those were sold. Gooding partnered with Harmony Sweepstakes producer John Neal (who took over from Lisa Murphy), and when they had a falling out, a second company was formed: Mainely A Cappella (based in Maine). Primarily A Cappella became Singers.com and continues to today, although nowhere near the dominant force it once was in the community (as iTunes, Spotify, and SheetMusicPlus.com now embrace a cappella), and Mainely A Cappella became Acappella.com, now defunct.

A cappella sheet music remained notoriously difficult to find, and my frustration from college that groups all sang the same music proved to be even more problematic within most adult groups, so when I started the Contemporary A Cappella Society (CASA) I created the arrangement trading library: a few hundred handwritten arrangements that people in the community could share (send in an arrangement or ask for copies of an arrangement). My thought was that if a group can get a copy of "The Lion Sleeps Tonight" and learn it easily, rather than laboriously transcribe it, they'll more quickly and easily move past it and develop their own sound and style. This happened but not quickly enough, so I sought out a sheet music company to publish a core repertoire of classic a cappella songs, much like the Barbershop Polecat repertoire but for popular music, but no one was interested until I found a small company—Voices Music Publishing in Tyler, Texas. We published the *Contemporary A Cappella Songbooks 1* and *2* as well as *A CASA Christmas* before the company folded, so Don Gooding stepped in and, along with myself and coarranger/music editor/notation expert extraordinaire Anne Raugh, formed Contemporary A Cappella Publishing. Hal Leonard Publishing noticed how well our songbooks were selling and offered to print and distribute our music, a relationship that continues through today.

Every hobby has its own conventions, including barbershop and choral music, so it was clear a cappella needed one as well, but building it from scratch would be expensive and risky. I approached John Neal about creating a convention. We decided to hold it in the fall, six months away from the Harmony Sweepstakes finals, and initially feature winners and favorites from the sweeps during a big Saturday Night Extravaganza after a day of workshops, classes, informal performances, and the like at nearby Dominican College. Thus the first A Cappella Summit was born in 1993. It was a joy to meet in person so many of the people that up to that point were merely voices in my headphones, including The Real Group's Anders Jalkeus who had flown all the way from Sweden.

Before long the summit became a major event, if not the major event in the professional and recreational a cappella community, and we expanded a few years later so we could have an East Coast A Cappella Summit, which allowed for more groups to be featured and people in the area to visit without a transcontinental plane ticket. The event grew until we were able to start featuring groups from outside the United States, most notably Vocal Sampling's first US performance, which required a cappella singers in various groups lobbying senators, as the Cuba embargo was in full effect. It was well worth the effort.

Meanwhile, my professional group the House Jacks ♪ had become a full-time endeavor and was performing as many as 250 shows each year. A couple of record labels (Tommy Boy Records, a rap label, owned at the time by Warner Brothers, and RCA) became interested in the original music on our debut album *Naked Noise*, and we signed with Tommy Boy in 1994. Three years of songwriting, demos, recordings, and marketing plans came and went, and in 1997 we were dropped, the label completely unable to figure out how to market an original pop/rock band that sounded as if it had instruments but didn't. Our college agent at the time, Denise Kirk, had it right: people needed to see us to understand what we were doing, which wasn't going to become an option until the next generation of a cappella groups went viral on YouTube twenty years later.

My *BOCA* partner, Adam Farb, was looking to find a way to become a full-time a cappella impresario, so I floated an idea I'd had for many years: to create a "March Madness" of a cappella. No one cares if some college students are playing basketball in the gym, but if there's a national tournament behind it all, you have the eyes of the nation. The name, National Championship of Collegiate A Cappella (NCCA), was a play on NCAA (at the time I never expected it to become international, resulting in the current clumsy acronym ICCA), with regional competitions culminating in a final at Carnegie Hall in New York for the first few years (starting in 1996) and then moving to Lincoln Center. When Adam Farb grew tired of spending the first five months of the year on airplanes and in hotel rooms, he sold the competition and *BOCA* to Don Gooding of Acappella.com who later sold it to Amanda Newman; she now oversees it and the International Championship of High School A Cappella (ICHSA) as well as *BOCA* under the company name Varsity Vocals. If you'd told us at the time that the competition would be the basis for a huge hit movie (*Pitch Perfect*) as well as a television show (*Sing It On*), we wouldn't have been surprised. That was the point, after all.

Around this time in the middle of the nineties there were a few fledgling local and collegiate radio stations with DJs creating a cappella radio shows on their own, but they often struggled to get enough copies of albums to augment their own private libraries and the copies of local groups that would drop by the studio. We would list all radio shows in every edition of the *CAN*, but that wasn't quite enough. Partnering with longtime barbershop singer and early member of Chanticleer Phil De-Bar and House Jacks a cappella engineer/coproducer Buddy Saleman, A Cappella Radio International was born. We created an hour-long show that featured new recordings, news, interviews, and the like, sending it out to stations around the world on CD-R, a new, very expensive technology (CD-Rs were at least five dollars each), thanks to a grant from the Barbershop Harmony Foundation, which was eager to hear their star group's recordings alongside many other styles.

2000s AND 2010s

At the end of 1999, the contemporary a cappella sound was just beginning to become noticed by the major media companies. I was contacted by Disney, which was interested in creating a new vocal group to be a modern counterpart to the Voices of Liberty at Epcot in Orlando, Florida, and together we created American Vybe ♪—eight-part vocals with upright bass—which performed all manner of twentieth-century music, from field hollers to jazz, pop, and R&B. Disneyland then wanted their own modern a cappella group for Disney's California Adventure, so I created Groove 66, ♪ a six-part a cappella rock band that performed as people entered the park.

Many a collegiate group was formed in the 1990s, and Indiana University's Straight No Chaser ♪ was a cut above, being formed at one of the nation's premier music schools. They became well known on their campus, and before the original members graduated they decided to don tuxedos and videotape their annual holiday concert. As is often the case with extracurricular collegiate endeavors, the footage was never edited or made public, but former member Randy Stein decided to upload some of the performances to YouTube in honor of the group's ten-year anniversary, and one of the songs—a hilariously convoluted version of the "12 Days of Christmas"—went viral. When receiving a phone call from the head of Atlantic Records, Randy was convinced it was a prank.

Several albums, awards, and international tours later, the group has a following that is the envy of most rock bands.

The Sing-Off ♪ was the result of two filmmakers—Sam Weisman and Bobby Newmyer—who approached Sony about making a film about a male collegiate group's many adventures and misadventures. Sony held off on the movie idea, unsure, but asked about the potential of a televised singing competition, and thus the show was born. Sadly, Bobby Newmyer passed away before the show was made, so his wife, Deb Newmyer, stepped in as one of the executive producers. The show was the highest-rated (viewership) new show on NBC in its first year, and the third highest rated overall in its second year. The show had five seasons in the United States and aired in many other countries; as well, it was remade with local groups in China, Holland, France, and South Africa. Perhaps the show's greatest legacy was that it showed the world what contemporary a cappella had become, while creating new opportunities for existing groups (the Tufts Beelzebubs became the voices of the Warblers on *Glee*), helping existing groups find their sound (Home Free went from pop group to country superstars), and inspiring many groups to form and rehearse, in hopes of making it on the show.

Of the many groups who were formed for *The Sing-Off*, Pentatonix ♪ is the most notable, having become the standard-bearers for the contemporary a cappella community with three Grammy Awards, multiple platinum albums, a Christmas special, and more followers on YouTube than Beyoncé. Although they were crowned champions of season three of *The Sing-Off*, their prospects were far from guaranteed. The previous two winners, Nota and Committed, had their fortunes tied up in management and label deals, both ostensibly prizes for winning the show but in reality anchors that kept them from going very far. Pentatonix also won a record deal but were dropped by the label the very next day and instead focused on generating their own fan base by releasing frequent videos of current pop hits. And as they say, the rest is history as they built a global fan base that drew record labels to them (they ultimately signed with RCA).

Sadly, Weisman and Newmyer never got a chance to make their a cappella movie because Gold Circle green-lighted a film before Sony, a comedic story about a female collegiate group who rebuild after an embarrassment in the International Championship of Collegiate A Cappella (ICCA) finals. *Pitch Perfect* was first a nonfiction book by *GQ* writer Mickey Rapkin, telling the tale of the current collegiate a cappella community by following three groups: the all-male Tufts Beelzebubs and the University of Virginia Hullabahoos, and the all-female University of Oregon Divisi. Divisi did make it to the ICCA finals and were widely expected to win, but a single judge (a female judge from Julliard, for the record) didn't like them at all and rated them in fifth place, causing an uproar that resulted in changes in ICCA judging rules.

Pitch Perfect was a sleeper hit, opening to modest crowds in a limited number of cities in the fall of 2012, but the word-of-mouth spread, and by the time it was released on DVD before Christmas it started to become well known. The soundtrack became the best-selling soundtrack the following year, one of only five platinum albums that year (a sign of ongoing diminishing album sales). The Cup Song, a 1938 bluegrass song sung by Anna Kendrick in the movie while flipping a plastic cup, became an international phenomenon, with the song selling over four million copies and sparking a seemingly endless variety of versions by everyone from Girl Scouts to gun enthusiasts. *Pitch Perfect 2* followed two years later and was a certified blockbuster, grossing over $287 million worldwide at the box office, making it the best-selling music comedy movie of all time and the third best-selling college comedy of all time (according to Box Office Mojo). PopTV, a new channel, created a show following the ICCA's called *Sing It On*. Lifetime Television got in on the action, creating *Pitch Slapped*, ♪ a television show about the high school a cappella world, and WGBH created *Sing That Thing*, a televised competition for Boston-area groups.

A cappella camps began appearing in 2012, the first being Camp A Cappella, ♪ which was held at Ohio State University and now finds its home at Wright State University in Dayton; and the second, A Cappella Academy ♪ in Los Angeles. Many smaller local and regional vocal music summer camps have incorporated or changed entirely to focus on contemporary a cappella. Many new a cappella festivals have also been born in the new millennium, including VoiceJam ♪ in Bentonville, Arkansas, and AcaWest in San Francisco (a comprehensive list of a cappella festivals worldwide can be found at the end of this book). The A Cappella Education Association, formed in 2014, is holding its third annual conference and continues to provide resources for educators who want to integrate a cappella into their curricula.

Broadway has had a cappella songs in its productions (such as *The Music Man*), but never a fully a cappella musical, until *In Transit ♪* opened in December 2016. The show had humble roots, as four members of a postcollegiate a cappella group started writing songs about the experiences they were having living in New York City. The songs grew into an off-Broadway show and then five years later opened at the Circle in the Square Theater, directed by three-time Tony winner Kathleen Marshall.

Speaking of postcollegiate groups, the Contemporary A Cappella League (aka CAL), ♪ which was formed as a part of CASA a decade ago, has grown so quickly that it branched off and became its own organization: a network of postcollegiate contemporary a cappella groups for the casual singer who wants to continue singing but doesn't want to pursue music full-time. And speaking of theatrical a cappella, performing arts centers have seen that individual groups such as Straight No Chaser and Pentatonix have been very lucrative, so they have opened their doors to new touring shows designed for their market, such as Vocalosity ♪ and Gobsmacked.

SNAPSHOT OF TODAY, EARLY 2017

Although a book about current events becomes out of date the moment it is printed, it's still valuable to have a snapshot of a moment in time: *Pitch Perfect 3* is in production (in fact I'm writing this book in Atlanta, during breaks from filming). The BBC just began production on a new competitive television singing show for choral and a cappella groups called *Pitch Battles*, created by the creator of global hit show *Dancing with the Stars* (I'll be joining them as soon as filming here ends). *In Transit* just celebrated its hundredth show, Vocalosity just finished its fiftieth of its current tour, and Straight No Chaser returned home after another epic three and a half months on the road. Both Pentatonix and Home Free are working on new albums in the studio. The college a cappella community has grown from around two hundred groups when CASA was formed to more than three thousand, and the ICCA/ICHSA season is under way with more competitors than ever (387 collegiate groups, 160 high school groups). Camp A Cappella sold out last year and is at record enrollment already for this coming year. CASA just announced the first AVAs (A Cappella Video Awards) at the Los Angeles A Cappella Festival, and the CARAs, going strong since 1992, will be announced in April. The California branch of the American Choral Directors' Association has its first contemporary a cappella repertoire and resources chair, and other states are following suit.

By any measure, a cappella continues to grow, and as a result there are more people making a living from a cappella than ever before. If you're excited and focused on careers right now, jump ahead to the "Where" section of this book, in which interviews with several successful a cappella professionals provide insight into career options within their various fields. If you're ready to dive into vocal techniques specific to contemporary a cappella, such as vocal percussion and instrumental imitation, leap ahead to "How." If instead you'd like to start with some fundamental insight into the mechanics of singing, general vocal technique, and vocal health, turn the page.

NOTES

1. Many years later, in the 2000s, I mentioned to Bobs founder Richard Greene that he and they were a huge inspiration to me and a major reason I'd chosen a cappella as a career, to which he said in his characteristically droll way, "Really? Wow. I'm so sorry."

2. One might take exception with the song's characterization as being a cappella when it clearly features an electronic drum machine after the extended slow introduction, but at the time, and since then, most a cappella fans and groups aren't completely dogmatic about the inclusion of various instrumental elements from time to time, most often some form of percussion.

3. The Bubs had the best collegiate database pre-Internet, and a great reputation, which meant we'd perform at something like twenty colleges a year when most groups would do one a semester. We took collegiate gigging very seriously, as it was the best part of being in the group: traveling to other colleges, "winning" the night by showing up the local favorites, and then partying till the wee hours with the coolest and cutest group and audience members.

WHAT

The Original and Most Powerful Instrument:
The Human Voice

3

SINGING AND VOICE SCIENCE

Scott McCoy

This chapter presents a concise overview of how the voice functions as a biomechanical, acoustic instrument. We will be dealing with elements of anatomy, physiology, acoustics, and resonance. But don't panic: the things you need to know are easily accessible, even if it has been many years since you last set foot in a science or math class!

All musical instruments, including the human voice, have at least four things in common, consisting of a power source, sound source (vibrator), resonator, and a system for articulation. In most cases, the person who plays the instrument provides power by pressing a key, plucking a string, or blowing into a horn. This power is used to set the sound source in motion, which creates vibrations in the air that we perceive as sound. Musical vibrators come in many forms, including strings, reeds, and human lips. The sound produced by the vibrator, however, needs a lot of help before it becomes beautiful music—we might think of it as raw material, like a lump of clay that a potter turns into a vase. Musical instruments use resonance to enhance and strengthen the sound of the vibrator, transforming it into sounds we identify as a piano, trumpet, or guitar. Finally, instruments must have a means of articulation to create the nuanced sounds of music. Let's see how these four elements are used to create the sounds of singing.

PULMONARY SYSTEM: THE POWER SOURCE
OF YOUR VOICE

The human voice has a lot in common with a trumpet: both use flaps of tissue as a sound source, both use hollow tubes as resonators, and both rely on the respiratory (pulmonary) system for power. If you stop to think about it, you quickly realize why breathing is so important for singing. First and foremost, it keeps us alive through the exchange of blood gases—oxygen in, carbon dioxide out. But it also serves as the storage depot for the air we use to produce sound. Most singers rarely encounter situations in which these two functions are in conflict, but if you are required to sustain an extremely long phrase, you could find yourself in need of fresh oxygen before your lungs are totally empty.

Misconceptions about breathing for singing are rampant. Fortunately, most are easily dispelled. We must start with a brief foray into the world of physics in the guise of Boyle's law. Some of you no doubt remember this principle: the pressure of a gas within a container changes inversely with changes of volume. If the quantity of a gas is constant and its container is made smaller, pressure rises. But if we make the container get bigger, pressure goes down. Boyle's law explains everything that happens when we breathe, especially when we combine it with another physical law: nature abhors a vacuum. If one location has reduced pressure, air flows from an area of higher pressure to equalize the two, and vice versa. So if we can create a zone of reduced air pressure by expanding our lungs, air automatically flows in to restore balance. When air pressure in the lungs is increased, it has no choice but to flow outward.

As we all know, the air we breathe goes in and out of our lungs. Each lung contains millions and millions of tiny air sacs called alveoli, where gases are exchanged. The alveoli also function like ultra-miniature versions of the bladder for a bagpipe, storing the air that will be used to set the vocal folds into vibration. To get the air in and out of them, all we need to do is make the lungs larger for inhalation and smaller for exhalation. Always remember this relationship between cause and effect during breathing: we inhale because we make ourselves large; we exhale because we make ourselves smaller. Unfortunately, the lungs are organs, not muscles, and have no ability on their own to accomplish this feat. For this reason, your bodies came from the factory with special muscles designed to enlarge and compress your entire thorax (rib cage), while simultaneously moving your lungs. We can classify these muscles in two main categories: any muscle that has the ability to increase the volume capacity of the thorax serves an inspiratory function; any muscle that has the ability to decrease the volume capacity of the thorax serves an expiratory function.

Your largest muscle of inspiration is called the diaphragm (figure 3.1). This dome-shaped muscle originates from the bottom of your sternum (breastbone) and completely fills the area from that point around your ribs to your spine. It's the second-largest muscle in your body, but you probably have no conscious awareness of it or ability to directly control it. When we take a deep breath, the diaphragm contracts and the cen-

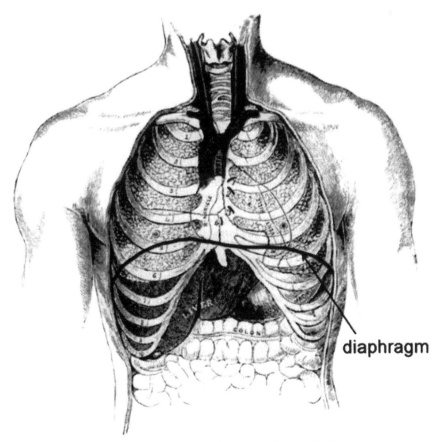

diaphragm

Figure 3.1.   Location of diaphragm. *Courtesy of Scott McCoy.*

tral portion flattens out and drops downward a couple inches into your abdomen, pressing against all of your internal organs. If you release tension from your abdominal muscles as you inhale, you will feel a gentle bulge in your upper or lower belly, or perhaps in your back, resulting from the displacement of your innards by the diaphragm. This is a good thing and can be used to let you know you have taken a good inhalation.

The diaphragm is important, but we must remember that it cannot function in isolation. After you inhale, it relaxes and gently returns to its resting position through an action called elastic recoil. This movement, however, is entirely passive and makes no significant contribution to generating the pressure required to sustain phonation. Therefore, it makes no sense at all to try to "sing from your diaphragm"—unless you intend to sing while you inhale, not exhale!

Eleven pairs of muscles assist the diaphragm in its inhalatory efforts, which are called the external intercostal muscles (figure 3.2). These muscles start from ribs one through eleven and connect at a slight angle downward to ribs two through twelve. When they contract, the entire thorax moves up and out, somewhat like moving a bucket handle. With the diaphragm and intercostals working together, you are able to increase the capacity of your lungs by about three to six liters, depending on your gender and overall physical stature; thus, we have quite a lot of air available to power our voices.

Eleven additional pairs of muscles are located directly under the external intercostals, which, not surprisingly, are called the internal intercostals (figure 3.2). These muscles start from ribs two through twelve and connect upward to ribs one through eleven. When they contract, they induce the opposite action of their external partners: the thorax is made smaller, inducing exhalation. Four additional pairs of expiratory muscles are located in the abdomen, beginning with the rectus (figure 3.2). The two rectus abdominis muscles run from your pubic bone to your sternum and are divided into four separate portions, called bellies of the muscle (lots of muscles have multiple bellies; it is coincidental that the bellies of the rectus are found in the location we colloquially refer to as our belly). Definition of these bellies results in the so-called ripped abdomen or six-pack of body builders and others who are especially fit.

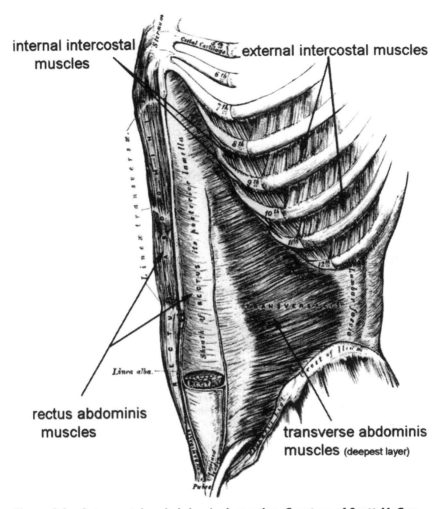

internal intercostal muscles

external intercostal muscles

rectus abdominis muscles

transverse abdominis muscles (deepest layer)

Figure 3.2.   Intercostal and abdominal muscles. *Courtesy of Scott McCoy.*

The largest muscles of the abdomen are called the external obliques (figure 3.3), which run at a downward angle from the sides of the rectus, covering the lower portion of the thorax, and extend all the way to the spine. The internal obliques lie immediately below, oriented at an angle that crisscrosses the external muscles. They are slightly smaller, beginning at the bottom of the thorax, rather than extending over it. The deepest muscle layer is the transverse abdominis (figure 3.2), which is oriented with fibers that run horizontally. These four muscle pairs com-

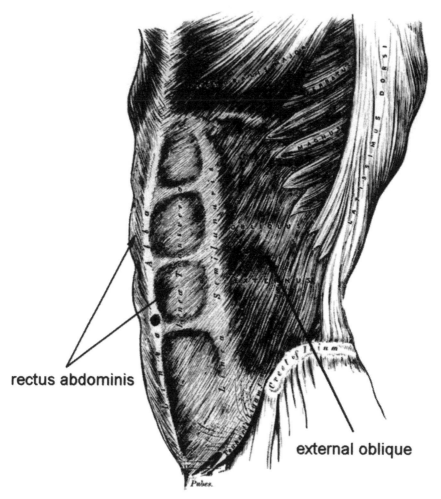

rectus abdominis

external oblique

Figure 3.3. External oblique and rectus abdominis muscles. *Courtesy of Scott McCoy.*

pletely encase the abdominal region, holding your organs and digestive system in place while simultaneously helping you breathe.

Your expiratory muscles are quite large and can produce a great deal of pulmonary or air pressure. In fact, they can easily overpower the larynx. Healthy adults generally can generate more than twice the pressure that is required to produce even the loudest sounds; therefore, singers must develop a system for moderating and controlling airflow and breath pressure. This practice goes by many names, including breath support, breath control, and breath management, all of which rely on the principle of muscular antagonism. Muscles are said to have an antagonistic relationship when they work in opposing directions, usually pulling on a common point of attachment, for the sake of increasing stability or motor control. You can see a clear example of muscular antagonism in the relationship between your biceps (flexors) and triceps (extensors) when you hold out your arm. In breathing for singing, we activate inspiratory muscles (e.g., diaphragm and external intercostals) during exhalation to help control respiratory pressure and the rate at which air is expelled from the lungs.

One of the things you will notice when watching a variety of singers is that they tend to breathe in many different ways. You might think that voice teachers and scientists, who have been teaching and studying singing for hundreds, if not thousands, of years, would have come to agreement on the best possible breathing technique. But for many reasons, this is not the case. For one, different musical and vocal styles place varying demands on breathing. For another, humans have a huge variety of body types, sizes, and morphologies. A breathing strategy that is successful for a tall, slender woman might be completely ineffective in a short, robust man. Our bodies actually contain a large number of muscles beyond those we've already discussed that are capable of assisting with respiration. For an example, consider your latissimi dorsi muscles. These large muscles of the arm enable us to do pull-ups (or pull-downs, depending on which exercise you perform) at the fitness center. But because they wrap around a large portion of the thorax, they also exert an expiratory force. We have at least two dozen such muscles that have secondary respiratory functions, some for exhalation and some for inhalation. When we consider all these possibilities, it is no surprise at all that there are many ways to breathe that can produce beautiful singing. Just remember to practice some muscular antagonism—maintaining a degree of inhalation posture during exhalation—and you should do well.

LARYNX: THE VIBRATOR OF YOUR VOICE

The larynx, sometimes known as the voice box or Adam's apple, is a complex physiologic structure made of cartilage, muscle, and tissue. Biologically, it serves as a sphincter valve, closing off the airway to prevent foreign objects from entering the lungs. When firmly closed, it is also used to increase abdominal pressure to assist with lifting heavy objects, childbirth, and defecation. But if we gently close this valve while we exhale, tissue in the larynx begins to vibrate and produce the sounds that become speech and singing.

The human larynx is a remarkably small instrument, typically ranging from the size of a pecan to a walnut for women and men, respectively. Sound is produced at a location called the glottis, which is formed by two flaps of tissue called the vocal folds (aka vocal cords). In women, the glottis is about the size of a dime; in men, it can approach the diameter of a quarter. The two folds are always attached together at their front point but open in the shape of the letter V during normal breathing, an action called abduction. To phonate, we must close the V while we exhale, an action called adduction (just like the machines you use at the fitness center to exercise your thigh and chest muscles).

Phonation is only possible because of the unique multilayer structure of the vocal folds (figure 3.4). The core of each fold is formed by muscle, which is surrounded by a layer of gelatinous material called the lamina propria. The vocal ligament also runs through the lamina propria, which helps to prevent injury by limiting how far the folds can be stretched for high pitches. A thin, hairless epithelial layer that is constantly kept moist with mucus secreted by the throat, larynx, and trachea surrounds all of this. During phonation, the outer layer of the fold glides independently over the inner layer in a wavelike motion, without which phonation is impossible.

We can use a simple demonstration to better understand the independence of the inner and outer portions of the folds. Explore the palm of your hand with your other index finger. Note that the skin is attached quite firmly to the flesh beneath it. If you poke at your palm, that flesh acts as padding, protecting the underlying bone. Now explore the back of your hand. You will observe that the skin is attached quite loosely—you easily can move it around with your finger. And if you poke at the back of your hand, it is likely to hurt; there is very little padding between the skin and your bones. Your vocal folds combine the best attributes of both sides of your hand. They provide sufficient padding to help reduce impact stress, while permitting the outer layer to slip like the skin on the back of your hand, enabling phonation to occur. When you are sick

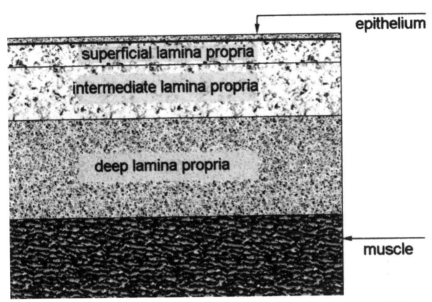

epithelium

superficial lamina propria

intermediate lamina propria

deep lamina propria

muscle

Figure 3.4. Layered structure of the vocal fold. *Courtesy of Scott McCoy.*

with laryngitis and lose your voice (a condition called aphonia), inflammation in the vocal folds couples the layers of the folds tightly together.
The outer layer can no longer move independently over the inner, and
phonation becomes difficult or impossible.

The vocal folds are located within the five cartilaginous structures
of the larynx (figure 3.5). The largest is called the thyroid cartilage,
which is shaped like a small shield. The thyroid connects to the cricoid
cartilage below it, which is shaped like a signet ring—broad in the back
and narrow in the front. Two cartilages that are shaped like squashed
pyramids sit atop the cricoid, called the arytenoids. Each vocal fold runs
from the thyroid cartilage in front to one of the arytenoids at the back.
Finally, the epiglottis is located at the top of the larynx, flipping backward each time we swallow to prevent food and liquid from entering our
lungs. Muscles connect between the various cartilages to open and close
the glottis and to lengthen and shorten the vocal folds for ascending
and descending pitch, respectively. Because they are sometimes used to
identify vocal function, it is a good idea to know the names of the muscles that control the length of the folds. We've already mentioned that
a muscle forms the core of each fold. Because it runs between the thyroid cartilage and an arytenoid, it is named the thyroarytenoid muscle

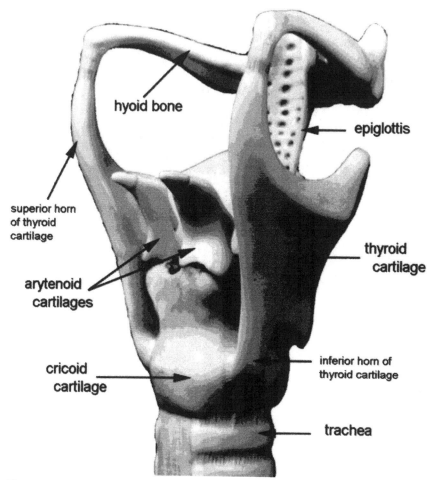

hyoid bone

epiglottis

superior horn
of thyroid
cartilage

thyroid
cartilage

arytenoid
cartilages

inferior horn of
thyroid cartilage

cricoid
cartilage

trachea

Figure 3.5. Cartilages of the larynx, viewed at an angle from the back.
Courtesy of Scott McCoy.

(formerly known as the vocalis muscle). When the thyroarytenoid, or TA muscle, contracts, the fold is shortened and pitch goes down. The folds are elongated through the action of the cricothyroid, or CT muscles, which run from the thyroid to cricoid cartilage.

Vocal color (timbre) is created by the combined effects of the sound produced by the vocal folds and the resonance provided by the vocal tract. While these elements can never be completely separated, it is useful to consider the two primary modes of vocal fold vibration and their resulting sound qualities. The main differences are related to the

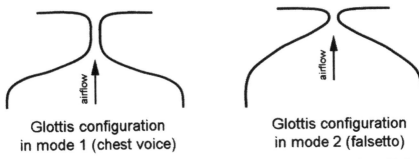

Glottis configuration
in mode 1 (chest voice)

Glottis configuration
in mode 2 (falsetto)

Figure 3.6.   Primary modes of vocal fold vibration. *Courtesy of Scott McCoy.*

relative thickness of the folds and their cross-sectional shape (figure 3.6). The first option depends on short, thick folds that come together with nearly square-shaped edges. Vibration in this configuration is given a variety of names, including mode 1, thyroarytenoid (TA) dominant, chest mode, or modal voice. The alternate configuration uses longer, thinner folds that only make contact at their upper margins. Common names include mode 2, cricothyroid (CT) dominant, falsetto mode, or loft voice. Singers vary the vibrational mode of the folds according to the quality of sound they wish to produce.

Before we move on to a discussion of resonance, we must consider the quality of the sound that is produced by the larynx. At the level of the glottis, we create a sound not unlike the annoying buzz of a duck call. That buzz, however, contains all the raw material we need to create speech and singing. Vocal or glottal sound is considered to be complex, meaning it consists of many simultaneously sounding frequencies (pitches). The lowest frequency within any tone is called the fundamental, which corresponds to its named pitch in the musical scale. Orchestras tune to a pitch called A-440, which means it has a frequency of 440 vibrations per second, or 440 hertz (abbreviated Hz). Additional frequencies are included above the fundamental, which are called overtones. Overtones in the glottal sound are quieter than the fundamental. In voices, the overtones are usually whole number multiples of the fundamental, creating a pattern called the harmonic series (e.g., 100 Hz, 200 Hz, 300 Hz, 400 Hz, 500 Hz, etc., or G2, G3, D4, G4, B4—note that pitches are named by the international system in which the lowest C of the piano keyboard is C1; middle C therefore becomes C4, the fourth C of the keyboard; figure 3.7).

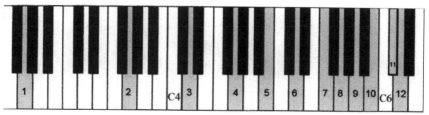

Figure 3.7. Natural harmonic series, beginning at G2. *Courtesy of Scott McCoy.*

Singers who choose to make coarse or rough sounds as might be appropriate for rock or blues often add overtones that are inharmonic, or not part of the standard numerical sequence. Inharmonic overtones are also common in singers with damaged or pathological voices.

Under most circumstances, we are completely unaware of the presence of overtones—they simply contribute to the overall timbre of a voice. In some vocal styles, however, harmonics become a dominant feature. This is especially true in throat singing or overtone singing, as is found in places like Tuva. Throat singers tune their vocal tracts so precisely that single harmonics are highlighted within the harmonic spectrum as a separate, whistle-like tone. These singers sustain a low-pitched drone and then create a melody by moving from tone to tone within the natural harmonic series. You can learn to do this too. Sustain a comfortable pitch in your range and slowly morph between the vowels [i] and [u]. If you listen carefully, you will hear individual harmonics pop out of your sound.

The mode of vocal fold vibration has a strong impact on the overtones that are produced. In mode 1, high-frequency harmonics are relatively strong; in mode 2, they are much weaker. As a result, mode 1 tends to yield a much brighter, brassier sound.

VOCAL TRACT: YOUR SOURCE OF RESONANCE

Resonance is typically defined as the amplification and enhancement (or enrichment) of musical sound through supplemental vibration. What does this really mean? In layman's terms, we could say that resonance makes instruments louder and more beautiful by reinforcing the original vibrations of the sound source. This enhancement occurs in two primary ways, which are known as forced and free resonance (there is nothing pejorative in these terms; free resonance is not superior to forced resonance). Any object that is physically connected to a vibrator can serve as a forced resonator. For a piano, the resonator is the soundboard (on the underside of a grand or on the back of an upright); the vibrations of the strings are transmitted directly to the soundboard through a structure known as the bridge, which also is found on violins and guitars. Forced resonance also plays a role in voice production. Place your hand on your chest and say [a] at a low pitch. You almost certainly felt the vibrations of forced resonance. In singing, this might best be considered your private resonance; you can feel it and it might impact your self-perception of sound, but nobody else can hear it. To understand why this is true, imagine what a violin would sound like if it were encased in a thick layer of foam rubber. The vibrations of the string would be damped out, muting the instrument. Your skin, muscles, and other tissues do the same thing to the vibrations of your vocal folds.

By contrast, free resonance occurs when sound travels through a hollow space, such as the inside of a trumpet, an organ pipe, or your vocal tract, which consists of the pharynx (throat), oral cavity (mouth), and nasal cavity (nose). As sound travels through these regions, a complex pattern of echoes is created; every time sound encounters a change in the shape of the vocal tract, some of its energy is reflected backward, much like an echo in a canyon. If these echoes arrive back at the glottis at the precise moment a new pulse of sound is created, the two elements synchronize, resulting in a significant increase in intensity. All of this happens very quickly—remember that sound is traveling through your vocal tract at more than seven hundred miles per hour.

Whenever this synchronization of the vocal tract and sound source occurs, we say that the system is in resonance. The phenomenon occurs at specific frequencies (pitches), which can be varied by changing the position of the tongue, lips, jaw, palate, and larynx. These resonant frequencies, or areas in which strong amplification occurs, are called formants. Formants provide the specific amplification that changes the raw, buzzing sound produced by your vocal folds into speech and singing. The vocal tract is capable of producing many formants, which are labeled sequentially by ascending pitch. The first two, F1 and F2, are used to create vowels; higher formants contribute to the overall timbre and individual characteristics of a voice. In some singers, especially those who train to sing in opera, formants three through five are clustered together to form a super formant, eponymously called the singer's formant, which creates a ringing sound and enables a voice to be heard in a large theater without electronic amplification.

Formants are vitally important in singing, but they can be a bit intimidating to understand. An analogy that works really well for me is to think of formants like the wind. You cannot see the wind, but you know it is present when you see leaves rustling in a tree or feel a breeze on your face. Formants work in the same manner. They are completely invisible and directly inaudible. But just as we see the rustling leaf, we can hear, and perhaps even feel, the action of formants through how they change our sound. Try a little experiment. Sing an ascending scale beginning at B♭3, sustaining the vowel [i]. As you approach the D♯ or E♭ of the scale, you will likely feel (and hear) that your sound becomes a bit stronger and easier to produce. This occurs because the scale tone and formant are on the same pitch, providing additional amplification. If you change to a [u] vowel, you will feel the same thing at about the same place in the scale. If you sing to an [o] or [e] and continue up the scale, you'll feel a bloom in the sound somewhere around C5 (an octave above middle C); [a] is likely to come into its best focus at about G5.

To remember the approximate pitches of the first formants for the main vowels, [i]–[e]–[a]–[o]–[u], just think of a C-major triad in first inversion, open position, starting at E4: [i] = E4, [e] = C5, [a] = G5, [o] = C5, and [u] = E4 (figure 3.8). If your music theory isn't strong, you could use the mnemonic "every child gets candy eagerly." These pitches

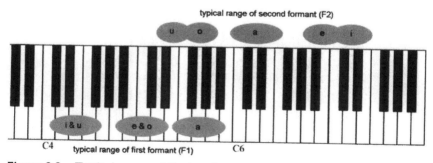

Figure 3.8. Typical range of first and second formants for primary vowels. Courtesy of Scott McCoy.

might vary by as much as a minor third higher and lower but no farther: once a formant changes by more than that interval, the vowel that is produced must change.

Formants have absolutely no preference for what they amplify—they are indiscriminate lovers, just as happy to bond with the first harmonic as the fifth. When men or women sing low pitches, there will almost always be at least one harmonic that comes close enough to a formant to produce a clear vowel sound. The same is not true for women with high voices, especially sopranos, who routinely must sing pitches that have a fundamental frequency higher than the first formant of many vowels. Imagine what happens if she must sing the phrase "and I'll leave you forever," with the word "leave" set on a very high, climactic note. The audience won't be able to tell if she is singing leave or love; the two will sound identical. This happens because the formant that is required to identify the vowel [i] is too far below the pitch being sung. Even if she tries to sing leave, the sound that comes out of her mouth will be heard as some variation of [a].

Fortunately, this kind of mismatch between formants and musical pitches rarely causes problems for anyone but opera singers, choir so-pranos, and perhaps ingénues in classic music theater shows. Almost ev-eryone else generally sings low enough in their respective voice ranges to produce easily identifiable vowels.

Second formants can also be important, but more so for opera singers than everyone else. They are much higher in pitch, tracking the pattern [u] = E5, [o] = G5, [a] = D6, [e] = B6, [i] = D7 (you can use the mne-monic "every good dad buys diapers" to remember these pitches; figure 3.8). Because they can extend so high, into the top octave of the piano keyboard for [i], they interact primarily with higher tones in the natural harmonic series. Unless you are striving to produce the loudest unam-plified sound possible, you probably never need to worry about the second formant; it will steadfastly do its job of helping to produce vowel sounds without any conscious thought or manipulation on your part.

If you are interested in discovering more about resonance and how it impacts your voice, you might want to install a spectrum analyzer on your computer. Free (or inexpensive) programs are readily available for download over the Internet that will work with either a PC or a Mac computer. You don't need any specialized hardware—if you can use

Skype or FaceTime, you already have everything you need. Once you've installed something, simply start playing with it. Experiment with your voice to see exactly how the analysis signal changes when you change the way your voice sounds. You'll be able to see how harmonics change in intensity as they interact with your formants. If you sing with vibrato, you'll see how consistently you produce your variations in pitch and amplitude. You'll even be able to see if your tone is excessively nasal for the kind of singing you want to do. Other programs are available that will help you improve your intonation (how well you sing in tune) or enhance your basic musicianship skills. Technology truly has advanced sufficiently to help us sing more beautifully.

MOUTH, LIPS, AND TONGUE: YOUR ARTICULATORS

The articulatory life of a singer is not easy, especially when compared to the demands placed on other musicians. Like a pianist or brass player, we must be able to produce the entire spectrum of musical articulation, including dynamic levels from hushed pianissimos to thunderous fortes, short notes, long notes, accents, crescendos, diminuendos, and so on. We produce most of these articulations the same way instrumentalists do, which is by varying our power supply. But singers have another layer of articulation that makes everything much more complicated; we must produce these musical gestures while simultaneously singing words.

As we learned in our brief examination of formants, altering the resonance characteristics of the vocal tract creates the vowel sounds of language. We do this by changing the position of our tongue, jaw, lips, and sometimes palate. Slowly say the vowel pattern [i]–[e]–[a]–[o]–[u]. Can you feel how your tongue moves in your mouth? For [i], it is high in the front and low in the back, but it takes the opposite position for [u]. Now slowly say the word "Tuesday," noting all the places your tongue comes into contact with your teeth and palate and how it changes shape as you produce the vowels and diphthongs. There is a lot going on in there—no wonder it takes so long for babies to learn to speak!

Our articulatory anatomy is extraordinarily complex, in large part because our bodies use the same passageway for food, water, air, and sound. As a result, our tongue, larynx, throat, jaw, and palate are all interconnected with common physical and neurologic points of attachment. Our anatomical Union Station in this regard is a small structure called the hyoid bone. The hyoid is one of only three bones in your entire body that do not connect to other bones via a joint (the other two are your patellae, or kneecaps). This little bone is suspended below your jaw, freely floating up and down every time you swallow. It is a busy place, serving as the upper suspension point for the larynx, the connection for the root of the tongue, and the primary location of the muscles that open your mouth by dropping your jaw.

Good singing—in any genre—requires a high degree of independence in all these articulatory structures. Unfortunately, nature conspires against us to make this difficult to accomplish. From the time we were born, our bodies have relied on a reflex reaction to elevate the palate and raise the larynx each time we swallow. This action becomes habitual: palate goes up, larynx also lifts. But depending on the style of music we are singing, we might need to keep the larynx down while the palate goes up (opera and classical) or palate down with the larynx up (country and bluegrass). As we all know, habits can be very hard to change, which is one of the reasons that it can take a lot of study and practice to become an excellent singer. Understanding your body's natural reflexive habits can make some of this work a bit easier.

There is one more significant pitfall to the close proximity of all these articulators: tension in one area is easily passed along to another. If your jaw muscles are too tight while you sing, that hyperactivity will likely be transferred to the larynx and tongue—remember, they all are interconnected through the hyoid bone. It can be tricky to determine the primary offender in this kind of chain reaction of tension. A tight tongue could just as easily be making your jaw stiff, or an elevated, rigid larynx could make both tongue and jaw suffer.

Neurology complicates matters even further. You have sixteen muscles in your tongue, fourteen in your larynx, twenty-two in your throat and palate, and another sixteen that control your jaw. Many of these are very small and lie directly adjacent to each other, and you are often required to contract one quite strongly while its next-door neighbor must remain totally relaxed. Our brains need to develop laser-like control, sending signals at the right moment with the right intensity to the precise spot where they are needed. When we first start singing, these brain signals come more like a blast from a shotgun, spreading the neurologic impulse over a broad area to multiple muscles, not all of which are the intended target. Again, with practice and training, we learn to refine our control, enabling us to use only those muscles that will help, while disengaging those that would get in the way of our best singing.

FINAL THOUGHTS

This brief chapter has only scratched the surface of the huge field of voice science. To learn more, you might visit the websites of the National Association of Teachers of Singing (NATS), the Voice Foundation (TVF), or the National Center for Voice and Speech (NCVS). You can easily locate the appropriate addresses through any Internet search engine. Remember: knowledge is power. Occasionally, people are afraid that if they know more about the science of how they sing, they will become so analytical that all spontaneity will be lost or they will become paralyzed by too much information and thought. In my forty-plus years as a singer and teacher, I've never encountered somebody who actually suffered this fate. To the contrary, the more we know, the easier—and more joyful—singing becomes.

ANATOMY OF AN A CAPPELLA GROUP

Deke Sharon

Just as the human voice is made up of various components that work together to create sound, so is an a cappella group. There are different ways in which an a cappella group's composition can be described, each important to the effective functioning of the ensemble.

Musical Anatomy

Melody. At the heart of any piece of music is the melody, and when you have a group of people singing, that melody needs to be pre-dominant. It might be that the entire ensemble sings the melody, a la Gregorian Chant, or Take 6's stunning rendition of "The Star Spangled Banner," the first half of which is sung in gorgeous unison. ♪ More common in contemporary a cappella is either to have a lead vocal sung by a section, such as the "lead" (second tenor) in a barbershop chorus, or most common, to have the melody sung by a single individual, which allows for the greatest amount of fluidity and therefore emotional and artistic expression.

The challenge, of course, is to make sure the melody is not drowned out by the other voices. This can be achieved physically (by having that person stand in the center, in front of the other singers), electronically (by using amplification—a microphone—and making sure that voice *is* louder in the mix), by using arranging techniques such as call-and-response so that the background singers clear space for the lead vocal, and so on. When arranging, when rehearsing, and when directing and performing, one of the most important parameters is to ensure that the melody is performed powerfully—musically and emotionally—and clearly heard.

Bass. After the melody, the second most important part is the bass line. Be it a Bach chorale or a techno dance tune, we want to hear the bass loud and clear. The biggest reason for this is that the bass in an a cappella group usually sings the root of each chord, and the harmonics he (it's usually a he) casts provide the scaffolding upon which all other parts can securely tune. A quiet bass line results in unclear harmonic progressions and shaky tuning.

To follow the harmonic series, you generally want your bass singer to be separated from the other voices by at least an octave, unless singing moments of close harmony. This makes it easier for the upper voices to tune to the overtones, and reduces "mud." There are times when a low fifth can be pleasing, such as the imitation of a driving hard rock guitar line, but a low third is a recipe for disaster.

Note that in professional a cappella ensembles, and generally any group with amplification, your bass line wants to be sung by just one individual. That's because of the physics of sound—having a single fundamental to tune to—and unless you're specifically going for a large, wide choral sound, you want a clear, single low note anchoring each chord. This can be challenging to collegiate a cappella groups who often sing off- and on-mic live (requiring several bass singers off-mic to be heard but then ideally only one when amplified). The solution to this is to have only one bass on-mic when performing with a sound system and when you record. Having the other basses move up to higher parts is better than having them muddy the tuning.

Upper Harmonies.   Above your bass line and behind your melody you can have any number of vocal parts in a wide array of parallel harmonies, contrapuntal lines, imitative instrumental textures, and the like. The sky's the limit, so long as they don't swamp the melody or bass line, and align in tune. The human voice is the most versatile instrument (if you'll allow the term), with an incredibly wide array of possible sound that we're only now beginning to explore (as through human history we've had people sing the lyrics and simple textures, using instruments to explore other timbres), so don't be afraid of taking risks. Granted, there are synthesizers that can create a wider array of pitches with more varied timbres, but they don't have the power to make you laugh or cry within seconds. Advantage: human voice.

Note that the highest voice in your background parts will be heard over the other parts, all else being equal, as the human ear gravitates to the highest part. As such, make sure that part is crafted to have its own melodic shape and character (sorry, inner voices; that's why you get the more difficult and less melodic leaps and lines). Also remember that whereas it is possible for the human voice to do incredible things, it's still human: remember to allow for breathing, don't keep people outside of their comfort zone for too long, and keep lines interesting, for if your singers become bored their performance will lose emotional focus.

Percussion. As rhythm has grown in importance in popular music, so has the role of vocal percussion in a cappella. Whereas it is certainly not required or ubiquitous, it is common enough to be considered its own category at this point, with members of many groups considering themselves the designated vocal percussionist (or beatboxer).

A few thoughts: vocal percussion should weave into the bass line, the two forming a unified rhythm section. Although the percussion should be present, it should never overwhelm the bass pitch, particularly when presenting a low kick drum or lip-buzz (lest the group's tuning and over-all harmonic structure fall apart). More than one vocal percussionist is rarely needed, especially with today's incredibly impressive techniques that allow one person to sound like an entire drum kit/machine. And most importantly, rhythmic precision should be favored over timbre, as a consistent beat is more important than tones that sound 100 percent like drums. Remember that whereas not everyone can identify if a note is out of tune (especially since our Western tuning system is fundamentally compromised, thanks to the well-tempered scale), even young children can tell if a steady rhythm lapses (as we all are surrounded by constant beats, from our heart to the ticking of a clock).

Logistical Anatomy

For an a cappella group to function there needs to be leadership of various kinds in place. As much as a democratic process allows for all opinions to be heard and vetted, it's impossibly slow when trying to run a rehearsal or business meeting, or design a social media campaign. Moreover, different individuals in a group bring different experiences and skills that afford them insight into the best ways to make decisions big and small.

One possible option with all leadership positions is that the individual in charge has the final say, but that can be overruled if a majority of other group members disagree. Any decision from who should be singing a solo to if a group should take a certain gig can be reversed, a cumbersome last resort in most cases. This ideally is rarely enacted and serves more as a safety valve and peace-of-mind clause if group members are worried about being stuck in a dictatorship. Leaders often like this even more than group members, as it effectively quiets an insistent minority. In addition, the more leaders you have in a group handling different aspects of the group's logistics and functioning, the better they will be at following, as they realize the paralyzing frustration that comes when others micromanage their tasks.

The most common leadership positions in an a cappella group are as follows.

Music Director/Conductor. Unless you're the rarest of small ensembles in which you're able to all give creative input without needing someone in charge, your group will need a musical leader. Someone to ultimately choose repertoire, run rehearsals, decide on the songs in a particular set or concert, choose soloists, and the like. Some of these can be done by democratic vote but not all and not always. Having a singular person in charge of music will make rehearsals more effective, efficient, and focused.

In choirs and large groups that individual may need to physically conduct to keep everyone in time together, whereas in smaller ensembles and generally when performing popular music with a steady beat it's best to eliminate a conductor and have the group connect directly with the audience.

Business Manager. It's the rare professional a cappella group that has outside management that takes care of all the business decisions and dealings for a group. For everyone else, a designated business manager is the way to go. This person functions as manager, agent, and accountant all in one, overseeing performances, gear rental, travel logistics, and so on. I'm not suggesting that only one person ever looks at the group's financial records, as that would be foolish. You should always have multiple signers on any bank account and different group members check over the books from time to time.

For an amateur or casual a cappella group, having one person handle all these tasks makes the most sense, as there may be no more than one or two performances a month. In a busier group you may want to assign a team to work together, or divide up the tasks in a way that makes the most sense (one person handles transportation logistics, another books gigs, a third handles the money, and so on).

President. In scholastic groups, particularly student-run collegiate groups, a president can serve a vital function. He or she can act as the liaison with various university departments and student organizations, provide general leadership and run group meetings, support the music director and business manager, and if those are the only two leadership roles, provide an important third perspective so you don't have ties when the officers are making general group decisions. In addition to providing support in peer-run groups, larger choral-sized ensembles benefit from having a charismatic figurehead to speak to the media, welcome new members, address audiences during major performances, and so on.

A president's specific duties can be spelled out and assumed to cover any topics and issues that aren't specifically music or business. There may be times during a rehearsal or meeting when additional support is needed, such as quieting various members, or keeping the group on task, and a strong leader with a gentle manner can be invaluable. Finally, there may come times in your group when difficult issues arise, such as having to reprimand a member for inappropriate behavior or too many missed rehearsals. A president is just the person to handle this kind of situation.

In addition to the "big three," other positions can be created as needed, such as social media coordinator, videographer, tour manager, accountant, wardrobe/costumer, music librarian, historian, and so on. The size and focus of your group will determine what is needed. In most situations it's beneficial to have different roles covered by different people, particularly in casual, amateur, or volunteer groups, where expecting too much of just a couple of unpaid leaders can eventually lead to burnout.

Physical Anatomy

The number of members in an a cappella group determines its baseline stance onstage. In-ear monitors can allow for complicated choreography, but short of that all of the members of a group need to hear each other, which results in some standard positioning onstage.

Two to Ten Members. A single arc onstage makes for your best basic formation. Have the people at the ends of the arc almost face each other; then cheat slightly out toward the audience, so they can both face others in the group and face most of the house. When a soloist sings, have the person step into the middle of the arc and a bit beyond, like the dot in the middle of a fermata. Place your lowest bass singers in the center middle of the group, both so all can hear and so they're facing the audience and any soloists directly, maximizing their volume and presence. Other upper harmonies can be intermixed or positioned by section. Vocal percussionists either can be beside the bass section or more commonly are off on one side of the group, and any singing directors often stand on the other side, able to turn inward and conduct briefly if needed.

Eleven to Nineteen Members. With this number, you're best off with two lines, forming the same arc (bass in the middle of the back row, perhaps with a shorter member in the middle of the front row, and other parts interspersed, with the vocal percussionist [VP] on one side and the director on the other), with the caveat that the front row should have fewer members in it. For instance, a thirteen-member arc might have five in the front row and eight in the back, as opposed to six and seven, which allows the director to be seen more clearly and the vocal percussionist more room to rock out. Groups with even numbers will want to shift the front row to the side one way or the other, so the back row can be seen between members ("find your windows!").

Twenty-Plus Members. Although a sixteen-member ensemble is able to stand on risers, spread apart, once you reach around twenty members or so your group will need risers. The primary reason for this is so that all faces can be seen and voices can be heard, lest they be lost, muffled by the back of the head of the person in front of them. There are many chapters in choral books on how to best position a group on risers so I won't belabor the point here, other than to mention that soloists should step down and vocal percussionists should be given a handheld microphone (as well as any other "specialty" singers, whether singing a duet line, guitar solo, etc.). Area mics (which are different than handheld stage mics) are likely wanted to amplify the rest of the singers, as the mixture of amplified (soloist and percussion) and unamplified (various sections) is very difficult to consistently balance, is coming from different places (onstage acoustics as opposed to speakers), and has a different range of EQ (just as an acoustic and electric guitar sound different). In general, as soon as a group introduces choreography, area micing becomes insufficient, with handheld or headphone microphones the only way to accurately capture all of the voices. For an in-depth look at amplification, of both individual voices and a cappella groups as a whole, turn to chapters 9 and 10.

4

VOCAL HEALTH FOR THE A CAPPELLA SINGER

Wendy LeBorgne

GENERAL PHYSICAL WELL-BEING

All singers, regardless of genre, should consider themselves as "vocal athletes." The physical, emotional, and performance demands necessary for optimal output require that artists consider training and maintaining their instrument as an athlete trains for an event. With increased vocal and performance demands, it is unlikely that a vocal athlete will have an entire performing career completely injury-free. This may not be the fault of the singer, as many injuries occur due to circumstances beyond the singer's control such as singing through an illness or being on a new medication seemingly unrelated to the voice.

Vocal injury has often been considered taboo to talk about in the performing world as it has been considered to be the result of faulty technique or poor vocal habits. In actuality, the majority of vocal injuries presenting in the elite performing population tend to be overuse or acute injury. From a clinical perspective over the past seventeen years, younger, less experienced singers with fewer years of training (who tend to be quite talented) are generally the ones who present with issues related to technique or phonotrauma (nodules, edema, or contact ulcers), while more mature singers with professional performing careers tend to present with acute injuries (hemorrhage) or overuse and misuse injuries (muscle tension dysphonia, edema, or GERD) or injuries following an illness. There are no current studies documenting use and training in correlation to laryngeal pathologies. However, there are studies that document that somewhere between 35 percent and 100 percent of professional vocal athletes have abnormal vocal fold findings on stroboscopic evaluation. Many times these "abnormalities" are in singers who have no vocal complaints or symptoms of vocal problems. From a performance perspective, uniqueness in vocal quality often gets hired, and perhaps a slight aberration in the way a given larynx functions may become quite marketable. Regardless of what the vocal folds look like, the most integral part of performance is that singers must maintain agility, flexibility, stamina, power, and inherent beauty (genre appropriate) for their current level of performance taking into account physical, vocal, and emotional demands.

Unlike sports medicine and the exercise physiology literature where much is known about the types and nature of given sports injuries, there is no common parallel for the vocal athlete model. However, because the vocal athlete utilizes the body systems of alignment, respiration, phonation, and resonance with some similarities to physical athletes, a parallel protocol for vocal wellness may be implemented or considered for vocal athletes to maximize injury prevention knowledge for both the singer and teacher. This chapter aims to provide information on vocal wellness and injury prevention for the vocal athlete.

CONSIDERATIONS FOR WHOLE BODY WELLNESS

Nutrition

You have no doubt heard the saying "You are what you eat." Eating is a social and psychological event. For many people, food associations and eating have an emotional basis resulting in either overeating or being malnourished. Eating disorders in performers and body image issues can have major implications and consequences for the performer on both ends of the spectrum (obesity and anorexia). Singers should be encouraged to reprogram the brain and body to consider food as fuel. You want to use high-octane gas in your engine, as pouring water in your car's gas tank won't get you very far. Eating a poor diet or a diet that lacks appropriate nutritional value will have negative physical and vocal effects on the singer. Effects of poor dietary choices for the vocal athlete may result in physical and vocal effects ranging from fatigue to life-threatening disease over the course of a lifetime. Encouraging and engaging in healthy eating habits from a young age will potentially prevent long-term negative effects from poor nutritional choices. It is beyond the scope of this chapter to provide a complete overview of all the dietary guidelines for pediatrics, adolescents, adults, and the mature adult; however, a listing of additional references to help guide your food and beverage choices for making good nutritional choices can be found online at websites such as Dietary Guidelines for Americans, Nutrition.gov's Guidelines for Tweens and Teens, and Fruits and Veggies Matter. See the online companion web page on the National Association of Teachers of Singing (NATS) website for links to these and other resources.

Hydration

"Sing wet, pee pale." This phrase was echoed in the studio of Van Lawrence regarding how his students would know if they were well hydrated. Generally, this rule of pale urine during your waking hours is a good indicator that you are well hydrated. Medications, vitamins, and certain foods may alter urine color despite adequate hydration. Due to the varying levels of physical and vocal activity of many performers, in order to maintain adequate oral hydration, the use of a hydration calculator based on activity level may be a better choice. These hydration calculators are easily accessible online and take into account the amount and level of activity the performer engages in on a daily basis. In a recent study of the vocal habits of musical theater performers, one of the findings indicated a significantly underhydrated group of performers.[1]

Laryngeal and pharyngeal dryness as well as "thick, sticky, mucus" are often complaints of singers. Combating these concerns and maintaining an adequate viscosity of mucus for performance has resulted in some research. As a reminder of laryngeal and swallowing anatomy, nothing that is swallowed (or gargled) goes over or touches the vocal folds directly (or one would choke). Therefore, nothing that a singer eats or drinks ever touches the vocal folds, and in order to adequately hydrate the mucous membranes of the vocal folds, one must consume enough fluids for the body to produce a thin mucus. Therefore, any "vocal" effects from swallowed products are limited to potential pharyngeal and oral changes, not the vocal folds themselves.

The effects of systemic hydration are well documented in the literature. There is evidence to suggest that adequate hydration will provide some protection of the laryngeal mucosal membranes when they are placed under increased collision forces as well as reducing the amount of effort (phonation threshold pressure) to produce voice. This is important for the singer because it means that with adequate hydration and consistency of mucus, the effort to produce voice is less and your vocal folds are better protected from injury. Imagine the friction and heat produced when two dry hands rub together and then what happens if you put lotion on your hands. The mechanisms in the larynx to provide appropriate mucus production are not fully understood, but there is enough evidence at this time to support oral hydration as a vital component of every singer's vocal health regime to maintain appropriate mucosal viscosity.

Although very rare, overhydration (hyperhidrosis) can result in dehydration and even illness or death. An overindulgence of fluids essentially makes the kidneys work "overtime" and flushes too much water out of the body. This excessive fluid loss in a rapid manner can be detrimental to the body.

In addition to drinking water to systemically monitor hydration, there are many nonregulated products on the market for performers that lay claim to improving the laryngeal environment (e.g., Entertainer's Secret, Throat Coat Tea, Grether's Pastilles, slippery elm, etc.). Although there may be little detriment in using these products, quantitative research documenting change in laryngeal mucosa is sparse. One study suggests that the use of Throat Coat when compared to a placebo treatment for pharyngitis did show a significant difference in decreasing the perception of sore throat.[2] Another study compared the use of Entertainer's Secret to two other nebulized agents and its effect on phonation threshold pressure (PTP).[3] There was no positive benefit in decreasing PTP with Entertainer's Secret.

Many singers use personal steam inhalers or room humidification to supplement oral hydration and aid in combating laryngeal dryness.

There are several considerations for singers who choose to use external means of adding moisture to the air they breathe. Personal steam inhalers are portable and can often be used backstage or in the hotel room for the traveling performer. Typically, water is placed in the steamer and the face is placed over the steam for inhalation. Because the mucus membranes of the larynx are composed of a saltwater solution, one study looked at the use of nebulized saline in comparison to plain water and its potential effects on effort or ease to sound production in classically trained sopranos.[4] Data suggested that perceived effort to produce voice was less in the saline group than the plain water group. This indicated that the singers who used the saltwater solution reported less effort to sing after breathing in the saltwater than singers who used plain water. The researchers hypothesized that because the body's mucus is not plain water (rather it is a saltwater—think about your tears), when you use plain water for steam inhalation, it may actually draw the salt from your own saliva, resulting in a dehydrating effect.

In addition to personal steamers, other options for air humidification come in varying sizes of humidifiers from room size to whole house humidifiers. When choosing between a warm-mist and a cool-air humidifier, considerations include both personal preference and needs. One of the primary reasons warm-mist humidifiers are not recommended for young children is due to the risk of burns from the heating element. Both the warm-mist and cool-air humidifiers act similarly in adding moisture to the environmental air. External air humidification may be beneficial and provide a level of comfort for many singers. Regular cleaning of the humidifier is vital to prevent bacteria and mold buildup. Also, depending on the hardness of the water, it is important to avoid mineral buildup on the device and distilled water may be recommended for some humidifiers.

For traveling performers who often stay in hotels, fly on airplanes, or are generally exposed to other dry-air environments, there are products on the market designed to help minimize drying effects. One such device is called a Humidflyer, which is a face mask designed with a filter to recycle the moisture of a person's own breath and replenish moisture on each breath cycle.

For dry nasal passages or to clear sinuses, many singers use Neti pots, which provide a homeopathic flushing of the nasal passages regularly.

Research supports the use of a Neti pot as a part of allergy relief and chronic rhinosinusitis control when utilized properly, sometimes in combination with medical management.[5] Conversely, long-term use of nasal irrigation (without taking intermittent breaks from daily use) may result in washing out the "good" mucus of the nasal passages, which naturally helps to rid the nose of infections. A study presented at the 2009 American College of Allergy, Asthma, and Immunology (ACAAI) annual scientific meeting reported that when a group of individuals who were using twice-daily nasal irrigation for one year discontinued using it, they had an increase in acute rhinosinusitis.[6]

Tea, Honey, and Gargle to Keep the Throat Healthy

Regarding the use of general teas (which many singers combine with honey or lemon), there is likely no harm in the use of decaffeinated tea (caffeine may cause systemic dryness). The warmth of the tea may provide a soothing sensation to the pharynx and the act of swallowing can be relaxing for the muscles of the throat. Honey has shown promising results as an effective cough suppressant in the pediatric population.[7] The dose of honey given to the children in the study was two teaspoons. Gargling with salt or apple cider vinegar and water are also popular home remedies for many singers with the uses being from soothing the throat to curing reflux. Gargling plain water has been shown to be efficacious in reducing the risk of contracting upper-respiratory infections. I suggest that when gargling, the singer only "bubble" the water with air and avoid engaging the vocal folds in sound production. Saltwater as a gargle has long been touted as a sore-throat remedy and can be traced back to 2700 BCE in China for treating gum disease. The science behind a saltwater rinse for everything from oral hygiene to sore throat is that salt (sodium chloride) may act as a natural analgesic (painkiller) and may also kill bacteria. Similar to the effects that not enough salt in the water may have on drawing the salt out of the tissue in the steam inhalation, if you oversaturate the water solution with excess salt and gargle it, it may act to draw water out of the oral mucosa, thus reducing inflammation.

Another popular home remedy reported by singers is the use of apple cider vinegar to help with everything from acid reflux to sore throats. Dating back to 3300 BCE, apple cider vinegar was reported as a medicinal remedy, and it became popular in the 1970s as a weight loss diet cocktail. Popular media reports apple cider vinegar can improve conditions from acne and arthritis to nosebleeds and varicose veins. Specific efficacy data regarding the beneficial nature of apple cider vinegar for the purpose of sore throat, pharyngeal inflammation, and reflux has not been reported in the literature at this time. Of the peer-reviewed studies found in the literature, one discussed possible esophageal erosion and inconsistency of actual product in tablet form.[8] Therefore, at this time, strong evidence supporting the use of apple cider vinegar is not published.

Medications and the Voice

Medications (over the counter, prescription, and herbal) may have resultant drying effects on the body and often the laryngeal mucosa. General classes of drugs with potential drying effects include antidepressants, antihypertensives, diuretics, ADD/ADHD medications, some oral acne medications, hormones, allergy drugs, and vitamin C in high doses. The National Center for Voice and Speech (NCVS) provides a listing of some common medications with potential voice side effects including laryngeal dryness. This listing does not take into account all medications, so singers should always ask their pharmacist of the potential side effects of a given medication. Due to the significant number of drugs on the market, it is safe to say that most pharmacists will not be acutely aware of "vocal side effects," but if dryness is listed as a potential side effect of the drug, you may assume that all body systems could be affected. Under no circumstances should you stop taking a prescribed medication without consulting your physician first. As every person has a different body chemistry and reaction to medication, just because a medication lists dryness as a potential side effect does not necessarily mean you will experience that side effect. Conversely, if you begin a new medication and notice physical or vocal changes that are unexpected, you should consult with your physician. Ultimately, the goal of medical management for any condition is to achieve the most benefits with the least side effects. Please see the companion page on the NATS website for a list of possible resources for the singer regarding prescription drugs and herbs.

In contrast to medications that tend to dry, there are medications formulated to increase saliva production or alter the viscosity of mucus. Medically, these drugs are often used to treat patients who have had a loss of saliva production due to surgery or radiation. Mucolytic agents are used to thin secretions as needed. As a singer, if you feel you need to use a mucolytic agent on a consistent basis, it may be worth considering getting to the root of the laryngeal dryness symptom and seeking a professional opinion from an otolaryngologist.

Reflux and the Voice

Gastroesophageal reflux (GERD) and laryngopharyngeal reflux (LPR) can have a devastating impact on the singer if not recognized and treated appropriately. Although GERD and LPR are related, they are considered slightly different diseases. GERD (Latin root meaning "flowing back") is the reflux of digestive enzymes, acids, and other stomach contents into the esophagus (food pipe). If this backflow is propelled through the upper esophagus and into the throat (larynx and pharynx), it is referred to as LPR. It is not uncommon to have both GERD and LPR, but they can occur independently.

More frequently, people with GERD have decreased esophageal clearing. Esophagitis, or inflammation of the esophagus, is also associated with GERD. People with GERD often feel heartburn. LPR symptoms are often "silent" and do not include heartburn. Specific symptoms of LPR may include some or all of the following: lump in the throat sensation, feeling of constant need to clear the throat/postnasal drip, longer vocal warm-up time, quicker vocal fatigue, loss of high frequency range, worse voice in the morning, sore throat, and bitter/raw/brackish taste in the mouth. If you experience these symptoms on a regular basis, it is advised that you consider a medical consultation for your symptoms. Prolonged, untreated GERD or LPR can lead to permanent changes in both the esophagus and the larynx. Untreated LPR also provides a laryngeal environment that is conducive for vocal fold lesions to occur as it inhibits normal healing mechanisms.

Treatments of LPR and GERD generally include both dietary and lifestyle modifications in addition to medical management. Some of the dietary recommendations include elimination of caffeinated and carbonated beverages, smoking cessation, no alcohol use, and limiting tomatoes, acidic foods and drinks, and raw onions or peppers, to name a few. Also, avoidance of high-fat foods is recommended. From a lifestyle perspective, suggested changes include not eating within three hours of lying down, eating small meals frequently (instead of large meals), elevating the head of your bed, avoiding tight clothing around the belly, and not bending over or exercising too soon after you eat.

Reflux medications fall in three general categories: antacids, H2 blockers, and proton pump inhibitors (PPI). There are now combination drugs that include both an H2 blocker and a proton pump inhibitor. Every medication has both associated risks and benefits, and singers should be aware of the possible benefits and side effects of the medications they take. In general terms, antacids (e.g., Tums, Mylanta, or Gaviscon) neutralize stomach acid. H2 (histamine) blockers, such as Axid (nizatidine),Tagamet (cimetidine), Pepcid (famotidine), and Zantac (ranitidine), work to decrease acid production in the stomach by preventing histamine from triggering the H2 receptors to produce more acid. Then there are the PPIs: Nexium (esomeprazole), Prevacid (lansoprazole), Protonix (pantoprazole), AcipHex (rabeprazole), Prilosec (omeprazole), and Dexilant (dexlansoprazole). PPIs act as a last line of defense to decrease acid production by blocking the last step in gastric juice secretion. Some of the most recent drugs to combat GERD/LPR are combination drugs (e.g., Zegrid [sodium bicarbonate plus omeprazole]), which provide a short-acting response (sodium bicarbonate) and a long release (omeprazole). Because some singers prefer a holistic approach to reflux management, strict dietary and lifestyle compliance is recommended and consultation with both your primary-care physician and naturopath are warranted in that situation. Efficacy data on nonregulated herbs, vitamins, and supplements is limited, but some data does exist.

Physical Exercise

Vocal athletes, like other physical athletes, should consider how and what they do to maintain both cardiovascular fitness and muscular strength. In today's performance culture, it is rare that a performer stands still and sings, unless in a recital or choral setting. The range of physical activity can vary from light movement to high-intensity chore- ography with acrobatics. As performers are being required to increase their onstage physical activity level from the operatic stage to the pop- star arena, overall physical fitness is imperative to avoid compromise in the vocal system. Breathlessness will result in compensation by the larynx, which is now attempting to regulate the air. Compensatory vocal behaviors over time may result in a change in vocal performance. The health benefits of both cardiovascular training and strength training are well documented for physical athletes but relatively rare in the literature for vocal performers.

Mental Wellness

Vocal performers must maintain a mental focus during performance and a mental toughness during auditioning and training. Rarely during vocal performance training programs is this important aspect of perfor- mance addressed, and it is often left to individual performers to develop their own strategy or coping mechanism. Yet, many performers are on antianxiety or antidepressant drugs (which may be the direct result of performance-related issues). If the sports world is again used as a parallel for mental toughness, there are no elite-level athletes (and few junior-level athletes) who don't utilize the services of a performance/ sports psychologist to maximize focus and performance. I recommend that performers consider the potential benefits of a performance psy- chologist to help maximize vocal performance. Several references that may be of interest to the singer include Joanna Cazden's *Visualization for Singers* (1992) and Shirlee Emmons and Alma Thomas's *Power Per- formance for Singers: Transcending the Barriers* (1998).

Unlike instrumentalists, whose performance is dependent on accu- rate playing of an external musical instrument, the singer's instrument is uniquely intact and subject to the emotional confines of the brain and body in which it is housed. Musical performance anxiety (MPA) can be career threatening for all musicians, but perhaps the vocal athlete is more severely impacted. The majority of literature on MPA is dedicated to instrumentalists, but the basis of definition, performance effects, and treatment options can be considered for vocal athletes. Fear is a natural reaction to a stressful situation, and there is a fine line between emotional excitation and perceived threat (real or imagined). The job of a performer is to convey to an audience through vocal production, physical gestures, and facial expression a most heightened state of emotion. Otherwise, why would audience members pay top dollar to sit for two or three hours for a mundane experience? There is not only the emotional conveyance of the performance but also the internal turmoil often experienced by the singers themselves in preparation for elite performance. It is well documented in the literature that even the most elite performers have experienced debilitating performance anxiety. MPA is defined on a continuum with anxiety levels ranging from low to high and has been reported to comprise four distinct components: affect, cognition, behavior, and physiology. Affect comprises feelings (e.g., doom, panic, and anxiety). Affected cognition will result in altered levels of concentration, while the behavior component results in postural shifts, quivering, and trembling. Finally physiologically the body's autonomic nervous system (ANS) will activate, resulting in the "fight-or-flight" response.

In recent years, researchers have been able to define two distinct neurological pathways for MPA. The first pathway happens quickly and without conscious input (ANS), resulting in the same fear stimulus as if a person were put into an emergent, life-threatening situation. In those situations, the brain releases adrenaline, resulting in physical changes of increased heart rate, increased respiration, shaking, pale skin, dilated pupils, slowed digestion, bladder relaxation, dry mouth, and dry eyes, all of which severely affect vocal performance. The second pathway that has been identified results in a conscious identification of the fear/threat and a much slower physiologic response. With the second neuromotor response, the performer has a chance to recognize the fear, process how to deal with the fear, and respond accordingly.

Treatment modalities to address MPA include psycho-behavioral therapy (including biofeedback) and drug therapies. Elite physical performance athletes have been shown to benefit from visualization techniques and psychological readiness training, yet within the performing arts community, stage fright may be considered a weakness or character flaw precluding readiness for professional performance. On the contrary, vocal athletes, like physical athletes, should mentally prepare themselves for optimal competition (auditions) and performance. Learning to convey emotion without eliciting an internal emotional response by the vocal athlete may take the skill of an experienced psychologist to help change ingrained neural pathways. Ultimately, control and understanding of MPA will enhance performance and prepare the vocal athlete for the most intense performance demands without vocal compromise.

VOCAL WELLNESS: INJURY PREVENTION

In order to prevent vocal injury and understand vocal wellness in the singer, general knowledge of common causes of voice disorders is imperative. One common cause of voice disorders is vocally abusive behaviors or misuse of the voice to include phonotraumatic behaviors such as yelling, screaming, loud talking, talking over noise, throat clearing, coughing, harsh sneezing, and boisterous laughing. Chronic or less-than-optimal vocal properties such as poor breathing techniques, inappropriate phonatory habits during conversational speech (glottal fry or hard glottal attacks), inapt pitch, loudness, rate of speech, and hyperfunctional laryngeal-area muscle tone may also negatively impact vocal function. Medically related etiologies, which also have the potential to impact vocal function, range from untreated chronic allergies and sinusitis to endocrine dysfunction and hormonal imbalance. Direct trauma, such as a blow to the neck or the risk of vocal fold damage during intubation, can impact optimal performance in vocal athletes depending on the nature and extent of the trauma. Finally, external irritants ranging from cigarette smoke to reflux directly impact the laryngeal mucosa and can ultimately lead to laryngeal pathology.

Vocal hygiene education and compliance may be one of the primary essential components for maintaining the voice throughout a career. This section will provide the singer with information on prevention of vocal injury. However, just like a professional sports athlete, it is unlikely that a professional vocal athlete will go through an entire career without some compromise in vocal function. This may be a common upper-respiratory infection that creates vocal fold swelling for a short time, or it may be a "vocal accident" that is career threatening. Regardless, the knowledge of how to take care of your voice is essential for any vocal athlete.

Train Like an Athlete for Vocal Longevity

Performers seek instant gratification in performance sometimes at the cost of gradual vocal building for a lifetime of healthy singing. Historically, voice pedagogues required their students to perform vocalises exclusively for up to two years before beginning any song literature. Singers gradually built their voices by ingraining appropriate muscle memory and neuromotor patterns through development of aesthetically pleasing tones, onsets, breath management, and support. There was an intensive master-apprentice relationship and rigorous vocal guidelines to maintain a place within a given studio. Time off was taken if a vocal injury ensued or careers were potentially ended, and students were asked to leave a given singing studio if their voices were unable to withstand the rigors of training. Training vocal athletes today has evolved and appears driven to create a "product" quickly, perhaps at the expense of the longevity of the singer. Pop stars emerging well before puberty are doing international concert tours, yet many young artist programs in the classical arena do not consider singers for their programs until they are in their mid- to late twenties.

Each vocal genre presents with different standards and vocal demands. Therefore, the amount and degree of vocal training are varied. Some would argue that performing extensively without adequate vocal training and development is ill advised, yet singers today are thrust onto the stage at very young ages. Dancers, instrumentalists, and physical athletes all spend many hours per day developing muscle strength, memory, and proper technique for their craft. The more advanced the artist or athlete, generally the more specific the training protocol becomes. Consideration of training vocal athletes in this same fashion is recommended. One would generally not begin a young, inexperienced singer on a Wagner aria without previous vocal training. Similarly, in nonclassical vocal music, there are easy, moderate, and difficult pieces to consider pending level of vocal development and training.

Basic pedagogical training of alignment, breathing, voice production, and resonance are essential building blocks for development of good voice production. Muscle memory and development of appropriate muscle patterns happen slowly over time with appropriate repetitive practice. Doing too much, too soon for any athlete (physical or vocal) will result in an increased risk for injury. When singers are being asked to do "vocal gymnastics," they must be sure to have a solid basis of strength and stamina in the appropriate muscle groups to perform consistently with minimal risk of injury.

Vocal Fitness Program

One generally does not get out of bed first thing in the morning and try to do a split. Yet many singers go directly into a practice session or audition without a proper warm-up. Think of your larynx as your knee, made up of cartilages, ligaments, and muscles. Vocal health is dependent upon appropriate warm-ups (to get things moving), drills for technique, and then cool-downs (at the end of your day). Consider vocal warm-ups a "gentle stretch." Depending on the needs of the singer, warm-ups should include physical stretching; postural alignment self-checks; breathing exercises to promote rib cage, abdominal, and back expansion; vocal stretches (glides up to stretch the vocal folds and glides down to contract the vocal folds); articulatory stretches (yawning and facial stretches); and mental warm-ups (to provide focus for the task at hand). Vocalises, in my opinion, are designed as exercises to go beyond warm-ups and prepare the body and voice for the technical and vocal challenges of the music they sing. They are varied and address the technical level and genre of the singer to maximize performance and vocal growth. Cool-downs are a part of most athletes' workouts. However, singers often do not use cool-downs (physical, mental, and vocal) at the end of a performance. A recent study looked specifically at the benefits of vocal cool-downs in singers and found that singers who used a vocal cool-down had decreased effort to produce voice the next day.[9]

Systemic hydration as a means to keep the vocal folds adequately lubricated for the amount of impact and friction that they will undergo has been previously discussed in this chapter. Compliance with adequate oral hydration recommendations is important and subsequently so is the minimization of agents that could potentially dry the membranes (e.g., caffeine, medications, and dry air). The body produces approximately two quarts of mucus per day. If not adequately hydrated, the mucus tends to be thick and sticky. Poor hydration is similar to not putting enough oil in the car engine. Frankly, if the gears do not work as well, there is increased friction and heat, and the engine is not efficient.

Speak Well, Sing Well

Optimize the speaking voice utilizing ideal frequency range, breath, intensity, rate, and resonance. Singers are generally vocally enthusiastic individuals who talk a lot and often talk loudly. During typical conversation, the average fundamental speaking frequency (times per second the vocal folds are impacting) for a male varies from 100 to 150 Hz and 180 to 230 Hz for women. Because of the delicate structure of the vocal folds and the importance of the layered microstructure vibrating efficiently and effectively to produce voice, vocal behaviors or outside factors that compromise the integrity of the vibration patterns of the vocal folds may be considered phonotrauma.

Phonotraumatic behaviors can include yelling, screaming, loud talking, harsh sneezing, and harsh laughing. Elimination of phonotraumatic behaviors is essential for good vocal health. The louder one speaks, the farther apart the vocal folds move from midline, the harder they impact, and the longer they stay closed. A tangible example would be to take your hands, move them only six inches apart, and clap as hard and as loudly as you can for ten seconds. Now, move your hands two feet apart and clap as hard, loudly, and quickly as possible for ten seconds. The farther apart your hands are, the more air you move and the louder the clap, and the skin on the hands becomes red and ultimately swollen (if you do it long and hard enough). This is what happens to the vocal folds with repeated impact at increased vocal intensities. The vocal folds are approximately 17 mm in length and vibrate at 220 times per second on A3, 440 on A4, 880 on A5, and more than 1,000 per second when singing a high C. That is a lot of impact for little muscles. Consider this fact when singing loudly or in a high tessitura for prolonged periods of time. It becomes easy to see why women are more prone than men to laryngeal impact injuries due to the frequency range of the voice alone.

In addition to the amount of cycles per second (cps) the vocal folds are impacting, singers need to be aware of their vocal intensity (volume). One should be aware of the volume of the speaking and singing voice and consider using a distance of three to five feet (about an arms-length distance) as a gauge for how loud to be in general conversation. Using cell phones and speaking on a Bluetooth device in a car generally results in greater vocal intensity than normal, and singers are advised to minimize unnecessary use of these devices.

Singers should be encouraged to take "vocal naps" during their day. A vocal nap would be a short period of time (five minutes to an hour) of complete silence. Although the vocal folds are rarely completely still (because they move when you swallow and breathe), a vocal nap minimizes impact and vibration for a short window of time. A physical nap can also be refreshing for the singer mentally and physically.

Avoid Environmental Irritants: Alcohol, Smoking, Drugs

Arming singers with information on the actual effects of environmental irritants so they can make informed choices on engaging in exposure to these potential toxins is essential. The glamour that continues to be associated with smoking, drinking, and drugs can be tempered with the deaths of popular stars such as Amy Winehouse and Cory Monteith who engaged in life-ending choices. There is extensive documentation about the long-term effects of toxic and carcinogenic substances, but here are a few key facts to consider when choosing whether to partake.

Alcohol, although it does not go over the vocal folds directly, does have a systemic drying effect. Due to the acidity in alcohol, it may increase the likelihood of reflux, resulting in hoarseness and other laryngeal pathologies. Consuming alcohol generally decreases one's inhibitions, and therefore you are more likely to sing and do things you would not typically do under the influence of alcohol.

Beyond the carcinogens in nicotine and tobacco, the heat at which a cigarette burns is well above the boiling temperature of water (water boils at 212 °F; cigarettes burn at over 1400 °F). No one would consider pouring a pot of boiling water on their hand, and yet the burning temperature for a cigarette results in significant heat over the oral mucosa and vocal folds. The heat alone can create a deterioration in the lining, resulting in polypoid degeneration. Obviously, cigarette smoking has been well documented as a cause for laryngeal cancer.

Marijuana and street drugs can cause permanent mucosal lining changes depending on the drug used and the method of delivery. If you or one of your singer colleagues is experiencing a drug or alcohol problem, research or provide information and support on getting appropriate counseling and help.

SMART PRACTICE STRATEGIES FOR SKILL DEVELOPMENT AND VOICE CONSERVATION

Daily practice and drills for skill acquisition are an important part of any singer's training. However, overpracticing or inefficient practicing may be detrimental to the voice. Consider practice sessions of athletes: they may practice four to eight hours per day broken into one- to two-hour training sessions with a period of rest and recovery in between sessions. Although we cannot parallel the sports model without adequate evidence in the vocal athlete, the premise of short, intense, focused practice sessions is logical for the singer. Similar to physical exercise, it is suggested that practice sessions do not have to be all "singing." Rather, structuring sessions so that one-third of the session is spent on warm-up; one-third on vocalises, text work, rhythms, character development, and so on; and one-third on repertoire will allow the singer to function in a more efficient vocal manner. Building the amount of time per practice session—increasing duration by five minutes per week and building to sixty to ninety minutes—may be effective (e.g., week 1: twenty minutes three times per day; week 2: twenty-five minutes three times per day, etc.).

Vary the "vocal workout" during your week. For example, if you do the same physical exercise in the same way day after day with the same intensity and pattern, you will likely experience repetitive strain–type injuries. However, cross-training or varying the type and level of exercise aids in injury prevention. So when planning your practice sessions for a given week (or rehearsal process for a given role), consider varying your vocal intensity, tessitura, and exercises to maximize your training sessions, building stamina, muscle memory, and skill acquisition. For example, one day you may spend more time on learning rhythms and translation and the next day you spend thirty minutes performing coloratura exercises to prepare for a specific role. Take one day a week off from vocal training, and give your voice a break. This does not mean complete vocal rest (although some singers find this beneficial) but rather a day without singing and limited talking.

Practice Your Mental Focus

Mental wellness and stress management are equally as important as vocal training for vocal athletes. Addressing any mental health issues is paramount to developing the vocal artist. This may include anything from daily mental exercises/meditation/focus to overcoming performance anxiety and more serious mental health issues and illness. Every person can benefit from improved focus and mental acuity.

VOCAL WELLNESS TIPS FOR A CAPPELLA SINGERS

General vocal wellness guidelines for all singers hold true for the a cappella singer. Because a cappella singing encompasses many styles—from barbershop to commercial a cappella (where artists' voices imitate instruments) and a cappella Broadway musicals—there is limited information on the vocal health and wellness specifically of a cappella singers. A study on the vocal health of collegiate level a cappella singers indicated that 36 percent of the population sampled reported a past or present vocal problem.[10] This number of reported vocal problems is consistent with other reported singing populations (such as classical and music theater). However, any vocal problem within this group presents a possible concern for a cappella artists as participants may or may not have formal vocal training. Within the commercial style of a cappella, singers must often learn to provide vocal percussion (which results in high vocal-fold collision forces), imitation of instruments (requiring the ability to manipulate human resonators to mimic the timbre and frequency range of musical instruments), and maximal vocal instrument flexibility. Due to the lack of a specific pedagogy for a cappella vocal training, much of the information on vocal wellness is implied from information on similar singing styles.

For the a cappella vocalist, the most common presentation in my voice clinic relates to vocal fatigue, acute vocal injury, and loss of high frequency range. Vocal fatigue complaints are generally related to the duration of their rehearsals, concert tours, and the vocal requirements to traverse their entire range (and occasionally outside of physiological comfort range). Specifically, many a cappella singers will sing for four to six hours at a time (either in rehearsal or performance) several times per week. This is considered a high vocal load with the associated risk of repetitive strain and collision force injuries. Acute vocal injuries within this population (as reported by a single voice clinic) include phonotraumatic lesions (hemorrhages, vocal fold polyps, vocal fold nodules, and general vocal fold edema/erythema). Direct correlation between a cappella singing and phonotraumatic lesions cannot be assumed. However, it is suspected that these types of injuries are generally consistent with high vocal load and high vocal demands combined. A cappella singers are likely consistent with their classical and music theater counterparts in terms of injury. Often these are injuries not related to problematic vocal technique but rather due to "vocal accidents."

Similar to contemporary pop singers, a cappella singers are required to connect with the audience from a vocal and emotional standpoint through their voices alone (no instruments). They also have to be able to vocally blend with the other members of their ensemble for a cohesive execution of the vocal performance. This genre is unique in that the voice is the only instrument, and therefore, both physical and vocal fitness should be foremost in the minds of anyone desiring to perform a cappella music today. These singers should be physically and vocally in shape to meet the necessary performance demands.

Performance of a cappella music requires that the singer has a flexible, agile, dynamic instrument with appropriate stamina. The singers must have a good command of their instrument as well as exceptional underlying intention to what they are singing as it is about relaying a message, having a characteristic sound, and connecting with the audience. The voices that convey a cappella music—regardless of the a cappella genre—must reflect the mood and intent of the composer requiring dynamic control, vocal control/power, and an emotional connection to the text.

Similar to other commercial music vocalists, a cappella singers use microphones and personal amplification to their maximal capacity (especially if imitating instruments using voice alone). If used correctly, amplification can be used to maximize vocal health by allowing the singer to produce voice in an efficient manner while the sound engineer is effectively able to mix, amplify, and add effects to the voice. Understanding both the utility and limits of a given microphone and sound system is essential for the singer for both live and studio performances. Using an appropriate microphone can not only enhance the singer's performance but also reduce vocal load. Emotional extremes (intimacy and exultation) can be enhanced by appropriate microphone choice, placement, and acoustical mixing, thus saving the singer's voice.

Not everything a singer does is "vocally healthy," sometimes because the emotional expression may be so intense it results in vocal collision forces that are extreme. Even if the singer does not have formal vocal training, the concept of "vocal cross-training" (which can mean singing in both high and low registers with varying intensities and resonance options) before and after practice sessions and services is likely a vital component to minimizing vocal injury.

FINAL THOUGHTS

Ultimately, the singer must learn to provide the most output with the least "cost" to the system. Taking care of the physical instrument through daily physical exercise, adequate nutrition and hydration, and focused attention on performance will provide a necessary basis for vocal health during performance. Small doses of high-intensity singing (or speaking) will limit impact stress on the vocal folds. Finally, attention to the mind, body, and voice will provide the singer with an awareness when something is wrong. This awareness and knowledge of when to rest or seek help will promote vocal well-being for the singer throughout his or her career.

A CAPPELLA GROUP HEALTH

Deke Sharon

To build on what has been said above, colds can ravage an ensemble, so as a precaution, water bottles shouldn't be shared, sick members should stay home from rehearsal, hands should be washed often, people should cough into their bent arms (behind their elbows), and all of the other recommendations that come from the CDC and other health organizations should be implemented.

However, when speaking about the health of an a cappella group, I'm not referring to viruses and the like. Rather, I'm referring to the relationships between the various members as well as the general character of the group. Why does this matter? As I explain in my book *The Heart of Vocal Harmony*, music without emotion is simply organized sound, and people are not able to be emotionally available and vulnerable onstage if they feel judged by their fellow singers or director. A group needs to be a place where people can share honest feelings, discuss difficult topics, and breathe life into a piece of music. When one sings a song alone no discussion is needed, but when many sing, they need to be on the same page, and open with each other. No safety means no openness, which means significantly diminished emotion.

The expression "harmony through harmony" can have multiple meanings (see chapter 18), but in this case it's meant to mean that one can't create musical harmony without having interpersonal harmony between a group's members. Why does this matter? If a director can't honestly critique members, a group won't be as technically good. If members won't look at each other while singing, they can't accurately match vowels, watch cutoffs, or reinforce each other's emotions. Extracurricular connection, outside of rehearsal, is also very beneficial as it knits together a group socially, which makes for greater cohesion, more openness, and so forth. People who aren't getting along won't opt to spend time together outside rehearsal, and less bonding ultimately means less effective harmony.

So, how can a group improve its relationships?

First, know that knowledge is power. Getting to know the other members of a group outside rehearsal, spending time bonding and enjoying each other's company, is always a good idea. Weekly or monthly dinners together or other regular social activities can bring together a group in ways that just can't happen in rehearsal. Weekend retreats are not just for rehearsing; the extra hours together between rehearsals are sometimes even more transformational.

Once people know each other casually, especially in small groups, greater insight can be found through various measures such as the Myers-Briggs Type Indicator (MBTI), which is used by many companies to create greater insight between teams. There are no right or wrong answers, but rather it's an opportunity to get a better understanding of one's own proclivities, as well as how those interface and interlace with others'. Some aspects might be obvious, such as how extroverts should not do all the talking, allowing for more introverted members' opinions to be aired, but others are subtle and very insightful.

It's important to deal with issues before they become problems and speak directly to people if there is conflict, rather than allow the group to become a maelstrom of people talking about others. Active listening is a very effective tool when the topic or situation becomes heated or loaded. Often used in times of conflict as well as marriage counseling, the process involves taking measured turns speaking, repeating back what is heard, and making it clear it has been understood. What sounds frustratingly slow when described is in action a transformational process that can help people move past impasses and learn how to better communicate difficult topics.

Speaking of marriage, many collegiate a cappella groups have as a part of their bylaws a "once a rock, always a rock" clause, stating that any member who is "sung in" to a group is always a member. Members never need to reaudition if they end up taking time away from the group, and they will be welcomed back as an alum for the rest of their lives. This element of eternal brotherhood/sisterhood may seem extreme or unnecessary, but like a marriage it creates a dynamic within which everyone knows they belong, and members need to work out their differences.

Having clear, agreed-upon goals is a great way to diminish problems down the road, be it agreeing on how often to rehearse or which songs to sing. It's not necessary to have every detail worked out, but it's good to have a general sense of what each member is hoping to get out of the group, and perhaps a contract with a specific amount of time so you don't need to worry about a revolving door or an unreasonable set of goals within varying timelines.

It used to be the case that businesses expected their workers to do everything well, and more recently they've learned that specialization is the most effective method of maximizing everyone's potential. Don't put someone who isn't good with details in charge of scheduling, and so forth. The diversity within every a cappella group is essential to its for-mat—you need low voices and high, creative and logical minds—and it's best if you as a group assign tasks to everyone based on each member's proclivities and strengths, and accept that everyone has shortcomings.

Finally, it's very important to celebrate successes. It is the very na-ture of music rehearsal in general that when you have 50 percent of the music learned you focus on the half you don't know, and then when you have 70, 80, 95 percent learned, you still focus on all the errors. The result can feel at times as if nothing is going well, or that people are fail-ing when in fact they're already in "A" range. Concerts are great ways to get positive feedback from audiences, and parties or other celebrations when the time is right is a good way to make sure people are aware of everything that's going right.

NOTES

1. W. LeBorgne et al., "Prevalence of Vocal Pathology in Incoming Fresh-man Musical Theatre Majors: A 10-Year Retrospective Study," Fall Voice Con-ference, New York, 2012.

2. J. Brinckmann et al., "Safety and Efficacy of a Traditional Herbal Medi-cine (Throat Coat) in Symptomatic Temporary Relief of Pain in Patients with Acute Pharyngitis: A Multicenter, Prospective, Randomized, Double-Blinded, Placebo-Controlled Study," *Journal of Alternative and Complementary Medi-cine* 9, no. 2 (2003): 285–98.

3. N. Roy et al., "An Evaluation of the Effects of Three Laryngeal Lubri-cants on Phonation Threshold Pressure (PTP)," *Journal of Voice* 17, no. 3 (2003): 331–42.

4. K. Tanner et al., "Nebulized Isotonic Saline versus Water following a Laryngeal Desiccation Challenge in Classically Trained Sopranos," *Journal of Speech Language and Hearing Research* 53, no. 6 (2010): 1555–66.

5. C. Brown and S. Graham, "Nasal Irrigations: Good or Bad?" *Current Opinion in Otolaryngology, Head and Neck Surgery* 12, no. 1 (2004): 9–13.

6. T. Nsouli, "Long-Term Use of Nasal Saline Irrigation: Harmful or Helpful?" American College of Allergy, Asthma and Immunology Annual Scientific Meeting, Abstract 32, 2009.

7. M. Shadkam et al., "A Comparison of the Effect of Honey, Dextromethorphan, and Diphenhydramine on Nightly Cough and Sleep Quality in Children and Their Parents," *Journal of Alternative and Complementary Medicine* 16, no. 7 (2010): 787–93.

8. L. Hill et al., "Esophageal Injury by Apple Cider Vinegar Tablets and Subsequent Evaluation of Products," *Journal of the American Dietetic Association* 105, no. 7 (2005): 1141–44.

9. R. O. Gottliebson, "The Efficacy of Cool-Down Exercises in the Practice Regimen of Elite Singers" (PhD diss., University of Cincinnati, 2011).

10. C. R. Watts, "The Prevalence of Voice Problems in a Sample of Collegiate A Cappella Singers," *Journal of Speech Pathology and Therapy* 1 (2016): 105.

HOW

Contemporary A Cappella's Extended
Vocal Techniques and Practices

❺

VOCAL TECHNIQUES AND VOCAL INSTRUMENTS

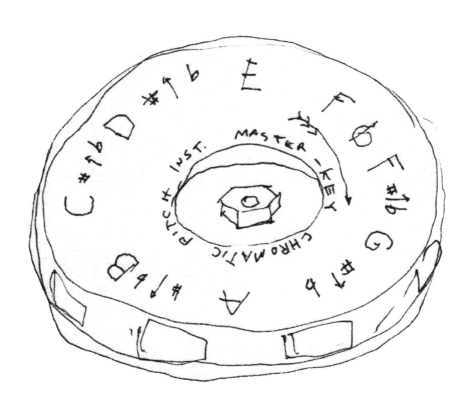

Perhaps the biggest question in your mind when purchasing this book was, What are the technical elements of a cappella singing that differ from singing other styles of music? It's a question often raised, particularly by educators who want to make sure they're preparing their students properly and approaching music with the correct technique.

First, it is important to note that most of music history has included a cappella, and very little of that history included a formal pedagogy, scholastic training, and the like. When cavemen sang around the campfire, sailors raised their voices in sea shanties, workers sang in fields or chain gangs, and they did so without a conductor, a book, or a degree. Perhaps you find this frustrating, but the fact is that pretty much all music throughout music history was created without rules; then later educators looked for common threads that could be applied to the formal teaching of the subject. This is a valuable process but only if you realize that music theory is only a theory and was formalized after the fact, and so on. If you struggle because you want to be right, if you stumble because the path forward is not always clear, know that you're making music exactly the way humans have since prehistoric times, and the best way forward is usually your instinct, honed by years of singing, listening, and creating.

Secondly, a cappella isn't a style; it's an instrumentation, for lack of a better word. (Elsewhere in the book, for ease of reading, the phrase "contemporary a cappella style" has been used with some consternation on my part. Know that it is meant as "a set of practices" rather than a specific musical style.) A cappella is or can be every style, and just as each style has its own best practices, so should you be approaching each song based on that individual style. To date, this book series (So You Want to Sing . . .) has volumes on a variety of styles, including rock and roll, jazz, music theater, country, gospel, sacred music, and folk music. Upcoming editions include light opera, blues, early music, chamber music, and barbershop. Each gives an in-depth look at the nature of vocal technique through the individual style, and I highly recommend you pick up a copy of any styles in which you anticipate your group will be performing.

It's also important to know that there are no rules when it comes to using your voice, other than not causing permanent damage. The human voice is the most versatile "instrument" in the world (no synthesizer can make you laugh or cry within seconds), and yet the incredible range of timbres and tones has only begun to be explored. We are akin to parrots that can mimic sounds they hear in their environment. We too can mimic instruments (more on this below) as well as other voices (the best celebrity impersonators make a living doing just this), but what of the myriad sounds that are mimicry? There are an infinite range of possible sounds and combinations of textures that lay before us, waiting to be explored.

That said, there are some techniques that are universal to most a cappella groups and styles, a result of the nature of people singing together:

- Reduce vibrato to end of long-held notes: most vibrato is the result of rapidly varying pitch and does not provide a firm foundation upon which to tune chords. Lead vocals can have vibrato, but background parts should be sung cleanly. Exceptions exist, such as in traditional choral and gospel settings.
- Avoid having singers slide to pitches on background parts, and when they do, make sure everyone slides as a unit: singers often slide to notes when singing without realizing it, because they're phrasing their part as if it were the melody. This is okay when they're alone and no other person is on their part or in parallel harmony, but if there is, make sure any sliding happens as a unit, as if all altos are the same guitarist's bent string, or a backing trio is one pedal steel player's sliding chord.
- Sing group melodies as solo lines: sheet music is imprecise, especially when it comes to notating popular music. When a group of singers read the notes off the page, there is a wealth of nuanced information that is lost, resulting in a wooden, blocky-sounding line. When this happens, have a single person sing a part with some personality (yes, sliding between notes is okay, pushing and pulling rhythms, adding flips, etc.), and then have all of the other people on the same part mimic that exact same phrasing.
- Use dynamics to mix various parts/layers: choral music is usually designed to balance the (primarily four) vocal parts such that all can be heard more or less equally. Contemporary a cappella, on the other hand, treats voices as instruments, and as such there can be many layers of sound all of which should be balanced based on

what sounds best as opposed to where it lands in a singer's voice (higher pitches tend to be louder; lower, quieter, etc.). Imagine a sound engineer at a sound board balancing levels; treat your various singers and sections the same way in rehearsal so that the end result sounds good without amplification.

- Embrace extended vocal techniques: forget much of what you've learned about the "proper" vocal ranges or standard voice parts. When singing contemporary a cappella you may find baritones above your tenors (lower voices generally have stronger and higher falsettos due to their thicker vocal chords), altos singing a part that's primarily rhythmic without pitch, sopranos each slowly morphing between vowel sounds (to cast a variety of harmonics, creating a flanged synthesizer effect), and so on. There's no right or wrong, so long as no one's voice hurts or is being damaged through overly high or loud singing (if you suspect harm, visit an ENT or vocal specialist).
- Use your singers where they sound best: no longer are most a cappella groups divided into four part SATB/SSAA/TTBB groupings, as a wise director will assign voices where they fit best based on tone color, vocal range, rhythmic acuity, blend, and so on.
- Make arrangements your own: just as a custom tailored suit will fit most people far better than a suit off the rack, so does a custom tailored arrangement fit a specific group's voices. Change form, chords, syllables, dynamics . . . anything. I have arranged over two thousand songs and am constantly urging people to alter my work. The arrangement isn't the music; what your singers create is the music, and the notes on the page are simply a road map. There are many ways to get to a destination; find the best one for your group.

This is by no means a comprehensive list of every best practice for contemporary a cappella groups. Learn from others, rely on your own skill and technique, and remember that unlike classical music idioms, you have been surrounded by popular music your entire life. You have heard that Beatles song at least fifty times, so you know how it goes, and you know your singers' voices, personalities, and talents. With your instinct as your guide, and a little trial and error, marrying the two is not as challenging as you may think.

VOCAL INSTRUMENTS

Years ago, a cappella was mostly lyrics, "ah," "bum," and "doo." Now
people are using their voices to imitate and represent a wide variety of
instruments. Instrumental imitation is by no means unique to contemporary a cappella, the Mills Brothers being an excellent example of its
use in the past. However, it is being used more now than ever before,
and yet with nowhere to study this, people have been figuring it out on
their own, sharing techniques in person and, more recently, online.

Here are a few things to know before you dive in:

- Learning unusual vocal techniques by reading about them is a bit
  like learning to tie your shoelaces via audio recording: it is at best
  incomplete information. I have recorded a number of tutorial videos that will help considerably. These can be found on the So You
  Want to Sing website.♪
- Even with an extremely accurate imitation, how you use a sound
  and what you express is more important than the specific timbre. A
  great deal of beatboxing doesn't quite sound like drums, but if the
  groove is tight, no one cares. On the other hand, just as perfectly
  imitative drum sounds in a lurching pattern are unsatisfying, so is
  a great trumpet timbre devoid of feeling and flow. Listen to the
  greats to learn phrasing, feel, and mood.
- You don't have to sound exactly like an instrument to trigger
  people's "wow" reaction. The human brain has several different
  regions in which information is processed (mathematic, kines-
  thetic, spatial, etc.), and when you sing lyrics the information is
  being processed in both the linguistic and the music centers. Even
  lyrics such as "bum" and "doo" sound like a person because they
  are words in the English language. When you cross the threshold
  out of linguistic sounds and into something new, even if you don't
  sound exactly like a particular instrument when people hear the
  sound, their brain will attempt to categorize it and likely lump it in
  with the closest instrument. Voila.
- Using your hands to mimic the way the instrument is played serves
  two functions: it helps you phrase the sound as played on the instrument, and it helps complete the illusion for the audience (and

key them in if they're thrown and unsure what that sound is or if it's indeed coming from you).

- Some instrumental sounds will come more easily to you than others, because everyone has a different vocal cavity and muscles and therefore sounds a little different when replicating various instruments. You can learn to make any sound, but not all will come right away. Expect some to be easy and some to take time. Focus initially on your strengths, the sounds you do best, and then circle back later to tackle the more elusive, frustrating ones.
- Once you master a sound, take it a step further by learning actual jazz solos the way instrumentalists do. Singing along with recordings is a great way to improve your sound and phrasing. By memorizing and singing classic instrumental solos, you'll be learning the way all great jazz musicians have since Louis Armstrong.
- There is more than one approach to each instrument. Moreover, there is no right or wrong way to sound like an instrument, other than one that damages your voice. If the sound you are making hurts, stop. There's a way to do it without pain, and that pain is your body's way of letting you know you're doing something damaging.
- Be sure to adjust each sound to your own vocal range and tessitura. Just as there are violins, violas, cellos, and double basses, most classes of instruments have a variety of sizes, so there's rarely a need for you to sing outside your comfort zone. That said, many of the sounds resonate particularly well in the upper register, meaning that men will sound great using their falsetto. Try each sound in different parts of your voice as some will resonate particularly well in a specific part of your range.
- As with any other endeavor, only practice and listening will bring improvement. For an accurate idea of your sound, record yourself and listen back, so you can hear what you sound like outside your body (the resonance inside your body is why you sound different when you hear your spoken voice recorded).
- This is hardly an exhaustive list of all potential sounds. Experimentation is the best way to find your own sounds. Sing along with the radio and play. There are some instruments that are very hard to replicate, such as the piano (technically a percussion *and* a string

instrument), but hard doesn't mean impossible. You may stumble on new sounds, timbres, and techniques, and if you do, please share with the rest of us!

- Just think of how much you're saving on instrument lessons!

Trumpet

So I had a couple of years of playing trumpet. I really enjoyed it, but it was not the kind of instrument you could whip out at a party. Let's face it.—Jackson Browne

The vocal trumpet is likely the most ubiquitous vocal instrumental sound, with many people stumbling on how to do it on their own, making it a good place to start. Sing "boo" or "too" through somewhat tight lips, keeping a bright, open palate even though your lips are closed—think "ta" so your palate is open and your lips are flat rather than pursed. Regulating the air burst to give just the right amount of lip flap takes practice. You can over- or underemphasize your t attack to vary your sound. Once you have the sound locked in, for a fast series of restruck notes (a la the beginning of the William Tell Overture) sing "tuh duh luh duh luh." Trumpet vibrato is most effective when it follows a clear straight tone and doesn't appear on short notes, so when in doubt sing straight tone.

Trombone

I chose the trombone because the trombone players in the marching band got to be up front with the majorettes (because of the slides) and I loved that!—Quincy Jones

You should master the vocal trumpet before moving to trombone as the same technique and principles apply. The difference is that the trombone is a bit lower, and notes are often approached by sliding from one to another, which is an easy addition to the trumpet sound. One major difference between the two is that trombone vibrato covers a wider pitch range than the trumpet and indeed most instruments. Using your hands as if you're holding a slide will help you get the feel for it.

Muted Trumpet

> I was minding my own business when something says to me, "you ought to blow trumpet." I have just been trying ever since.
>
> —Miles Davis

This sound requires you to sound "ugly" if that makes sense. So much of vocal technique is about approaching the purest of tones, most open of vowels, most resonant of timbres, whereas this specific sound requires you to move in the opposite direction at times. Reminder: if at any time your voice hurts, stop singing. This is perhaps the most difficult of the sounds, and my voice hurt until I could figure out how to get it.

The best way I can describe how to make this sound is that you want to approach it as though you're gagging, choking, or throwing up. This is not how you're going to make the sound, but to have that suite of sounds in your mind starts you on a very different path than the one you usually use. From there, see if you can imitate the sounds of Cartman, the *South Park* character with a distinctive voice (if you don't know whom I am referring to, you can find many links online). Both low register and falsetto work, with falsetto being more effective. Start with a big, ugly, gaggy "ah" that borders on "eh" and then slowly close your mouth while keeping the back of your throat open, much like a German umlaut. Having the sound start or end with breath or a sloppy glottal attack only improves the character. While making this sound you can vary your mouth shape a bit, reflecting moving the plunger (keeping it dark sounds more like a Harmon mute), but don't open your mouth too much or else it will tip your hand and make it clear that the sound is vocal not instrumental. Less is more.

In addition, you can get a different (and simpler) 1930s recording muted trumpet by doing a normal trumpet while you pinch your nose, or for a more extreme thirties sound, pinch nose and sing "wa wa wa" with trumpet phrasing.

Saxophone

> Don't play the saxophone, let the saxophone play you.—Charlie Parker

For this sound, you want to sing through your teeth, almost as if you were singing "fur fur fur" or more precisely "fr fr fr" since you don't want a clear vowel sound, just the *f* attack followed by "rrrrr." Start the sound with too much air, "fffff," and then let your vocal chords engage, the way Dexter Gordon attacks notes breathily when playing ballads. Keep your mouth relaxed, and never take your teeth off your lower lip, which gives you a resonant, somewhat muted overall sound.

Horn Section

I stole everything I ever heard, but mostly I stole from the horns.

—Ella Fitzgerald

Once you and your cohorts have begun to master various horns, you can begin to put them into your arrangements. Stack chords the way a big band arranger does (usually in close voicing), and try singing them as instruments: trumpet, sax, and trombone, top to bottom, like the band Chicago. If you can muster five horn-voiced singers, you can create the Tower of Power horns. There is no limit; just play with your voices in various configurations and timbres until you find something you like, using instrumental arranging and phrasing as your guide.

Flute

A flute with no holes is not a flute, and a doughnut with no hole is a Danish.—Chevy Chase

Although the flute may be one of the least frequently used instruments, it is a rather easy one to master. Start by singing "thoo" then repeat with more breath. Keep adding breath until you find you're not able to make a tone, so you know where your voice gives out and remain on the tonal side of the line—but only barely. Although every voice teacher and choral director instructs singers to eliminate breathy tone, you want the extra breath here to mimic the breathy sound of a flute. The best attack is somewhere between a *t* and a *th*, and you should be singing between barely opened lips, a very tight "oo" that closely resembles the embouchure (mouth shape a flautist uses). For the characteristic flute vibrato, gently waver your lips during the "oo."

Plucked/Pizzicato Violin

> The difference between a violin and a viola is that a viola burns longer.—Victor Borge

If you've made it this far, you deserve a break, so here's the simplest of all vocal instrumental sounds: a simple "tm" or "thm" is all you need to replicate the sound of a plucked string on a violin. Make sure the first *t* is rather explosive—not soft—and lean toward *th*—to get the sound of the string slapping the neck of the instrument. You don't want a vowel sound, just a pluck and a string resonance: "mmmm." The lower in your range you go, the larger the string instrument.

Bass

> I play bass. I don't have to go out there and screech.—Tina Weymouth

An upright bass is nothing more than a giant violin, so it stands to reason that the violin sound will be all you need. Well, all you need besides a low, resonant voice (sorry, tenors). Tessitura (where the sound lands in your range) is important as well, and you'll find the deeper you get into your chest register the more compelling the sound (which is why a woman singing low in her register can sound more bass-like than an actual bass high in his). Other upright bass tones include a short, per-cussive "duh" or "doo" sound. To weave a little vocal percussion into a walking bass line, try alternating "thm, tm, thm, tm," the "tm" resulting in a sound like a hi-hat on two and four.

Theremin and Kazoo

> There was one man who was interested in the color of music, the connection between light and music, and that was Einstein.
>
> —Leon Theremin

Before we can make a bowed violin sound, we need to start by turning your mouth into a kazoo. This will be the most frustrating of sounds because it's binary: either you have it or you don't. Before you have it, you'll try singing a *v* sound to replicate the buzzy nature of the kazoo, but that's not right. As with Luke learning to use the force, you just have to trust that the sound will eventually arrive once the conditions are right (like whistling) and then once you get it you can work with it.

Start by singing "nn"—a simple resonant, open-mouthed sound with your tongue touching the roof of your mouth. Next, close your mouth with your teeth exposed a bit, touching your lower lip gently, not unlike the vocal saxophone sound. If the tension is just right between your teeth and lower lip, and if there is a complete seal so that no air can escape around the sides of your teeth, when you pull your tongue away from the roof of your mouth, you should get a buzzy spaceship noise. Be patient, it takes time, and it's worth getting. Once you have that sound, you can learn to sing through it with vibrato, and you have a theremin (a la "Good Vibrations" by the Beach Boys, or the *Star Trek* theme).

Bowed Violin

> Singing has always seemed to me the most perfect means of expression. It is so spontaneous. And after singing, I think the violin. Since I cannot sing, I paint.—Georgia O'Keeffe

A more delicate approach to the kazoo/theremin sound results in a good bowed violin sound (which sounds even more effective when sung by multiple people at once). This violin takes very little air, almost like humming. Both pitch and volume vibrato work well with a vocal violin, but know that this bowed violin sound requires that your mouth remain very still regardless of pitch or volume (if you move your mouth too much, the overtones shift and it starts to sound like a synthesizer). Head voice/falsetto resonates like a violin; chest voice, like a cello. When arranging, I usually spell the violin sound "nv" and for those who can't get the sound; singing either a "nnnn" or "vvvv" usually blends in well enough that it all sounds like one unit. This vocal violin works well in place of "oo" or a hum.

Electric Guitar

> You don't have to be singing about love all the time in order to give love to the people. You don't have to keep flashing those words all the time.—Jimi Hendrix

On the other side of the theremin/kazoo scale is an electric guitar, which wants all the grit and attitude you stripped away from the bowed violin. Don't be afraid to make an ugly sound, as the best guitar sounds require volume and a gonzo attitude (and, ideally, amplification that emphasizes the best parts of the sound). Guitar vibrato (fingered or whammy bar) modulates pitch, not volume, so like a guitarist strike a straight guitar-held tone and then add vibrato. It is not necessary to use only this sound for electric guitars, as some good sounds can be made using syllables such as "jg," "zhm," "wao," "wawa," and "o–ka–ch–ka." Sing along with recordings, and see what sounds work best for you. When arranging power chords, use the same sound/tone in low parallel fifths or fourths.

Synthesizers

> I was never worried that synthesizers would replace musicians. First of all, you have to be a musician in order to make music with a synthesizer.—Robert Moog

Considering how synthesizers and sampling keyboards can sound like almost anything nowadays, it seems almost unnecessary to attempt to imitate one, and yet there are times when you want a classic 1970s or 1980s synth sounds. Start by creating a vocal flange, which is nothing more than sweeping between exaggerated vowel sounds. Starting with the vowel "oo," begin to shift and morph between different vowel sounds slowly, focusing on maintaining resonance, and you'll find you begin to sound like a synthesizer. Restrike the note every quarter or eighth ("mo," "meh," "ma," "me," "mih," etc.), and you'll sound like someone restriking the synth keyboard. From there you're on your own, as each keyboard patch sounds different. Try replicating the core vowel sound first and then work on the attack and decay of the sound. Listen and experiment.

Harmonica

> "Love Me Do," the first song we recorded, John was supposed to sing the lead, but they changed their minds and asked me to sing lead because they wanted John to play harmonica.—Paul McCartney

This sound needs a little bit of honk in it, almost like a goose, so some-where between "huh" and "hwaaa" is a good way to approach (and spell) this sound. First make the sound and then augment it by pinching your nose (which changes the resonance) and cupping your hands over your mouth, much as a harmonica player does while playing. For vibrato, take one hand and pull it away from your nose, which varies the volume as well as timbre of the sound (and approximates closely how a harmonica player creates vibrato). If making this sound while on a sound system, it's possible to hold a mic and double-cup your mouth for a harmonica sound, but it takes practice. Try wedging the microphone between your ring finger and pinky on your dominant hand (because it's stronger), which gives you the flexibility to use your other three fingers to press against your nose and shape the sound.

Additional Instruments: Mandolin, Steel Drums, Didgeridoo, and Bagpipe

> I get a lot of joy from playing instruments, and I have a different personality on each instrument. I like to let that come out. I get kind of selfish.—Lenny Kravitz

A steel drum and mandolin have a very similar approach vocally. Start by singing "bl–l–l–l–l" as a child playing with her tongue outside her mouth, slapping it up and down on her upper and lower lip quickly. Restrike with a clean *b* when hitting a new note. Tighten your mouth, and hide your lips for the mandolin sound. The sound is a bit more of a *m* than a *b*, so try starting from a hum until you become comfortable with the attack. A good mandolin takes some tongue dexterity—keep a constant speed if possible—as the pick hits the strings at a constant rate.

Didgeridoo is a traditional Australian instrument that sounds almost like a very low human voice. Take the synthesizer sound, add some grit (make it ugly), and start with a deep breath as a didgeridoo player uses circular breathing to keep the sounds going indefinitely.

For vocal bagpipe you want to start with a low similar drone sound leaning toward an "reeeee" and then build a fifth and octave upon it (this one takes multiple people, ideally a room full); then for the melody you can gently "karate chop" your throat/voice box while you restrike notes, but be careful as you don't want to hurt yourself. Admittedly there's not a huge market for a cappella bagpipe.

Final Thoughts

The imitation of instruments with your voice is not a goal but rather a path that allows you to express more as you'll have a more diverse and colorful palate of tonal colors and timbres to use when you sing. Instrumental imitation is merely a stepping-stone on a path toward creating new sounds and textures with voices. For thousands of years our world's musical traditions have usually been content with the vocalist in front, singing the melody, with an ever-increasing array of varied instruments in the back creating all the layers of sound. No longer: now we can do it all.

I have only ever been able to find one book on this topic: *Mouth Sounds* by Fred Newman (whom you may know from the PBS television show *Between the Lions*). This book was originally published in the 1980s and then came back into print briefly in 2004 but is sadly now back out of print. It originally included a thin, square vinyl record with demonstrations of the sounds. Used copies of the book can be found online. Most of the sounds in the book aren't instrumental (train whistles and the like), but it's all fun and more importantly is a great exercise in expanding your vocal range and timbre.

6

VOCAL PERCUSSION FOR EVERYONE

Kari Francis

Whether you've been immersed in a cappella for the longest time or you're newly exploring contemporary a cappella territory, learning vocal percussion can seem like a daunting task. In literal terms, the vocal percussionist creates varied, rhythmic sounds through manipulating air using the lips, tongue, throat, and body, often operating in tandem with the bass singers and as a counterpoint or added emphasis to the other textures in a vocal arrangement. The birth of vocal percussion represents an intersection of urban arts, instrumental playing traditions, and grassroots performing that has since become a staple of the contemporary a cappella style.

VOCAL PERCUSSION AND BEATBOXING

Though similar, vocal percussion and beatboxing are not synonymous. Beatboxing is a form of music making that can include vocally imitating electronic sampling, sound effects, and other synthesized sounds and production methods. Beatboxing performances and competitions ("battles") typically feature individuals, and sometimes duos, rather than groups. Vocal percussion is a broader term that usually refers to imitating acoustic drum sounds with a focus on replicating the grooves and functions of a drum kit player. The term originated in the midnineties to delineate beatboxing from the percussive sounds used for keeping time in vocal bands such as the House Jacks and Rockapella, and today is often used to describe the type of vocal drumming that occurs in ensemble settings such as contemporary a cappella groups.

HISTORICAL OVERVIEW

The human voice has a stunning capacity for producing and manipulating a vast number of sounds and tones. It is perhaps no surprise that the voice has played a large role in drumming traditions from Ghana[1] to India[2] and Japan, as the use of vocal syllables (even those without semantic value) still allow for nuanced transmission of tonal and timbral information. Beatboxing and vocal percussion continue these traditions in the context of modern, popular styles, linking current vocal practice with otherwise distant instrumental traditions.

As with any practice, pinpointing the exact beginnings of beatboxing is difficult:

> Beatboxing, like graffiti, began its life as an urban art form. The beginnings of hip-hop are well known—DJs spinning the breakbeats in records with MCs rapping over the top. When MCs starting to rap over drum machine (beat box) beats in the urban communities of New York City, especially in the Bronx, drum machines and synthesizers were not very affordable. Samplers were well out of reach even for well-paid musicians.
>
> Necessity is the mother of invention, and without machine-supplied beats to rap over, a new, more accessible instrument was adopted—the mouth—and thus human beatboxing was born.[3]

The term "beatbox" likely derives from a description of commercial drum machines, the first of which included the Chamberlin Rhythmate[4] and Wurlitzer Sideman. These models gave way to the ELI Compu-Rhythm CR-7030 "Beat Box" and the Roland series of drum machines and synthesizers. Rapper and self-proclaimed "Original Human Beatbox" Doug E. Fresh claims to have coined the term "beatbox" in 1980. Performers such as Biz Markie and Buffy Robinson are credited with growing the beatbox vocabulary with new techniques developed while part of performing acts, such as Markie with Roxanne Shanté.[5]

The nineties saw a period of beatboxing moving to hip-hop's underground scene, while performers such as Dana Elaine Owens ("Queen Latifah") and Leonardo Roman ("Wise") incorporated beatboxing in their live group acts—Ladies Fresh and Stetsasonic, respectively. At the same time, beatboxing had moved outside of hip-hop circles. Multivocalist entertainers such as Bobby McFerrin and Michael Winslow popularized and adapted vocal sound effects to new musical genres and audiences. Vocal groups also began to incorporate dedicated beatboxers such as Andrew Chaikin ("Kid Beyond") of the House Jacks, Jeff Thacher of Rockapella, Matthew Selby of m-pact, Wes Carroll of Five o'Clock Shadow, and others.

Beatboxing saw a renewed push back to the mainstream in the late nineties and the first decade of the twenty-first century with albums such as Rahzel's *Make the Music 2000* and Björk's mostly vocal *Medulla*. Increased access to and understanding of studio production techniques meant that vocal groups could more easily manipulate drum sounds on recordings, creating intricately layered and rhythmically accurate vocal percussion. PBS highlighted a plethora of vocal bands in its 1990 special *Spike and Co.: Do It A Cappella*, including what is likely the first full-time vocal percussionist in the group True Image. Rockapella would continue to showcase their vocal percussionist as part of their act on PBS's *Where in the World Is Carmen Sandiego?* bringing contemporary a cappella to a national television audience.

Since then, both beatboxing and vocal percussion have been show-cased as part of televised shows and movies such as *American Idol*, *America's Got Talent*, *The X-Factor*, *The Sing-Off*, *Sing It On*, *Pitch Perfect*, *TEDTalks*, numerous commercials, and more, providing twenty-first-century outlets for solo performers such as Joel Turner, Blake Lewis, Antoinette Clinton ("Butterscotch"), Harry Yeff ("Reeps One"), Darren Foreman ("Beardyman"), Simon Kahn ("Shlomo"), Belle Ehresmann ("Bellatrix"), Kevin Olusola ("K.O."), Tom Thum, and myriad others to display individual performance styles synthesizing beatbox techniques with other musical forms. With concerts, collaborations, and competitions occurring in cities across the world and Internet, vocal percussion and beatboxing are thriving, interdependent practices thanks to supportive practitioners and fans.

THE ROLE OF THE VOCAL PERCUSSIONIST

The vocal percussionist keeps the group in time, right? Well, rhythmic feel and a consistent tempo should be a group effort for which every member—from soloist down to baritone and bass—is responsible. Like a drummer in an instrumental band, the vocal percussionist's primary focus is to be a rhythmic anchor for the rest of the group: a steady, "in the pocket" reference for the other singers (figure 6.1). The fluidity of live performance and the elasticity among each performer's perception of time usually results in moment-to-moment compromises between each singer, and often between the vocal percussionist and soloist as the de facto "rhythmic leaders" of a given song.

Creating a groove that has stylistically appropriate sounds and tempo—and maintaining the quality of those sounds at that tempo—is perhaps the most important facet of the vocal percussionist's role both in and out of group settings. Except in the case of an intentional percussion solo or feature, the percussionist plays as much a supportive role

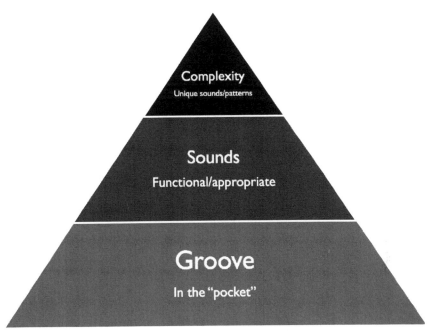

Figure 6.1. A vocal drummer's hierarchy of priorities for group settings.
Courtesy of Kari Francis.

as any other group member. Similarly, the vocal percussionist typically shouldn't put on a separate visual show of gesticulations or choreography unless it is in tandem with the rest of the group's movements. Simply put, it's often when the percussionist goes somewhat unnoticed that she has done her job correctly, as this typically signifies a rhythmically unified ensemble performance wherein the vocal percussion constitutes one integrated layer within the entire arrangement texture.

In the category of "Rhythmic Accuracy/Vocal Percussion," the Varsity Vocals ICCA/ICHSA judging rubric reads,

Rhythmic precision, tempo consistency, or effective use of non-metered time

If using vocal percussion:
Contribution to the musicality of the performance
Use of advanced techniques[6]

These are reasonable expectations, though "Use of advanced techniques" might be treated as a bonus: percussionists have still walked away from competition with the "Best Vocal Percussion" award because they provided consistent support to the ensemble and arrangement with their choice and placement of sounds, even when those sounds were relatively simple. "Advanced techniques," if employed haphazardly and at the expense of the tempo, can hurt a performance more than help it.

It is important to note that the vocal percussion may affect other categories on the judging sheet, as it can be the gateway through which sung rhythms, dynamics, and other textures are perceived by the audience. Many of these aspects must be rated by the judges in terms of being "rhythmically interesting," and it can be creative use of the vocal percussion part that "sells" these elements in that way.

Ultimately, know your craft: be your group's groove expert, always working in tandem with the director, arranger, and bass singer to make sure the percussion truly adds to the performance. Additionally, if you have a unique sound or beat you've just mastered, talk to your arranger about incorporating it in your group's next chart.

SOUNDS AND SOUND PRODUCTION

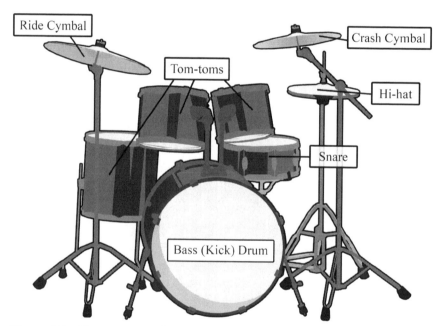

Figure 6.2. Components of a standard drum set. *Courtesy of Kari Francis.*

As with practicing any instrument, vocal percussion requires building strength, dexterity, and familiarity with the body's regulatory systems (specifically for breath, spit, and physical stamina). As you practice, pay attention to which methods work best for your physical abilities, keeping in mind that they may differ from what works for someone else.

Most grooves combine sounds that occupy a spectrum of high (hi-hat), middle (snare), and low (kick/bass drum; see table 6.1).

Table 6.1. A typical eight-pulse breakdown of high-medium-low sounds in a groove

I	&	2	&	3	&	4	&
	high		high				high
		middle				middle	
low				low	low		
B	t	K	t	B	B	K	t

TECHNIQUES

Table 6.2. Common vocal percussion techniques for beginners

Technique	Letter Representation	Description
Kick/bass drum	B, Bm, Dmp, Db	Tight, high-pressure expulsion of air through articulated "b." Typically nonvocalized but with some exceptions (see *vocalization* in "Sound Production" section). Think "buh," "dub."
Snare	Pf, Psh	Created with lips, combines kick drum attack *p* with fricative *f* to imitate snare rattle. Nonvocalized, typically outward. Think "piff."
	K, ^K, ^Kl	Nonvocalized, can be outward or inward (as indicated by ^—see *breath control* in "Sound Production" section). The outward sound typically passes through the middle of the top and bottom teeth, whereas the inward sound relies on space created around the back molars on one or both sides of the mouth. Think "keh," "kuh."
Hi-hat	t, ts, ^t, ^ts	Dentalized *t* stopped by tongue touching soft palate. Relies on metallic "sweet spot" between top and bottom teeth for realistic ring. Nonvocalized, can be inward or outward. Think "tee," "tiss."

While not usually necessary for basic grooves, many of the sounds in tables 6.2 and 6.3 can be produced by novice vocal percussionists and, when used judiciously, can add interest and variety to simple drumming patterns.

Table 6.3. Additional vocal percussion techniques

Technique	Letter Representation	Description
Crash or ride cymbal	Ksh, Psh, Ks, Ps	Sharply articulated *k* or *p* followed by sustained decay on fricative *sh* or *s*.
Tom-toms	Gm, Gv; "buh-bih-duh," "dih-bih-duh" triplet combinations	Consonant into *v* (more aggressive) or *m* (more mellow), with larynx lowered to create deeper, more realistic sound. Usually voiced to delineate between drum pitches.
Rimshot snare	k	Unlike *K* snare, this is unforced, unaspirated, and unvoiced. Create pressure at back of jaw and release on *k* while dropping jaw. No audible air; quickly cut off.
Bongo	k + "um"	Combine *k* rimshot snare attack with vocalized "um" at higher and lower pitches to emulate shifts between differently sized drums.
Fast hi-hat	tktk, tftf	Unforced plosives in light, quick succession behind teeth.
Breath	h, ^h	Aspirated *h* both outward and inward, in either a soft or harsh tone. Can be vocalized. Can allow the performer to breathe normally while utilizing the breath rhythmically in a pattern.
Vocal scratch	"ibidda," "dibidda," "igada," "owi," "ara," "awa"	Imitates a DJ record scratch, usually interrupts a groove or spoken phrase. Cricothyroid-dominant production (head voice, falsetto) with sound determined by tongue and mouth shape.
Lip buzz/bass	PP	Tightened lip oscillation. High pressure creates higher resulting pitch; lower pressure, lower pitch.

These lists are by no means exhaustive but should provide the stable footing for vocal percussionists to begin learning their craft. Additionally, numerous tutorial videos and websites can be found online, such as at http://www.humanbeatbox.com.

SOUND PRODUCTION

Breath control refers to the use of grooves that incorporate sounds that intake or expel air in order for the vocal percussionist to maintain an uninterrupted groove without stopping to breathe.[7] Inward sounds are denoted by the caret (^) next to its respective letter in table 6.2. Common inward sounds for managing breath control include ^K (snare) and ^ts (hi-hat).

Color and placement. The vocal percussionist can use space in the mouth to affect different "colors" (not far from the concept of "brightness" and "darkness" of sung tone color) of any sound. For example, an inward ^K snare can be created by intaking air through the teeth with the mouth in a wide, smiling "kih" shape, or a tall "koh" shape. Similarly, one can modify a sound by intaking air primarily around the teeth on one side of the mouth, rather than inhaling equally on both sides (or vice versa).

Vocalization (also phonation) refers to the vibration of the vocal folds to create sound, as in speaking or singing. While many vocal percussion sounds rely heavily on the manipulation of air through the lips, teeth, and tongue, vocalization can also be used to add pitch information to a sound, such as assigning three discrete, high-to-low pitches for the tom-tom fill "gv-gv-gv." When performing without a microphone and depending on the venue's acoustics, it may make sense to vocalize certain sounds that would otherwise be too quiet, such as a voiced "Db" for the kick drum rather than an unvoiced "B."

Auditory illusions. Just as an optical illusion may trick your eyes into seeing something that isn't really there, auditory illusions can trick the brain into inferring sounds that are not actually being produced.[8] One common example of this is the implied continuation of a hi-hat line through a groove that alternates between hi-hat and kick drum—despite the fact that the vocal percussionist usually produces only one sound at a time. Mastery of this concept is demonstrated in Bobby McFerrin's "Drive" routine, wherein his seamless transitions between different textural elements imply the continuation of the bass line and percussive sounds behind the melody. Consequently, the vocal percussionist needs to be able to create not simultaneous sounds but rather enough sound to promote the illusion of that simultaneity.

NOTATION

A handful of notation systems have emerged to illustrate vocal percussion and beatbox sequences in cases where verbal coaching is not possible. Some play on existing Western percussion notation, while others derive from the phonetic qualities of the sounds themselves. There is not currently a formal, universal standard, and different groups, arrangers, and performers often rely on different methods suited to their personal preferences.

WESTERN NOTATION

Sounds are usually distributed across the staff from low to high to reflect their (approximate) pitch in relation to other sounds (see figure 6.3).

Figure 6.3. A sample drum set notation legend. More detailed notational conventions can be found in Norman Weinberg's *Guide to Standardized Drumset Notation*.⁹ Courtesy of Kari Francis.

When presented in the context of a contemporary a cappella arrangement, the percussion part might present traditional drum set notation with syllable suggestions (see figure 6.4).

Figure 6.4. Conventional percussion notation featuring kick drum, snare drum, and hi-hat, followed by a potential vocal version. Courtesy of Kari Francis.

STANDARD BEATBOX NOTATION (SBN)

Developed by Mark Splinter and Gavin Tyte of the Human Beatbox online community, Standard Beatbox Notation (SBN) relies on combinations of letters related to the production of a given sound to illustrate rhythmic sequences and grooves.¹⁰ Here is an example of a drum-and-bass groove written in Standard Beatbox Notation:

{ B t t t / Psh t t B / t B B t / Psh t t t }

In this row of sixteen consecutive, equally spaced sounds, a typical 4/4 time signature translates to four large macrobeats (each divided by the forward slash [/]), with sounds occurring during each of the four smaller microbeats. Uppercase letters indicate forced—audibly accented or exhaled—sounds, whereas lowercase delineates unforced sounds, or sounds not audibly ejected (usually because they have an inherent plosive quality, such as an unaspirated t or k).[11] Expelling additional air—aspiration—can be demonstrated by adding an h to a sound, as in "Bh" for an aspirated kick drum, while combination with a fricative sound (a soft continuant such as f, sh, or s)[12] can by shown by "P" + "sh" = "Psh."

Rests are shown by horizontal dashes, as in the following:

{ B—t k / Psh—B—/ t k B—/ Psh—t k }

For the group director or music educator seeking to connect vocal percussion with a form of notation, SBN can be a helpful starting point. One can combine SBN with conventional drum set notation as in the examples above, or in a single percussion line, such as in figure 6.5.

B t K t B B K t   B t t t K t t t B t B t K t t t

Figure 6.5.   Single line notation sample. *Courtesy of Kari Francis.*

GROOVES AND PLAYING STYLES

Groove can be defined as a pattern of sounds repeated in time.[13] Though a vocal percussionist may create a part by imitating the percussion in the original song, the ability to discriminate between sounds that are appropriate to omit and those that are "required" relies on a familiarity with the tenets of that musical style. Additionally, the vocal percussionist can bring new flair to an arrangement through acquired knowledge of other drumming styles and traditions. Recommendations for style-specific drum rudiment texts can be found in the "Resources and Further Reading" section at the end of this chapter.

It is important to consider vocal percussionists as creative, expressive interpreters who take inspiration from many drum set playing styles but add their own characteristics in the process of deciding how to make polyphonic lines—normally executed using four appendages—into a linear, monophonic sequence. It is in this decision-making process that the vocal percussionist has a unique duty as a soloist and accompanist.

The main groove in Earth, Wind and Fire's funk-disco classic "September" illustrates the need for consistency between sounds and tempo (performance speed) on the part of the vocal percussionist. Here, the groove serves as a steady, unornamented anchor for other syncopated figures swirling around it in the form of the rhythm guitar, bass line, and horn hits. For the "September" chorus drum set part and potential vocal percussion interpretation, see figure 6.6.

Figure 6.6. "September" funk groove sample. *Courtesy of Kari Francis.*

The same type of straightforward beat can also be heard in other classic funk songs such as "Superstition" by Stevie Wonder and "Stayin' Alive" by the Bee Gees. For added authenticity, try to find a moment—such as a fill or interlude—to showcase a cowbell sound.

"I Got You (I Feel Good)" by James Brown offers a variation on a funk groove at a higher tempo, where the shift between closed and open hi-hat determines much of the groove's feel—the latter represented by the small circle above the notehead as well as a "ts" in the SBN (the + above the notehead indicates a return to the closed hi-hat; see figure 6.7). Figure 6.8 shows a reduction of the figure 6.7 part for vocal percussion.

Figure 6.7. James Brown, "I Got You (I Feel Good)" drum set part. *Courtesy of Kari Francis.*

Figure 6.8. A possible vocal percussion interpretation of James Brown's "I Got You (I Feel Good)." *Courtesy of Kari Francis.*

The prominent two-bar groove in "Roxanne" by the Police begins with a cymbal crash, focuses on the interplay between kick and snare, and ends with an open/closed hi-hat tradeoff. With the backbeat (beats two and four of a measure written in 4/4) consistently emphasized by the snare, it is drummer Stewart Copeland's creative use of open and closed hi-hat that adds special timbral character to the chorus (see figure 6.9). Without losing the backbeat, the vocal percussionist can still incorporate closed hi-hats throughout to contrast with the open hi-hats at the end of the phrase (see figure 6.10).

Figure 6.9.   The Police's "Roxanne" chorus drum set part. *Courtesy of Kari Francis.*

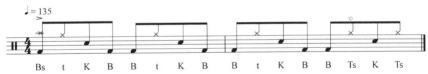

Figure 6.10.   A potential vocal percussion interpretation of the chorus for "Roxanne" by the Police. *Courtesy of Kari Francis.*

In pop and rock styles, the kick (bass) drum and snare drum serve as primary focal points of the groove, with the snare maintaining the backbeat, the kick drum contributing much of the groove-specific variety, and the hi-hat providing a steady eighth or sixteenth subdivision. The hi-hat is typically quieter than the kick and snare, and should not overpower either element (see figure 6.11). A groove with a sixteenth subdivided feel might look like figure 6.12.

Figure 6.11.   Two versions of a simple, steady rock groove. *Courtesy of Kari Francis.*

B t t t K t t t B t B t K t t t   Bs t t t K t t t B t B B t K t t t

Figure 6.12. A simple rock groove followed by a drum-and-bass accent pattern. *Courtesy of Kari Francis.*

Another common feature of popular music has been the four-on-the-floor (or four-to-the-floor) pattern, where the groove is dominated by multiple, sequential kick drum hits (see figure 6.13). This can be reinforced by the snare, hi-hat, or claps but ultimately emphasizes the larger macrobeat without significant attention to microbeat subdivisions. This pattern features prominently in many popular songs, including Carly Rae Jepson's "Call Me Maybe" and Ed Sheeran's "Castle on the Hill."

B   B   B   B   Db   Db   Db   Db

Figure 6.13. Four-on-the-floor pattern. *Courtesy of Kari Francis.*

A common accent pattern is the 3+3+2 division of eight microbeat pulses. This motif is found in both popular and folk music around the world and is known in Latin American musics as the tresillo rhythm.[14] This can be heard in drum and guitar motifs in popular songs such as "What You Wanted" by OneRepublic. The tresillo rhythm also comprises the first half of the 3:2 son clave rhythm, which was adapted by blues artist Bo Diddley early in the rock 'n' roll era to become the "Bo Diddley" beat (see figure 6.14). This can be heard in the snare accent pattern of "Mickey's Monkey" by Smokey Robinson and the Miracles, the tom-tom rhythm of "I Want Candy" by the Strangeloves, and in the rhythm guitar riff in "Black Horse and a Cherry Tree" by KT Tunstall—and in many of Bo Diddley's own songs.

♩ = 120

Figure 6.14. Bo Diddley pattern. *Courtesy of Kari Francis.*

Latin American patterns reflect the influences including Brazilian, Afro-Cuban, African, and island drumming styles. Superimposing the 3+3+2 tresillo rhythm over a four-on-the-floor kick drum results in variants relating to calypso and reggaeton patterns (see figure 6.15). This groove can be heard in the backing groove of songs such as Sia's "Cheap Thrills," DJ Snake's "Let Me Love You (feat. Justin Bieber)," and Ed Sheeran's "Shape of You."

Figure 6.15. Sample reggaeton groove. *Courtesy of Kari Francis.*

Though it may look similar to the eighth rock groove, the feel of the bossa nova groove in figure 6.16 is completely different.

Figure 6.16. Sample bossa nova groove. *Courtesy of Kari Francis.*

Compared to rock and pop grooves, a different sonic hierarchy is at play as the kick drum is low but soft (without the aggressive punch of other drum kit styles), the hi-hat is lighter and tighter, and the key element is the crisp, cross-stick snare, noted here by the inward ^K (see figure 6.17).

Figure 6.17. Bossa nova groove sample. *Courtesy of Kari Francis.*

In jazz styles, the swing feel (eighth notes "swung" over a triplet subdivision) is dependent upon the ride cymbal and hi-hat as constants around which the kick and snare provide embellishments to complement other parts of the texture or arrangement. Don't be fooled by the notation—these eighth notes are played in a "swung," triple-meter feel, rather than "straight" duple.

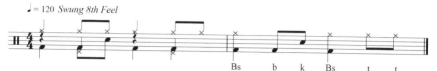

Figure 6.18. Swing groove sample. *Courtesy of Kari Francis.*

The swing feel is similarly relevant in pop and rock songs such as "Sunday Morning" by Maroon 5, or "Are You Gonna Be My Girl" by JET, where the nuance of the triplet-based swing beat might be misinterpreted by the novice drummer as being in duple meter (see figure 6.19). The first measure depicts the "un-swung" groove as it might appear in writing. The second measure shows the same groove as it would be performed with a swing feel.

Figure 6.19. Comparison between duple- and triple-feel swing grooves. *Courtesy of Kari Francis.*

FILLS

Fills are brief, improvisatory passages that connect a phrase or section of a song to another, such as a verse to the chorus, chorus to bridge, or four- and eight-bar phrases to each other. Fills add rhythmic and textural variety, and help maintain the flow of the song while transferring energy to the next musical idea. Measure one represents the groove; measure two contains the fill leading to the next phrase, which culminates in a crash on the downbeat of measure three to begin the next phrase and the reiteration of the original groove.

Figure 6.20. Sample rock fill. *Courtesy of Kari Francis.*

A fill should reflect the underlying subdivisions of a song, drawing its content from the style and overall feel. In the example in figure 6.20, the fill occupies an entire four-macrobeat measure, but fills can take up smaller or greater durations depending on the needs of the song. Fills that deviate too far from a song's established rhythmic vocabulary may sound jarring. And, as is often the case, simplicity—especially the creative use of space—is key.

VOCAL PERCUSSION IN AN A CAPPELLA ARRANGEMENT

So you've got your sounds and basic grooves—now what? Just as the vocal percussionist shouldn't visually distract from the rest of the group, the percussion part shouldn't distract from the vocal writing. Perhaps the biggest mistake young vocal percussionists and beatboxers make is trying to do too much with too many sounds (and too loudly!), muddling the arrangement and the other group members' performances. Ideally, a basic outline of the percussion part should be conceived as part of the arranging process, rather than being added as an afterthought. Table 6.4 provides some suggestions for best practices.

Table 6.4. Suggestions and best practices

Do	Don't
Create a part that supports the style and feel of the arrangement.	Upstage the soloist or rest of the group with sounds or grooves outside of the song's style.
Plan ahead to regulate breath/spit in order to maintain tempo and quality of sounds.	Let anything—sound, choreography, adrenaline, or other—interrupt the tempo.
Keep it simple and effective. Less is more!	Overextend yourself at the expense of the music.
Listen to the rest of ensemble, and react accordingly in your percussion part.	Concern yourself with only the percussion part. (After all, no part of an arrangement exists in a vacuum!)

SONG BREAKDOWNS

To provide additional insight into elements such as sound choice, stamina, and style, vocal percussionists Adam Heimbigner, Courtney Jensen, and Beejul Khatri have graciously shared their groove-creation processes in the context of songs each has performed. The following accounts are adapted or paraphrased from conversations and written messages.

"Good Time" as Performed by Owl City Feat. Carly Rae Jepsen

Vocal Point (Brigham Young University)— Adam Heimbigner

A large part of why "Good Time" sounded the way it did came from how it fit into the show flow. This song was going to take over as the show opener, typically a very upbeat song that doesn't take a lot of risks but introduces the audience to the classic Vocal Point sound that many people love. The percussion style of Vocal Point has always leaned on a precise drum kit feel rather than a very contemporary or flashy beatbox style. A much safer—yet still driving—touch was needed. This was further warranted by needing to showcase all the vocalists at the very beginning of the show, to let the audience "meet" everyone. Any exaggerated percussion would have distracted from the soloist, who was constantly rotating.

Knowing those goals, let's look at the song (in table 6.5). In the end, the goals were met: this song is simple and familiar yet still very "Vocal Point" with a bit of Adam mixed in.

Table 6.5. Vocal percussion breakdown of "Good Time" by section

Intro (0:00–0:10)	All vocalists introduce the chorus for the first time with no perc. Only when the bass singer starts his slide to transition to the first verse do we get a strong hit and playful scratches.
Verse 1 (0:11–0:41)	Four-on-the-floor kick hits to provide motion and establish the tempo, punctuated by breathing noises (a bit of a departure from VP's typical drum kit flavor and more in line with my own style—peppering the main beat keeps it interesting but not distracting). Halfway through we add a snare on beats two and four, further adding motion to our basic beat.
Prechorus 1 (0:41–0:56)	Remove the snare, back to four-on-the-floor with a variation on the intermittent punctuation to coincide with the drop in energy by the background vocals without losing drive. Add snares halfway through again. Also, adding a nice swell and a sharp cutoff on three, again accenting the vocals, yet coming back with a snare on four to not lose the tempo and transition seamlessly to the chorus.
Chorus 1 (0:56–1:12)	Establishment of our main beat, which strongly echoes what the verse introduced: four-on-the-floor kick, snare on beats two and four, this time with strong hi-hat rides on the "ands" between all four beats, alternating between inhaling and exhaling. (Why alternating? I knew the choreography would be killer, so working breaths into the beat would give some reprieve when performing live.) Halfway through the chorus, a simple tom-tom fill and cymbal crash further provide motion while the background vocals repeat their rhythms.
Postchorus (1:12–1:15)	Back to a simple four-on-the-floor to match energy until the last measure where multiple kick drum hits echo the vocals. Add a scratch to call back to the beginning of the song to ease the transition.
Verse 2 (1:15–1:31)	Halftime, with a twist! The background vocals make it feel like halftime, yet the percussion "speeds up," adding more intricate bass hits around a playful cymbal pattern. The energy is brought down, and the feeling changes while still adding something new to the perc.
Prechorus (1:31–1:46)	Swap to a halftime feel, big bass hits, powerful snare, which complements the halftime the background parts are doing. Swap back to a four-on-the-floor with snare when vocals revert from halftime to provide more motion in anticipation of the next chorus.
Chorus 2 (1:46–2:01)	Big, yet simple: very similar to the first chorus. Only the "seasoning" has slightly changed.
Bridge (2:01–2:17)	Four-on-the-floor punctuated by the breathing sounds introduced earlier, along with a harsher tom fill—familiar, yet different.
Chorus 3 (2:17 to end)	Same as chorus 2 (although this would be the loudest chorus when performed live), returning the audience to the "familiar" while punctuated by cymbal fills. This continues to the end of the song where a sharp cutoff is met by a large kick hit to articulate the bass slide.

"Breakeven" as Performed by the Script

The Backbeats—Courtney Jensen

My process of creating vocal percussion parts has evolved over time with the groups I've been in. As a member of Noteworthy (at Brigham Young University), the beats were a direct reflection of the original song, which I would practice until memorized, and through that I learned different sound and groove combinations.

With the Backbeats, I had developed the command of sounds and grooves to a point of independence and artistry that I could let go of the original song entirely. When we did "Breakeven" by the Script, I listened to the arrangement in rehearsal and created a part in reaction to hearing the flow of what Ben Bram had written—and I didn't listen to, or base the part on, the drums in the original song. The percussion part has a journey in terms of changing timbres and increasing complexity: it starts with a crisp hi-hat that turns into a basic beat to drive the arrangement along in its slower, more vocally spaced sections. This becomes a heavier groove when the chorus arrives, providing a firm rhythmic grounding under the sustains in the background parts. The groove adds more sounds and becomes busier during the bridge, emphasizing group accents before dropping out for the reiteration of the opening material.

That may be the truest mark of a mature beatbox artist: knowing when to drop out because your sounds won't add anything to the arrangement or performance at that moment. After singing with the group in that gap, a fill following the descending bass line leads back into the final chorus, where the groove features more subdivisions than the previous chorus and carries the song to its conclusion.

In the Riveters, I had the opportunity to collaborate with an incredibly talented arranger in Lisa Forkish. Despite not being a vocal percussionist, Lisa usually had an idea about the type of sounds or groove that would work well within the sonic world of her arrangement. The process of creating the percussion part was a tandem effort that generated something greater than what either of us started with.

"Don't You Worry Child" (Featuring John Martin) as performed by Swedish House Mafia

The Nor'easters (Northeastern University)— Beejul Khatri

Though the style, instrumentation, and form of the Nor'easters' arrangement of "Don't You Worry Child" were fundamentally different from the original, I began the writing process by examining the structure, rhythmic patterns, and percussive elements present in the original song. By familiarizing myself with the original percussion, I gave myself a starting point for grooves and sounds I could use in our cover. By thinking critically about the percussive choices in the original song, I was more informed as to which of those elements would be effective to reference in our arrangement, and where I would have to change things completely.

For example, a variation of the four-on-the-floor beat present in the original version's verses was appropriate for our cover, but our arrangement's first chorus was substantially gentler than that of the original, so minimal vocal percussion was warranted. Our music director and I frequently engaged in discussions about the intent behind my percussion choices and his arrangement choices, and their desired effects musically, emotionally, and sonically. This enabled us to fulfill his initial vision for the arrangement and then surpass that vision by collecting the best of both of our ideas.

The clearest instance of this can be heard in the second verse, where the percussion changes from a familiar four-on-the-floor club beat to a dubstep build midway through the verse. The lyrics at this point in the song are, "We were so young, I think of it now and then. / I still hear the songs reminding me of a friend." These lyrics reminded me of heartbreak I was experiencing at the time. Though these lyrics aren't intended to be angry, they inspired some anger in me, so one day during rehearsal I asked the group if we could try a more aggressive dubstep build during that section of the song, and it turned out to be an unexpected but effective change of pace. This illustrates that, no matter how irrelevant an idea may seem, it is worth exploring all ideas to find the best options. However, this is only possible in a group environment that encourages such spontaneity and outward collaboration.

VOCAL PERCUSSION IN A CONCERT

Whether your performance spans twelve minutes or two hours, use different songs to showcase a variety of grooves and rhythmic moments—but fight the urge to make too many changes within a single song. Stated differently, if your material is too redundant from song to song, both you and the audience will fatigue over time, and the audience may eventually tune you out. Even with a small collection of sounds, you can incorporate different types of rhythms, volumes, groove styles, and space (!) to keep the percussion sounding fresh across longer performances.

Whether it occurs within an arrangement or between songs, the beatbox "feature" can be a fun opportunity to interact with the audience, show off your skills that don't fit elsewhere in the concert, and ultimately break up the show with a shift in energy and communication style. Some performers prefer to do an extended solo, whereas others teach the audience some basic sounds so they can join in the fun.

Finally, be creative with your water breaks. Your strength and your body's capacity for regulating air and spit will develop endurance with practice—even so, try to avoid running offstage after every song to rehydrate. Additionally, adrenaline and anxiety may drain your stamina more quickly during a concert than in rehearsal—counter this by performing for audiences (of any size) as often as possible in order to recognize and better control these changes.

SUGGESTIONS FOR PRACTICE

Above all other tips for practice—be it in rehearsal or at home—make sure to stay hydrated, and if it hurts, stop! No technique is worth potentially damaging your mouth or vocal chords.

Use your resources. With YouTube, Spotify, *Wikipedia*, and the vastness of the Internet at your disposal, now more than ever you can discover great beatboxers and musical acts. Expand your drumming vocabulary by listening to a wide variety of musics, paying special attention to the genres your group most often performs. Conversely, exploring songs in styles outside of your group's typical fare may yield inspiration for different rhythms and grooves you can bring to your group's arrangements or your own solo practice.

Use a metronome. As of this writing, 120 beats per minute (bpm) is one of the most popular tempos for Billboard Top 100 songs, with "highly danceable" pop hits ranging from 95 bpm to 140 bpm.[15] Use the metronome to sharpen your sense of subdivision, physical endurance, and consistency of sound quality. More importantly, use it as a helpful reference when improvising new grooves. French beatboxer Mael Gayaud ("Alem") offers a creative take on metronome-centric practice with his "Work Your Beatbox" series of call-and-response videos.

The following is from Rockapella's Jeff Thacher:

> Try practicing to a steady, commercially released, non–a cappella recording. Instrumental drummers practice this way, "shedding" in private to funky beats or songs, with headphones on, until they learn and improve their own performance. It's all muscles and brain learning to work together.
>
> The benefits to this technique are many. When you're held to a steady tempo over the course of a song recording, you're forced to find the best way to breathe. You're also able to zero in on minute ways to be "in the pocket" using your mouth and body. Figure out why, for example, a classic James Brown song recording is so funky . . . listen very, very carefully and drum along with it. Find the pocket . . . the spirit of it. Find out what *isn't* happening, as much as what is. Essentially there's "no escape" as the music plays on.

Record yourself. It can be difficult to self-assess consistency and accuracy while practicing. Using a low-budget microphone or even a smartphone audio recorder can be a wonderful boon to your practice by providing an objective perspective from which to assess your strengths and areas for improvement you may not otherwise hear. As any professional vocal percussionist doing two-hour concerts can affirm, mouth drumming is an athletic activity: you will get better as you challenge yourself!

Good luck, have fun, and keep practicing!

APPENDIX

Ksh, Psh

Gm, Gv

Ksh, Psh, Ks, Ps

t, ts, ^t, ^ts

Pf, Psh, K, ^K, ^Kl

B, Bm, Dmp, Db

Figure 6.21. Common percussion sounds and their drum set analogues.
Courtesy of Kari Francis.

NOTES

1. "An Analysis of Oral Tradition in African Music," *Pitlane Magazine*, accessed February 12, 2017, http://www.pitlanemagazine.com.

2. Donovan Andru Arthen, "If You Can Say It, You Can Play It: An Investigation into the Use of Oral and Aural Pedagogy in New England Liberal Arts Colleges and Universities, Centering on Wesleyan University in Connecticut and Saint Michael's College in Vermont" (honor's thesis, Wesleyan University, April 15, 2011), 730, http://wesscholar.wesleyan.edu.

3. "History of Beatbox: Old School," Human Beatbox, April 20, 2005, accessed February 11, 2017, http://www.humanbeatbox.com.

4. "Chamberlin 'Rhythmate,' Harry Chamberlin, USA, 1947," 120 Years of Electronic Music, accessed February 11, 2017, http://www.120years.net.

5. "History of Beatbox," Human Beatbox.

6. "Varsity Vocals Judging Category Summary Sheet," *Varsity Vocals*, November 2015, accessed February 10, 2017, http://www.varsityvocals.com.

7. Jon Park, "Breath Control," Human Beatbox, October 20, 2016, accessed February 14, 2017, http://www.humanbeatbox.com.

8. "Lesson 2: My First DnB Beat," Human Beatbox, October 1, 2014, accessed February 13, 2017, http://www.humanbeatbox.com.

9. Norman Weinberg, *Guide to Standardized Drumset Notation* (Lawton, OK: Percussive Arts Society, 1998).

10. Mark Splinter and Gavin Tyte, "Standard Beatbox Notation," Human Beatbox, September 18, 2014, accessed February 15, 2017, http://www.human beatbox.com.

11. "Lesson 2," Human Beatbox.

12. "Fricative," Human Beatbox, September 18, 2014, accessed February 12, 2017, http://www.humanbeatbox.com.

13. Benjamin Stevens, "Beginning Vocal Percussion," SoJam A Cappella Festival, November 13, 2010.

14. David Peñalosa, *The Clave Matrix: Afro-Cuban Rhythm; Its Principles and African Origins* (Redway, CA: Bembe, 2010), 43.

15. Eric Strom, "Anatomy of a Hit Song: Tempo," *Pop Music Theory*, March 13, 2016, accessed February 10, 2017, http://www.popmusictheory.com.

RESOURCES AND FURTHER READING

Castellano, John. *Drummers Collective: Afro-Caribbean and Brazilian Rhythms for the Drumset*. Ethnic Style Series. New York: Carl Fischer, 2002.

Corniola, Frank. *Rhythm Section Drumming: Play-Along for Drums*. Milwaukee, WI: Hal Leonard, 1985.

Gordon, Edwin E. *Learning Sequences in Music: A Contemporary Music Learning Theory*. 2012 ed. Chicago: GIA Publications, 2012.

Hoffman, Richard, William Pelto, and John W. White. "Takadimi: A Beat-Oriented System of Rhythm Pedagogy." *Journal of Music Theory Pedagogy* 10 (1996): 7–30.

Igoe, Tommy. *Groove Essentials*. New York: Hudson Music, 2006.

Kew, Charlie. "Toward a Beatboxology." Human Beatbox, April 10, 2016. http://www.humanbeatbox.com.

"Konnakol: The Art of South Indian Vocal Percussion." Konnakol. http://www .konnakol.org.

Titon, Jeff T., ed. *Worlds of Music: An Introduction to the Music of the World's Peoples*. 4th ed. Belmont, CA: Schirmer, 2002.

Werbock, Jeffrey. "Oral Tradition in the Transmission of Ancient Music." *Gurdjieff International Review*, February 14, 2011.

SPECIAL THANKS

Thank you to Jeff Thacher, Ross Karre, Adam Heimbigner, Courtney Jensen, Beejul Khatri, Scott Cobban, Peter Huang, Steve Ryan, Mike Park, and Craig Simonetti for their feedback and contributions to this chapter.

7

BLEND

The concept of vocal blend is complex and nuanced, a confluence of multiple factors. To understand what goes into a great vocal blend one must understand the four fundamental elements of sound: pitch, timbre, duration, and loudness. Why those four elements? The physics of sound can be distilled down to those and only those components: the frequency of the wave (which is its pitch), the amplitude of the wave (volume/loudness), the length of the wave (duration), and the various overtones (higher frequencies) within a specific sound wave (tone color/timbre).

PITCH

When addressing vocal blend the first thing you should consider is pitch. Are your unisons precise (is one person flat or sharp)? Are they being approached and released in the same way (is one person sliding up to the note while another striking it directly)? If your voices are singing harmony, are the chord factors in tune (might the third be sharp or the fifth be flat)?

If your singers are not aware of the sound of two notes slightly out of tune, have one hold a note while you start on the exact pitch and slowly slide up or down a half step. The "beating" they hear (once they're able to hold the note steady; they'll likely try to follow you initially) will help them get used to the sound of a note that is slightly out of tune and learn to adjust themselves.

When you're looking to blend multiple pitches, start with the root of the chord (which hopefully is the lowest pitch), adding next the fifth, then third, and then color notes, each aligning with the initial singer's overtones. Your singers should be aware of the bass note and focusing on tuning to the fundamental of the chord, locking into its overtones.

There will be times during performance, particularly in a suboptimal setting such as an outdoor festival or a bad sound system, when your singers should use any and all tricks to lock down their tuning, which often means tuning to what they can hear, which will most likely be the solo or highest voice. Other groups, particularly young ones, may have more luck if they all stay focused on their own sense of the tonic as opposed to listening to the lowest part, whose voice may have just changed. My suggestion of tuning to the bass/root of the chord is not one that should be followed slavishly to the detriment of a performance. As always, do what works best for your group and circumstance.

It's important to realize that our entire Western tonal system is fundamentally out of tune, except for our octaves. Bach's "Well Tempered Clavier" was written to popularize what became our standard tuning system, with each pitch compromised a bit, which allows us to modulate keys easily but results in our instruments being slightly out of tune. A cappella, however, does not have this limitation, and some styles (especially barbershop) focus on locking and tuning chords, which results in additional over- and undertones.

Anytime a single vocal part moves, the other parts should move in parallel, like the Blue Angels flying in formation. The sound of a tight blend includes "singing in the cracks" together, even if it means they are all out of tune with the rest of the group from time to time, the way a pedal steel guitar will slide between chords. Don't spend too long between notes, and be sure to resolve together to chord factors, or else the pleasing motion will eventually sound out of tune. If a duet or trio is following a solo singer's melodic shape, they should follow it precisely, perhaps starting by mimicking the soloist in unison and then breaking out into the harmony lines with the same phrasing.

It is likely that you have been addressing tuning when rehearsing your group, so your blend issues may be a result of another deeper musical element.

TIMBRE

When we speak of vowels we're speaking of overtones, since the difference between different vowels is the result of emphasizing different harmonics. To this end, vowel matching is crucial.

As a warm-up or exercise, have your group members sing a standard vowel ("oo," "oh," "ah") and notice the differences. There is no right or wrong in contemporary a cappella, and in fact you will likely be singing a variety of different vowels in different songs, as you for instance want brighter, flatter vowels in bluegrass, and rounder, taller vowels when singing a piece within a more traditionally classical choral idiom. By practicing matching each group member's natural vowels, your singers will learn that there is no single correct sound but rather that they need to learn to listen and come together to align their vowels just as they do their pitches.

The people who will likely have the most difficulty with this vowel matching will be members of the group who are from other nationalities with different native languages or even different pronunciations of English (an American, Brit, Australian, and South African naturally sing the same vowels differently, based on the way they speak). American English is a common default for pop music (which is why the Beatles often sound like "Yanks"), but even within American English you'll find different pronunciations and dialects popping up, be it a country twang or lazy California vowels.

Whatever the choice, vowel matching is crucial within a section, be they on a unison or singing parallel parts. Just as you had singers mimic one another's phrasing on a solo line, have them listen to and copy one another, almost the way an impersonator would. Don't exaggerate the differences; simply strive to sound like the same person. Pay special attention to diphthongs, which are the morphing from one vowel sound to another: on a long-held note make sure your singers are sweeping through the vowel together such that you could freeze the chord at any moment and their vowels would align. As an exercise, have a group of singers say "Eight Days Sound Swell" together slowly, listening for the way they move through vowel sounds. Once they can speak it together, give them pitches and have them sing in alignment. When this happens well, with the emphasized overtones moving together just as pitches do, the result is spectacular. Watching each other's mouths in rehearsal can be a very effective way to align.

If you have your pitches and vowels/overtones in alignment, you likely have a great blend in hand, but there is still more that can be done to polish and perfect.

DURATION

Although it may seem obvious, each note should be attacked and released at the same time. The slight variance in note lengths, especially the end of notes, results in a "frayed" sound. The best way to get groups of singers to end notes together is to give them a specific beat on which to cut off, but this can occasionally result in a stilted sound, in which case they should follow their collective instincts and breathe when it feels natural, practicing while facing each other and watching each other's mouths so they can end together.

The duration of various notes combined with silence is what gives us rhythm, so this is also the time when you should make sure that all of your intricate inner rhythms are precise and aligned. For instance, sometimes a triplet and a dotted eighth + dotted eighth + eighth are sung interchangeably when in fact they are distinctly different.

At this point you may think everything's as tight as it can be, but there is one additional element that has the potential to throw off tuning completely.

LOUDNESS

In the absence of any other information, all notes comprising a unit (background "ooh," melodic trio, and so on) should have relatively the same volume level. However, there is other information that needs to be taken into consideration:

- Each part needs to be balanced based on importance, with the root of the chord generally loudest, then fifth, and then third.
- Color notes (the seventh, ninth, sixth, etc.) should be quieter, especially when stacked in seconds against major chord factors.
- Doubled chord factors should be quieter—less is needed.
- The human ear naturally gravitates to the highest voice (which is why Bach put the melodies in the top voice of his four-part chorales, and the sopranos have had the melody ever since), and for that reason the highest voice wants to be a hair quieter than the other parts to sound balanced.
- The major exception to all of this: the melody should always be loudest, regardless of chord factor and function.

If all of these nuances sound as if they are a lot to consider, well, they are. Luckily this level of detail isn't always needed. If things are sounding well blended, then you don't need to go in and do microsurgery on every note, analyzing its chord factor and assessing its relative importance and therefore volume. However, if you're having difficulty locking down the blend, if chords sound unbalanced, and if notes appear to be out of tune when they aren't, the reason is balance.

One final thought when it comes to balance and tuning: people's ears aren't perfect so there's no perfect tuning; it's just a matter of getting it "close enough for jazz" as they say. Too many times educators describe something as "in tune" or "out of tune" as though it is a binary either/or, black or white situation when in fact it's all a continuum and people have different thresholds within which things sound in or out of tune. Moreover, as a result of our intentionally compromised equal-tempered Western tuning system, we have a higher threshold for tuning variances, which is especially beneficial in a cappella. The point of music is not precision any more than the point of a great speech is grammar. The technique is important but not the point. What you have to say, how well you connect with the audience, and how well the audience receives your message emotionally and intellectually by the end of a concert is the point. Blend is merely one element that helps you reach that goal.

8

REHEARSAL TECHNIQUES

With apologies to Gertrude Stein, a rehearsal is a rehearsal is a rehearsal, and if you're reading this book you have likely been in many, know what works, know what doesn't work, and so on. Contemporary a cappella rehearsals are like any other vocal music rehearsal more or less, with the understanding that your singers will likely be called upon to be a bit more creative in their interpretations of the music (unlike a Bach motet or choral work, you will likely want them to put their own spin on certain vocal lines, vocal percussion, etc.), and as such a rehearsal requires more back-and-forth than the "sit down and shut up" choral rehearsals of your youth.

There is no single proper rehearsal process that must be followed by every director. To each his own. Through many a decade of running rehearsals I've come upon a process that works well for me, and may for you as well.

REHEARSAL ORDER

1. Warm-ups

- Start rehearsal exactly on time to the minute, which makes the most of your time together and provides an effective silent cue to late members that they are late (it is awkward to enter a room of people already singing).

- Spend minimal time warming vocal range, unless it's early morning, and instead focus on elements that engage your singers' minds as well as voices. You can create warm-ups to work on difficult elements: rhythms, blending, singing modes, intervals, or (shameless plug alert) just purchase my book *A Cappella Warmups for Pop and Jazz Choirs*, which has fifty different exercises designed to focus on different elements and skills. Most important: don't just do the same warm-ups every rehearsal as it trains your singers to "zone out" and sing without thought and focus, which results in more instinctual "autopilot" when singing your performance numbers.
- Ideally keep your warm-ups brief, no more than five to ten minutes, unless your rehearsal time isn't at a premium (perhaps you're doing a weekend retreat).
- If your rehearsal time is limited and you're not rehearsing first thing in the morning, tell your singers to arrive warmed up so you can dive right into music.

2. New Music

- It's best to start a new song while people are fresh and focused, and as learning new music is exciting to most singers, it engages them right away and inspires them to ensure they show up to rehearsal on time or even early, so they don't miss anything.
- Ideally your new music has been circulated in advance, perhaps with parts recordings, so that you're spending minimal time "note plunking," but don't be afraid to repeat difficult passages as needed. Start with a run-through of the entire song to assess; then move methodically through the song fixing notes as needed.
- Make sure to teach dynamics and articulation from the beginning (so they're "hardwired" into the notes), and take the time to get it all right during this first rehearsal, as it's much harder to unlearn the wrong notes later on.
- Emotion being central to music, don't just teach the technical elements of the music. Instead, be sure your singers understand why you have chosen a particular song, what it means, and what you are

bringing as a group to the performance. There should be a clear reason for your musical choices, from dynamics to phrasing, and they should all align with the song's higher purpose, message, and mood.

- Reinforce the behavior that you want your singers to "come clean" when they need extra time on a passage, are having trouble with a specific interval, and so on. You want them telling you when they're confused or uncertain, rather than having to spend your time and energy rooting it out. A raised hand should be used as a positive example and rewarded, not met with an eye roll or derision. Your slowest singers are doing you a favor by getting it right.
- Encourage the use of recording devices, such as cell phones, so your singers can record passages, archive the learning process, and listen to it all just before the next rehearsal so you can start where you left off.
- Don't "overstay your welcome"—move on after twenty to forty minutes, based on your singers' attention spans.

3. Songs in Progress

- Provide time to go back into pieces that need some polishing, stopping to work on specific sections as needed.
- Start with a run-through of the entire song (if possible), remembering what passages need focus. This gives singers a sense of progress, and some sight-singing/memory practice.
- Never "just run it from the top." Every time through a song should be fully engaged, with dynamics and emotions (shameless plug alert 2: see my book *The Heart of Vocal Harmony*). Anytime you sing through a song after having learned the notes you should be singing it with emotion. To repeatedly sing without emotion makes it increasingly unlikely that your singers will be able to perform appropriately, compellingly, and emotionally when they are onstage. Actors run lines in character, dancers move with their entire bodies, and singers need to sing with emotion, as it's why people come to hear them in the first place.
- Try not to spend much time with any one section of the song or section of your group. If needed call a sectional rehearsal, so you can keep the entire group focused and engaged.

- Let your singers know when the song is beyond this step and ready to be memorized (which should happen as soon as possible, so they're not relying on sheet music as a crutch).

4. Songs the Group Knows Well

- Sing through a song with no stopping and no excuses. Each time through the song should be performance-level singing, from memory, fully engaged, and fully emotive.
- Take a couple of moments before starting to remind your singers of the song's emotional focus, encouraging them to focus on the message not the notes and rhythms, which should be second nature at this point. It's okay if there is a moment or two in which they need to consciously focus on an interval or tempo shift, but for the most part they should be emoting, not analyzing.
- After the performance give an honest assessment, and a couple pointers, but don't belabor every single error. You can give notes to individuals on the side, instead of in front of the entire group, which will save time and bruised egos.
- If you have a larger group and don't think your singers are fully engaged or fully memorized, consider having people sing in small ensembles (one on a part) with others listening and watching.

5. Business

- Save business discussions for the last few minutes of rehearsal (or, if it's a long rehearsal, as a break in the middle, but with a time limit).
- Have an agenda and stick to it, as discussions can spiral out of control and take up valuable rehearsal time. Invite engaged singers to remain after rehearsal to continue discussion.
- Topics that can be handled via e-mail (such as T-shirt color or which logo people prefer) should be only discussed in rehearsal if they become emotionally charged or contentious. Spend your time together as a group doing things that require everyone to be together, and anything else should happen in a different forum.
- Delegate tasks, form committees to handle logistics/projects, and handle issues in smaller groupings whenever possible.

- Distribute hard data via paper and e-mail so no time is lost writing down/entering in calendar during rehearsal.

To facilitate this rehearsal process, it is helpful to describe your progress in terms of the four stages of song preparation.

- Learning: This encompasses everything from the first time your singers are seeing or hearing the arrangement to their ability to correctly sing all of the notes. Ideally much of this will be done outside of entire group rehearsal time, as it's the only stage that can be done individually on people's own time, and it's the stage in which people's skills can vary wildly (some being quick learners, others needing lots of repetition).
- Polishing: This is the process of turning a chain of notes and markings into a song. Focus on theme of song and emotional content throughout so there is a higher purpose to each musical choice and moment.
- Memorization: Once a song is memorized, which should happen as soon as possible, not much time should need to be spent on a song, other than singing once or twice through a song at the end of a rehearsal, with a few group notes each time. Make each time through the song as though it's a performance, exercising the "muscle" of your singer's full engagement.
- Performance: Once a song has been performed, no more rehearsal time should be needed unless it has been a while since the performance, or you noticed some element that needs fixing. Ideally, you'll have enough ongoing performances to keep these songs fresh while providing motivation to get songs through the memorization stage into your repertoire. To this end, a performance every couple of weeks is highly recommended, even if it's casual. To perform only a few times a year makes ongoing motivation in rehearsal difficult.

There will be times when you will want to break your group into smaller groups and have sectional rehearsals.

- These will ideally happen outside of your standard rehearsal time, perhaps just before or after existing rehearsals, so your singers won't have additional travel time.
- If you have a larger ensemble, it's a good idea to identify section leaders (traditionally four) who can teach the music and act as field marshals during rehearsal as well as provide you with updates as to how the section is doing, record rehearsals (note plunking and run-throughs) and share them with absent members, and so on.
- If you will be having sectionals before working on a song as a group, you should meet with section leaders so they know the song's emotional focus, dynamics, articulation, and how all the parts fit together.
- When you do take the time to have extended sectional rehearsals (perhaps at a retreat), give them multiple songs to work on so they're able to set their own pacing: learning some songs from scratch, polishing some learned songs, and making sure they have others properly memorized.

Learning tracks are an incredible tool, allowing notes to be learned outside of rehearsal, and are especially helpful to your slowest music learners (those that don't read sheet music well).

- They are best if sung, but it's still acceptable if the parts are played on piano or via MIDI file (distilled from Finale, Sibelius, or other music-notation program).
- If existing recordings are not available for music you've purchased, it's okay if you make your own. They can be as simple as recording a video of you sitting at the piano singing and playing through each part.
- As much as possible, infuse them with the feel, mood, and meaning you're planning for the song (dynamics, phrasing, etc.).

If you want to get the best out of your singers and make the most of every rehearsal, a director should treat a rehearsal as though it is a performance. Check your mood at the door and make the experience a fun and productive one for everyone.

- Plan some unexpected surprises for your group at noncritical rehearsals (e.g., just after a big concert) so it's not all regimented and predictable.
- Move as quickly as you can through any part teaching, and move on just as they have it (unless it's a "dangerous passage"). Fast is exciting and demands focus, and a focused rehearsal moves quickly (people enjoy time well spent).
- Everyone likes to sing, so maximize singing; minimize your speaking and note giving. Some directors like to talk a bit too much. Say what needs saying, perhaps make a quick joke, and dive back in. Don't exhaust your singers, but do keep them engaged and on their toes.
- Smile, and have fun yourself. Your genuine joy will positively impact everyone in the room, as you are the focus.

Here are a few other tips for directors to create a productive rehearsal and group environment:

- Find opportunities for each member to shine onstage, be it a solo, an introduction to a song, a choreographic moment, or other part.
- Take calculated creative risks, try new ideas, and find new sounds.
- Keep an open relationship with all members so they feel comfortable coming to you with problems and issues and are comfortable emoting onstage.
- Express your goals to everyone in advance, so they know what to expect and will feel a sense of accomplishment at the end of a rehearsal.
- Don't rely on the talents of any one member too much, as it can create resentment within a group, a power imbalance, and an illness can render you incapable of performing.
- When modifying arrangements in rehearsals, involve the singers. It can be overwhelming at times addressing many ideas, but the best ones will rise to the top and the end result will be a performance that is very much your own.
- Make sure singers all have pencils at rehearsal and take notes in their music. An arrangement is only a road map to connect your

singers with the audience, and when you decide on a detour they should all make sure to write it down so it becomes the new map.

- Keep the big picture in mind, and don't get lost in the details, be they musical, choreographic, or logistical.
- Build a repertoire with enough variety to address a variety of performing situations and moods. This makes your group more versatile and also expands the emotional impact of your performances.
- Directors should remain focused onstage, but don't forget you're performing too. A complete focus on details and imperfections will result in a blank face or worse yet a grimace that will impact the performers and the audience.
- Listen to live or rehearsal tapes from time to time to analyze and critique in a way that's impossible while in the middle of creating.
- Don't let imperfections erode your sense of joy and accomplishment. Live music is by its very nature imperfect, and one of the problems with modern recorded music is that it has frequently been tuned and polished to the point of sounding robotic and inhuman. A cappella is compelling because it is human, and imperfect.
- Remember that rehearsals are all about focusing on mistakes so that even if your group is 95 percent perfect you'll spend most of the time addressing the 5 percent that isn't right, resulting in the potential perception that your group isn't as good as they are. Celebrate successes and maintain a balanced perspective that appreciates all that is going well.

9

USING AUDIO
ENHANCEMENT TECHNOLOGY

Matthew Edwards

In the early days of popular music, musicians performed without electronic amplification. Singers learned to project their voices in the tradition of vaudeville performers with a technique similar to operatic and operetta performers who had been singing unamplified for centuries. When microphones began appearing onstage in the 1930s, vocal performance changed forever since the loudness of a voice was no longer a factor in the success of a performer. In order to be successful, all a singer needed was an interesting vocal quality and an emotional connection to what he or she was singing. The microphone would take care of projection.

Vocal qualities that sound weak without a microphone can sound strong and projected when sung with one. At the same time, a singer with a voice that is acoustically beautiful and powerful can sound harsh and pushed if he or she lacks microphone technique. Understanding how to use audio equipment to get the sounds a singer desires without harming the voice is crucial. The information in this chapter will help the reader gain a basic knowledge of terminology and equipment commonly used when amplifying or recording a vocalist as well as providing tips for singing with a microphone.

THE FUNDAMENTALS OF SOUND

In order to understand how to manipulate an audio signal, you must first understand a few basics of sound including frequency, amplitude, harmonics, and resonance.

Frequency

Sound travels in waves of compression and rarefaction within a medium, which for our purposes is air (see figure 9.1). These waves travel through the air and into our inner ears via the ear canal. There they are converted via the eardrums into nerve impulses that are transmitted to the brain and interpreted as sound. The number of waves per second is measured in hertz (Hz), which gives us the frequency of the sound that we have learned to perceive as pitch. For example, we hear 440 Hz (440 cycles of compression and rarefaction per second) as A4, the pitch A above middle C.

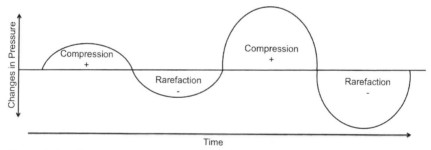

Figure 9.1. Compression and rarefaction. *Creative Commons.*

Amplitude

The magnitude of the waves of compression and rarefaction determines the amplitude of the sound, which we call its "volume." The larger the waves of compression and rarefaction, the louder we perceive the sound to be. Measured in decibels (dB), amplitude represents changes in air pressure from the baseline. Decibel measurements range from zero decibels (0 dB), the threshold of human hearing, to 130 dB, the upper edge of the threshold of pain.

Harmonics

The vibrating mechanism of an instrument produces the vibrations necessary to establish pitch (the fundamental frequency). The vibrating mechanism for a singer is the vocal folds. If an acoustic instrument, such as the voice, were to produce a note with the fundamental frequency alone, the sound would be strident and mechanical like the emergency alert signal used on television. Pitches played on acoustic instruments consist of multiple frequencies, called overtones, which are emitted from the vibrator along with the fundamental frequency. For the purposes of this chapter, the overtones we are interested in are called harmonics. Harmonics are whole number multiples of the fundamental frequency. For example, if the fundamental is 220 Hz (A3), the harmonic overtone series would be 220 Hz, 440 Hz (fundamental frequency times two), 660 Hz (fundamental frequency times three), 880 Hz (fundamental frequency times four), and so on. Every musical note contains both the fundamental frequency and a predictable series of harmonics, each of which can be measured and identified as a specific frequency. This series of frequencies then travels through a hollow cavity (the vocal tract) where they are attenuated or amplified by the resonating frequencies of the cavity, which is how resonance occurs.

Resonance

The complex waveform created by the vocal folds travels through the vocal tract, where it is enhanced by the tract's unique resonance characteristics. Depending on the resonator's shape, some harmonics are amplified and some are attenuated. Each singer has a unique vocal tract shape with unique resonance characteristics. This is why two singers of the same voice type can sing the same pitch and yet sound very different. We can analyze these changes with a tool called a spectral analyzer as seen in figure 9.2. The slope from left to right is called the spectral slope. The peaks and valleys along the slope indicate amplitude variations of the corresponding overtones. The difference in spectral slope between instruments (or voices) is what enables a listener to aurally distinguish the difference between two instruments playing or singing the same note.

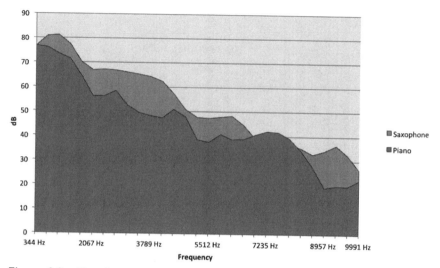

Figure 9.2. Two instruments playing the same pitch. The peak at the far left is the fundamental frequency, and the peaks to the right are harmonics that have been amplified and attenuated by the instrument's resonator, resulting in a specific timbre. *Courtesy of Matthew Edwards.*

Because the throat and mouth act as the resonating tube in acoustic singing, changing their size and shape is the only option for making adjustments to timbre for those who perform without microphones. In electronically amplified singing, the sound engineer can make adjustments to boost or attenuate specific frequency ranges, thus changing the singer's timbre. For this and many other reasons discussed in this chapter, it is vitally important for singers to know how audio technology can affect the quality of their voice.

SIGNAL CHAIN

The signal chain is the path an audio signal travels from the input to the output of a sound system. A voice enters the signal chain through a microphone, which transforms acoustic energy into electrical impulses. The electrical pulses generated by the microphone are transmitted through a series of components that modify the signal before the speakers transform it back into acoustic energy. Audio engineers and producers understand the intricacies of these systems and are able to make an infinite variety of alterations to the vocal signal. While some engineers strive to replicate the original sound source as accurately as possible, others use the capabilities of the system to alter the sound for artistic effect. Since more components and variations exist than can be discussed in just a few pages, this chapter will discuss only basic components and variations found in most systems.

Microphones

Microphones transform the acoustic sound waves of the voice into electrical impulses. The component of the microphone that is responsible for receiving the acoustic information is the diaphragm. The two most common diaphragm types that singers will encounter are dynamic and condenser. Each offers advantages and disadvantages depending on how the microphone is to be used.

Dynamic.   Dynamic microphones consist of a dome-shaped Mylar diaphragm attached to a free-moving copper wire coil that is positioned between the two poles of a magnet (figure 9.3). The Mylar diaphragm moves in response to air pressure changes caused by sound waves. When the diaphragm moves, the magnetic coil that is attached to it also moves. As the magnetic coil moves up and down between the magnetic

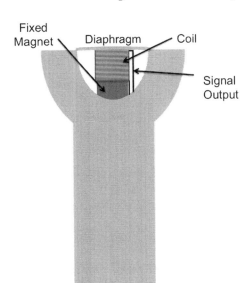

Fixed
Magnet   Diaphragm   Coil

Signal
Output

Figure 9.3.   This is the basic design of a dynamic microphone. *Courtesy of Matthew Edwards.*

poles, it produces an electrical current that corresponds to the sound waves produced by the singer's voice. That signal is then sent to the soundboard via the microphone cable.

The Shure SM58 dynamic microphone is the industry standard for live performance because it is affordable, nearly indestructible, and easy to use. Dynamic microphones such as the Shure SM58 have a lower sensitivity than condenser microphones, which makes them more successful at avoiding feedback. Because of their reduced tendency to feedback, dynamic microphones are the best choice for artists who use handheld microphones when performing.

Condenser. Condenser microphones are constructed with two parallel plates: a rigid posterior plate and a thin, flexible anterior plate (figure 9.4). The anterior plate is constructed of either a thin sheet of metal or a piece of Mylar that is coated with a conductive metal. The plates are separated by air, which acts as a layer of insulation. In order to use a condenser microphone, it must be connected to a soundboard that supplies "phantom power." A component of the soundboard, phantom power sends a 48-volt power supply through the microphone cable to the microphone's plates. When the plates are charged by phantom power,

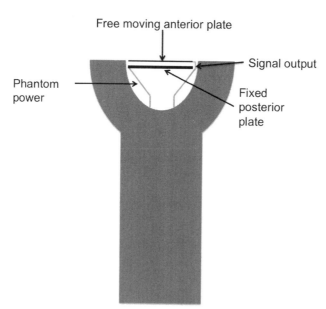

Figure 9.4. This is the basic design of a condenser microphone. *Courtesy of Matthew Edwards.*

they form a capacitor. As acoustic vibrations send the anterior plate into motion, the distance between the two plates varies, which causes the capacitor to release a small electric current. This current, which corresponds with the acoustic signal of the voice, travels through the microphone cable to the soundboard where it can be enhanced and amplified.

Electret condenser microphones are similar to condenser microphones, but they are designed to work without phantom power. The anterior plate of an electret microphone is made of a plastic film coated with a conductive metal that is electrically charged before being set into place opposite the posterior plate. The charge applied to the anterior plate will last for ten or more years and therefore eliminates the need for an exterior power source. Electret condenser microphones are often used in head-mounted and lapel microphones, laptop computers, and smartphones.

Recording engineers prefer condenser microphones for recording applications due to their high level of sensitivity. Using a condenser microphone, performers can sing at nearly inaudible acoustic levels and obtain a final recording that is intimate and earthy. While the same vocal effects can be recorded with a dynamic microphone, they will not have the same clarity as those produced with a condenser microphone.

Frequency Response. Frequency response is a term used to define how accurately a microphone captures the tone quality of the signal. A "flat response" microphone captures the original signal with little to no signal alteration. Microphones that are not designated as "flat" have some type of amplification or attenuation of specific frequencies, also known as cut or boost, within the audio spectrum. For instance, the Shure SM58 microphone drastically attenuates the signal below 300 Hz and amplifies the signal in the 3 kHz range by 6 dB, the 5 kHz range by nearly 8 dB, and the 10 kHz range by approximately 6 dB. The Oktava 319 microphone cuts the frequencies below 200 Hz while boosting everything above 300 Hz with nearly 5 dB between 7 kHz and 10k Hz (see figure 9.5). In practical terms, recording a bass singer with the Shure SM58 would drastically reduce the amplitude of the fundamental frequency while the Oktava 319 would produce a slightly more consistent boost in the range of the singer's formant. Either of these options could be acceptable depending on the situation, but the frequency response must be considered before making a recording or performing live.

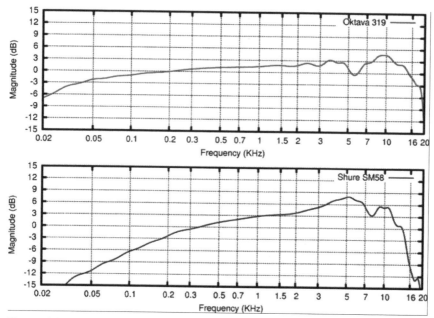

Figure 9.5. Example frequency response graphs for the Oktava 319 and the Shure SM58. *Wikimedia Commons.*

Amplitude Response. The amplitude response of a microphone varies depending on the angle at which the singer is positioned in relation to the axis of the microphone. In order to visualize the amplitude response of a microphone at various angles, microphone manufacturers publish polar pattern diagrams (also sometimes called a directional pattern or a pickup pattern). Polar pattern diagrams usually consist of six concentric circles divided into twelve equal sections. The center point of the microphone's diaphragm is labeled 0° and is referred to as "on-axis" while the opposite side of the diagram is labeled 180° and is described as "off-axis."

Although polar pattern diagrams appear in two dimensions, they actually represent a three-dimensional response to acoustic energy. You can use a round balloon as a physical example to help you visualize a three-dimensional polar pattern diagram. Position the tied end of the balloon away from your mouth and the inflated end directly in front of your lips. In this position, you are singing on-axis at 0° with the tied end of the balloon being 180°, or off-axis. If you were to split the balloon in half vertically and horizontally (in relationship to your lips), the point at which those lines intersect would be the center point of the balloon. That imaginary center represents the diaphragm of the microphone. If you were to extend a 45° angle in any direction from the imaginary center and then draw a circle around the inside of the balloon following that angle, you would have a visualization of the three-dimensional application of the two-dimensional polar pattern drawing.

The outermost circle of the diagram indicates that the sound pressure level (SPL) of the signal is transferred without any amplitude reduction, indicated in decibels (dB). Each of the inner circles represents a –5 dB reduction in the amplitude of the signal up to –25 dB. Figures 9.6 and 9.7 are examples. Figures 9.8, 9.9, and 9.10 show the most commonly encountered polar patterns.

When you are using a microphone with a polar pattern other than omnidirectional (a pattern that responds to sound equally from all directions), you may encounter frequency response fluctuations in addition to amplitude fluctuations. Cardioid microphones in particular are known for their tendency to boost lower frequencies at close proximity to the

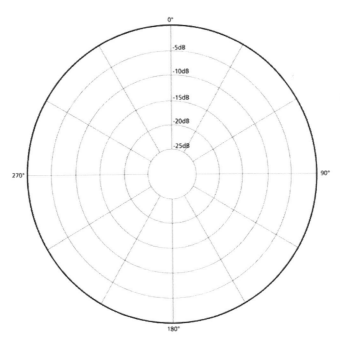

Figure 9.6.   An example of a microphone polar pattern diagram. *Wikimedia Commons.*

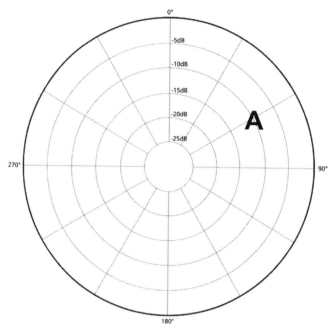

Figure 9.7. If the amplitude response curve intersected with point A, there would be a −10dB reduction in the amplitude of frequencies received by the microphone's diaphragm at that angle. *Wikimedia Commons.*

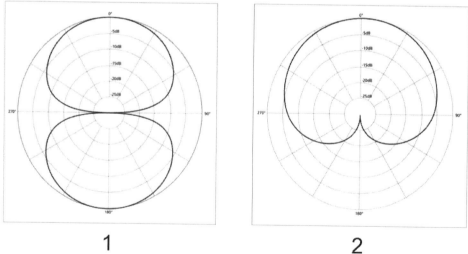

1   2

Figure 9.8. Diagram one represents a bidirectional pattern; diagram two represents a cardioid pattern. *Creative Commons.*

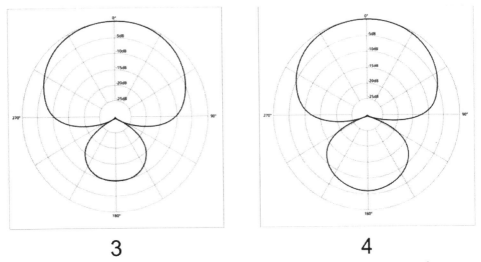

3

4

Figure 9.9.   Diagram three represents a super-cardioid pattern; diagram four represents a hyper-cardioid pattern. *Creative Commons.*

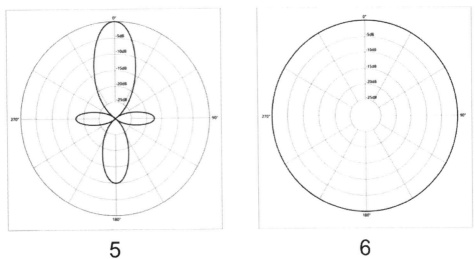

5

6

Figure 9.10.   Diagram five represents a shotgun pattern; diagram six represents an omnidirectional pattern. *Creative Commons.*

sound source while attenuating those same frequencies as the distance between the sound source and the microphone increases. This is known as the "proximity effect." Some manufacturers will notate these frequency response changes on their polar pattern diagrams by using a combination of various lines and dashes alongside the amplitude response curve.

Sensitivity. While sensitivity can be difficult to explain in technical terms without going into an in-depth discussion of electricity and electrical terminology, a simplified explanation should suffice for most readers. Manufacturers test microphones with a standardized 1 kHz tone at 94 dB in order to determine how sensitive the microphone's diaphragm will be to acoustic energy. Microphones with greater sensitivity can be placed farther from the sound source without adding excessive noise to the signal. Microphones with lower sensitivity will need to be placed closer to the sound source in order to keep excess noise at a minimum. When shopping for a microphone, the performer should audition several next to each other, plugged into the same soundboard, with the same volume level for each. When singing on each microphone, at the same distance, the performer will notice that some models replicate the voice louder than others. This change in output level is due to differences in each microphone's sensitivity. If a performer has a loud voice, he or she may prefer a microphone with lower sensitivity (one that requires more acoustic energy to respond). If a performer has a lighter voice, he or she may prefer a microphone with higher sensitivity (one that responds well to softer signals).

Equalization (EQ)

Equalizers enable the audio engineer to alter the audio spectrum of the sound source and make tone adjustments with a simple electronic interface. Equalizers come in three main types: shelf, parametric, and graphic.

Shelf. Shelf equalizers cut or boost the uppermost and lowermost frequencies of an audio signal in a straight line (see figure 9.11). While this style of equalization is not very useful for fine-tuning a singer's tone quality, it can be very effective in removing room noise. For example, if an air conditioner creates a 60 Hz hum in the recording studio, the shelf can be set at 65 Hz, with a steep slope. This setting eliminates

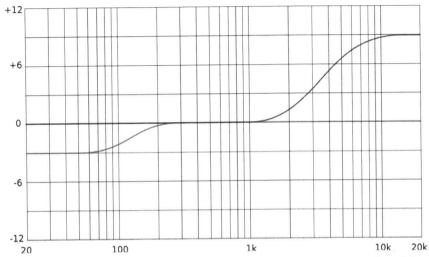

Figure 9.11.   These frequency amplitude curves show the affect of applying a shelf EQ to an audio signal. *Wikimedia Commons.*

frequencies below 65 Hz and effectively removes the hum from the microphone signal.

Parametric. Parametric units simultaneously adjust multiple frequencies of the audio spectrum that fall within a defined parameter. The engineer selects a center frequency and adjusts the width of the bell curve surrounding that frequency by adjusting the "Q" (see figure 9.12). He or she then boosts or cuts the frequencies within the bell curve to alter the audio spectrum. Parametric controls take up minimal space on a soundboard and offer sufficient control for most situations. Therefore, most live performance soundboards have parametric EQs on each individual channel. With the advent of digital workstations, engineers can now use computer software to fine-tune the audio quality of each individual channel using a more complex graphic equalizer in both live and recording studio settings without taking up any additional physical space on the board. However, many engineers still prefer to use parametric controls during a live performance since they are usually sufficient and are easier to adjust midperformance.

Parametric adjustments on a soundboard are made with rotary knobs similar to those in figure 9.13. In some cases, you will find a button labeled "low cut" or "high pass" that will automatically apply a shelf

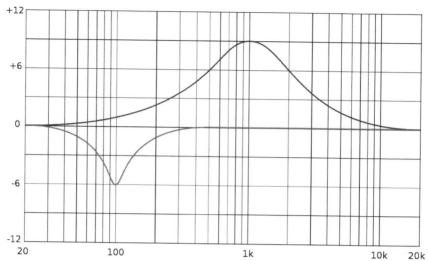

Figure 9.12. These frequency amplitude curves display two parametric EQ settings. The top curve represents a boost of +8 dB set at 1 kHz with a relatively large bell curve—a low Q. The lower curve represents a high Q set at 100 Hz with a cut of −6 dB. *Wikimedia Commons.*

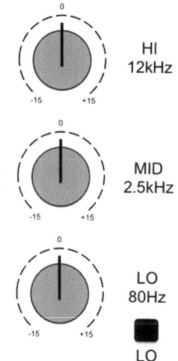

Figure 9.13. This is an example of a parametric EQ interface. The "LO CUT" button applies a shelf EQ at 80 Hz when depressed. *Courtesy of Matthew Edwards.*

filter to the bottom of the audio spectrum at a specified frequency. On higher-end boards, you may also find a knob that enables you to select the high pass frequency.

Graphic.   Graphic equalizers enable engineers to identify a specific frequency for boost or cut with a fixed frequency bandwidth. For example, a ten-band equalizer enables the audio engineer to adjust ten specific frequencies (in Hz): 31, 63, 125, 250, 500, 1K, 2K, 4K, 8K, and 16K. Graphic equalizers are often one of the final elements of the signal chain, preceding only the amplifier and speakers. In this position, they can be used to adjust the overall tonal quality of the entire mix.

Utilizing Equalization.   Opinions on the usage of equalization vary among engineers. Some prefer to only use equalization to remove or reduce frequencies that were not a part of the original sound signal. Others will use EQ if adjusting microphone placement fails to yield acceptable results. Some engineers prefer a more processed sound and may use equalization liberally to intentionally change the vocal quality of the singer. For instance, if the singer's voice sounds dull, the engineer could add "ring" or "presence" to the voice by boosting the equalizer in the 2–10 kHz range. See figure 9.14 for an example of a graphic equalizer interface.

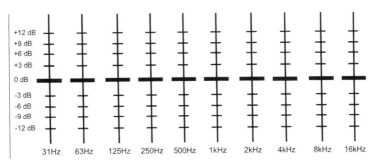

Figure 9.14.   This is an example of a graphic equalizer interface. *Courtesy of Matthew Edwards.*

Compression

Many singers are capable of producing vocal extremes in both frequency and amplitude levels that can prove problematic for the sound team. To help solve this problem, engineers often use compression.

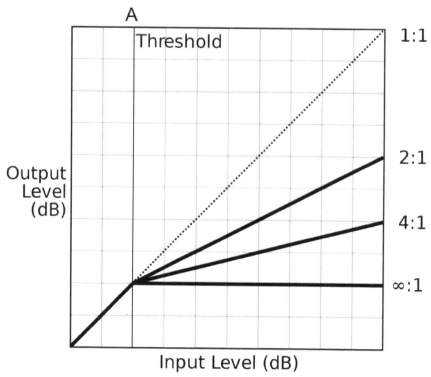

Figure 9.15. This graph represents the effects of various compression ratios applied to a signal. The 1:1 angle represents no compression. The other ratios represent the effect of compression on an input signal with the threshold set at line A. *Wikimedia Commons.*

Compressors limit the output of a sound source by a specified ratio. The user sets the maximum acceptable amplitude level for the output, called the "threshold," and then sets a ratio to reduce the output once it surpasses the threshold. The typical ratio for a singer is usually between 3:1 and 5:1. A 4:1 ratio indicates that for every 4 dB beyond the threshold level, the output will only increase by 1 dB. For example, if the singer went 24 dB beyond the threshold with a 4:1 ratio, the output would only be 6 dB beyond the threshold level (see figure 9.15).

Adjusting the sound via microphone technique can provide some of the same results as compression and is preferable for the experienced artist. However, compression tends to be more consistent and also gives the singer freedom to focus on performing and telling a story. The additional artistic freedom provided by compression is especially beneficial to singers who use head-mounted microphones, performers who switch between vocal extremes such as falsetto and chest voice, and those who are new to performing with a microphone. Compression can also be helpful for classical singers whose dynamic abilities, while impressive live, are often difficult to record in a manner that allows for consistent listening levels through a stereo system.

If a standard compressor causes unacceptable alterations to the tone quality, engineers can turn to a multiband compressor. Rather than affecting the entire spectrum of sound, multiband compressors allow the engineer to isolate a specific frequency range within the audio signal and then set an individual compression setting for that frequency range. For example, if a singer creates a dramatic boost in the 4 kHz range every time they sing above an A4, a multiband compressor can be used to limit the amplitude of the signal in only that part of the voice. By setting a 3:1 ratio in the 4 kHz range at a threshold that corresponds to the amplitude peaks that appear when the performer sings above A4, the engineer can eliminate vocal "ring" from the sound on only the offending notes while leaving the rest of the signal untouched. These units are available for both live and studio use and can be a great alternative to compressing the entire signal.

Reverb

Reverb is one of the easier effects for singers to identify; it is the effect you experience when singing in a cathedral. Audience members experiences natural reverberation when they hear the direct signal from the singer and then, milliseconds later, they hear multiple reflections as the acoustical waves of the voice bounce off the side walls, floor, and ceiling of the performance hall (figure 9.16).

Many performance venues and recording studios are designed to inhibit natural reverb. Without at least a little reverb added to the sound, even the best singer can sound harsh and even amateurish. Early reverb units transmitted the audio signal through a metal spring, which added supplementary vibrations to the signal. While some engineers still use spring reverb to obtain a specific effect, most now use digital units.

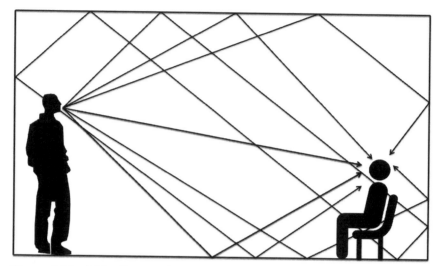

Figure 9.16. This diagram illustrates the multiple lines of reflection that create reverb. *Courtesy of Matthew Edwards.*

Common settings on digital reverb units include wet/dry, bright/dark, and options for delay time. The wet/dry control adjusts the amount of direct signal (dry) and the amount of reverberated signal (wet). The bright/dark control helps simulate the effects of various surfaces within a natural space. For instance, harder surfaces such as stone reflect high frequencies and create a brighter tone quality while softer surfaces such as wood reflect lower frequencies and create a darker tone quality. The delay time, which is usually adjustable from milliseconds to seconds, adjusts the amount of time between when the dry signal and wet signals reach the ear. Engineers can transform almost any room into a chamber music hall or concert stadium simply by adjusting these settings.

Delay

Whereas reverb blends multiple wet signals with the dry signal to replicate a natural space, delay purposefully separates a single wet signal from the dry signal to create repetitions of the voice (figure 9.17). With delay, you will hear the original note first and then a digitally produced repeat of the note several milliseconds to seconds later. The delayed note may be heard one time or multiple times, and the timing of those repeats can be adjusted to match the tempo of the song.

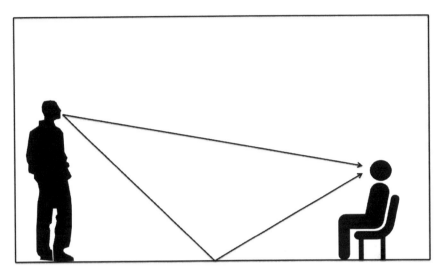

Figure 9.17. **This diagram illustrates how a direct line of sound followed by a reflected line of sound creates delay.** *Courtesy of Matthew Edwards.*

Auto-Tune

Auto-Tune was first used in studios as a useful way to clean up minor imperfections in otherwise perfect performances. Auto-Tune is now an industry standard that many artists use, even if they are not willing to admit it. Auto-Tune has gained a bad reputation in the past few years, and whether or not you agree with its use, it is a reality in today's market. If you do not understand how to use it properly, you could end up sounding like T-Pain.

Both Antares and Melodyne have developed Auto-Tune technology in both "auto" and "graphical" formats. "Auto" Auto-Tune allows the engineer to set specific parameters for pitch correction that are then computer controlled. "Graphical" Auto-Tune tracks the pitch in the selected area of a recording and plots the fundamental frequency on a linear graph. The engineer can then select specific notes for pitch correction. They can also drag selected pitches to a different frequency, add or reduce vibrato, and change formant frequencies above the fundamental. To simplify, the "auto" function makes general corrections while the "graphic" function makes specific corrections. The "auto" setting is usually used to achieve a specific effect (for instance, "I Believe" by Cher), while the "graphic" setting is used to correct small imperfections in a recorded performance.

Digital Voice Processors

Digital voice processors are still relatively new to the market and have yet to gain widespread usage among singers. While there are several brands of vocal effects processors available, the industry leader as of this printing is a company called TC-Helicon. TC-Helicon manufactures several different units that span from consumer to professional grade. TC-Helicon's premier performer-controlled unit is called the VoiceLive 3. The VoiceLive 3 incorporates more than twelve vocal effects, eleven guitar effects, and a multitrack looper with 250 factory presets and 250 memory slots for user presets. The VoiceLive 3 puts the effects at the singer's feet in a programmable stomp box that also includes phantom power, MIDI in/out, a USB connection, guitar input, and monitor out. Onboard vocal effects include equalization, compression, reverb, and "auto" Auto-Tune. The unit also offers μMod (an adjustable voice modulator), a doubler (for thickening the lead vocal), echo, delay, reverb, and several other specialized effects.

One of the most impressive features of digital voice processors is the ability to add computer-generated harmonies to the lead vocal. After the user sets the musical key, the processor identifies the fundamental frequency of each sung note. The computer then adds digitized voices at designated intervals above and below the lead singer. The unit also offers the option to program each individual song, with multiple settings for every verse, chorus, and bridge.

THE BASICS OF LIVE SOUND SYSTEMS

Live sound systems come in a variety of sizes from small practice units to state-of-the-art stadium rigs. Most singers only need a basic knowledge of the components commonly found in systems that have one to eight inputs. Units beyond that size usually require an independent sound engineer and are beyond the scope of this chapter.

Following the microphone, the first element in the live signal chain is usually the mixer. Basic portable mixers provide controls for equalization, volume level, auxiliary (usually used for effects such as reverb and compression), and on some units, controls for built-in digital effects processors. Powered mixers combine an amplifier with a basic mixer, providing a compact solution for those who do not need a complex system. Since unpowered mixers do not provide amplification, you will need to add a separate amplifier to power this system.

The powered mixer or amplifier connects to speaker cabinets, which contain a "woofer" and a "tweeter." The woofer is a large round speaker that handles the bass frequencies while the tweeter is a horn-shaped speaker that handles the treble frequencies. The crossover, a component built into the speaker cabinet, separates high and low frequencies and sends them to the appropriate speaker (woofer or tweeter). Speaker cabinets can be either active or passive. Passive cabinets require a powered mixer or an amplifier in order to operate. Active cabinets have an amplifier built in and do not require an external amplifier.

If you do not already own a microphone and amplification system, you can purchase a simple setup at relatively low cost through online vendors such as Sweetwater.com and MusiciansFriend.com. A dynamic microphone and a powered monitor are enough to get started. If you would like to add a digital voice processor, Digitech and TC-Helicon both sell entry-level models that will significantly improve the tonal quality of a sound system.

Monitors are arguably the most important element in a live sound system. The monitor is a speaker that faces the performers and allows them to hear themselves and the other instruments onstage. Onstage volume levels can vary considerably, with drummers often producing sound levels as high as 120 dB. Those volume levels make it nearly impossible for singers to receive natural acoustic feedback while performing. Monitors can improve aural feedback and help reduce the temptation to oversing. Powered monitors offer the same advantages as powered speaker cabinets and can be a great option for amplification when practicing. They are also good to have around as a backup plan in case you arrive at a venue and discover they do not supply monitors. In-ear monitors offer another option for performers and are especially useful for those who frequently move around the stage.

MICROPHONE TECHNIQUE

The microphone is an inseparable part of the contemporary commercial music singer's instrument. Just as there are techniques that improve singing, there are also techniques that will improve microphone use.

Understanding what a microphone does is only the first step to using it successfully. Once you understand how a microphone works, you need hands-on experience.

The best way to learn microphone technique is to experiment. Try the following exercises to gain a better understanding of how to use a microphone when singing:

- Hold a dynamic microphone with a cardioid pattern directly in front of your mouth, no farther than one centimeter away. Sustain a comfortable pitch, and slowly move the microphone away from your lips. Listen to how the vocal quality changes. When the microphone is close to the lips, you should notice that the sound is louder and has more bass response. As you move the microphone away from your mouth, there will be a noticeable loss in volume and the tone will become brighter.
- Next, sustain a pitch while rotating the handle down. The sound quality will change in a similar fashion as when you moved the microphone away from your lips.
- Now try singing breathy with the microphone close to your lips. How little effort can you get away with while producing a marketable sound?
- Try singing bright vowels and dark vowels and notice how the microphone affects the tone quality.
- Also experiment with adapting your diction to the microphone. Because the microphone amplifies everything, you may need to underpronounce certain consonants when singing. You will especially want to reduce the power of the consonants [t], [s], [p], and [b].

FINAL THOUGHTS

Since this is primarily an overview, you can greatly improve your comprehension of the material by seeking other resources to deepen your knowledge. There are many great resources available that may help clarify some of these difficult concepts. Most important, you must experiment. The more you play around with sound equipment on your own, the better you will understand it and the more comfortable you will feel when performing or recording with audio technology.

⑩

A CAPPELLA AUDIO TECH

Tony Huerta

When engineering audio for a cappella artists, everything that applies to a single voice generally remains true for groups. However, because of the various extended vocal techniques, such as instrumental imitation and vocal percussion, and the fact that only voices fill the sonic space, there are some specific acoustic strategies engineers can use to effectively showcase an a cappella group performing live with microphones. Disclaimer: This chapter presumes the reader is somewhat familiar with technical audio equipment and terminology and serves as a basic instructional guide for working specifically with a cappella performers. It also references equipment that is state of the art at the time of this writing.

SONIC ELEMENTS: THE BUILDING BLOCKS OF SOUND

Sound is what we hear and what our brains perceive when vibrations travel through the air or other medium. Sounds are sine waves characterized by frequency, amplitude, speed, and direction. To understand audio engineering concepts, you must first start with equalization (EQ) of frequencies, which is adjusting the volume of various frequency components, or sonic elements, of the sound to achieve a desired overall result.

Over the years, I developed an advanced theory on sonic elements, and it all started when a high school teacher with an a cappella group in her school e-mailed me with one simple question. She asked, "What settings do you use to EQ a bass singer?" I started to e-mail her back and realized that I couldn't answer her question. Then I had to ask myself the same question. How *do* I know what settings to use on a bass singer?

It's important to remember that every voice has different qualities. Those qualities dictate what settings to use. But how do I explain how to do that to someone in an e-mail? I developed a "Frequency Cheat Sheet" (refer to figure 10.1), which will help you translate what you hear into real numbers, so you can more easily adjust the EQ of your mix to achieve your desired result.

Across the top are frequencies labeled in hertz from 20 Hz to 20,000 Hz (20 kHz). Each section identifies a descriptor that people usually use when trying to describe sound in that frequency range to an audio engineer. Artists will say that the sound is tinny, honky, thumpy, or muddy. You can use this chart to see the actual frequencies that match the sound descriptions. Knowing where to find them will greatly enhance your ability to adjust EQ on the spot. I recommend getting a real-time analyzer (RTA) app for your smartphone. It will help you understand what different frequencies sound like. Most of the apps can play a sine wave sound with an adjustable frequency. Use the app in conjunction with my cheat sheet to experiment with various frequencies and their descriptors. You may even come up with a few of your own descriptors to refine even further—give it a try!

The next section on the exhibit is my theory on sonic elements: what specific frequencies make specific instruments sound the way they do. When I'm using EQ on a channel during sound check, what am I listening for? What knobs do I turn and why? Why does the snare drum sound bad, and how do I fix it? It may be helpful to break down the elements of first some popular instruments and then we'll move on to the human voice. Let's start with some of the most basic instruments you might end up mixing.

First, let's look at the kick drum. The kick drum has only two sonic elements. The first is the thump or very low sound, or "tone," and the

FREQUENCY CHEAT SHEET

	20 HZ	80 HZ	160 HZ	350 HZ	800 HZ	2.0 KHZ	5.0 KHZ	10.0 KHZ	20.0 KHZ
Descriptors	Thumpy	Bassy	Muddy	Wonky	A.M. Radio	Harshness	Too Bright	Air	
	Thuddy	Too much "low end"	Too warm	Honky	Megaphone	Hurts ears	Sibilant		
	Woofy		Not clear		Nasal		Tinny		
Sonic Elements									
Kick Drum		55Hz - 70Hz Thump					4.0 KHz - 5.5KHz Beater Attack		
Snare			200 Hz — — — — — — Tone — — — — — — 900 Hz			2.5KHz - 3.5KHz Stick Smack		8KHz & up Snares	
Vocal Sonic Elements									
Bass		60Hz—70Hz Thump	80Hz— — — — — 240Hz Tone (actual notes)		900 Hz — 1.2KHz Nasal ('dm')	2.5KHz - 5KHz Bite/Harshness/Mask		10KHz & Up Air	
Bari/Tenor			110Hz— — — — 400Hz Tone (actual notes)		900 Hz - 1.2KHz Nasal	2.5KHz - 5KHz Bite/Harshness		10KHz & Up Air	
Tenor 1			130Hz— — — — 440Hz Tone (actual notes)		900 Hz - 1.2KHz Nasal	2.5KHz - 5KHz Bite/Harshness		10KHz & Up Air	
Alto			195Hz— — — — 600Hz Tone (actual notes)		900 Hz - 1.2KHz Nasal	2.5KHz - 5KHz Bite/Harshness		10KHz & Up Air	
Soprano			260Hz— — — — — —900Hz Tone (actual notes)		900 Hz - 1.2KHz Nasal	2.5KHz - 5KHz Bite/Harshness		10KHz & Up Air	

Figure 10.1. Frequency Cheat Sheet. Courtesy of Tony Huerta.

second is the high attack or smack sound (labeled "stick smack"). The drum is made up of a membrane stretched over a large round wooden cylinder. The tone of the drum is in direct correlation to the size of the drum. The attack sound is from the beater that the musician "kicks." It is a felt or plastic beater that strikes the membrane and creates the smack sound you hear. The frequency of the tone of the drum is usually between 55 and 70 Hz. The typical frequency of the smack is usually between 4 kHz and 5.5 kHz. The two elements need to be present and equal or the drum will not sound good. As the sound engineer, you will need to listen for each element and adjust accordingly.

Next, let's look at the snare drum, which has three sonic elements. First is the tone of the drum, related to the size of the cylinder, and with typical frequencies between 200 and 900 Hz. The second is the stick smacking the skin or membrane, whose frequencies are generally in the 2.5kHz–3.5 kHz range. And lastly, there is the sound of the snares, the little wires that run across the bottom of the drum, with frequencies 8 kHz and higher.

The bass guitar is next, with only two sonic elements. The first sonic element, the tone, will be specific: the actual frequency of the note being played, between 50 and 400 Hz. Get out your RTA and play along so you can hear. Use headphones for lower frequencies because phone speakers rarely play tones lower than 180 Hz. The second sonic element of the bass guitar is the pluck or attack of the fingers on the strings. It gives the guitar definition and has a frequency range of 3kHz–5 kHz.

The next section of the exhibit moves into the human voice and helps illustrate why a cappella music is so hard to mix live. All human voices have at least four sonic elements, and some have five. Let's start with the bass singer. There are five sonic elements of the human bass voice. In order from lowest to highest, they are thump, tone, nasal, harshness, and air. Just as with instruments, if the sonic elements of the human voice are not balanced, we perceive their voice to not be so good. Have you ever heard a very nasally singer? Or one that is so harsh that it's ear piercing? Or a swallowed, woofy, bass sound? Each of those sonic elements can be adjusted in the sound console to make the overall voice sound more pleasing.

As a side note, the human voice only sings tones between 50 and 800 Hz in a typical performance. You might wonder how we could have to deal with sonic elements above those frequencies. The answer is that our voices create overtones and nasal vibrations through our faces. We also have the simple sound of the air moving out of our mouth. Table 10.1 shows the typical frequencies of each sonic element and a description of each, for the bass voice.

Table 10.1. Bass vocal sonic elements

Bass Sonic Element	Frequency Range	Description
Bass thump	50–70 Hz	The plosive "thump" heard when saying a B or P sound
Bass tone	80–240 Hz	The actual frequency of the note they are singing
Bass nasal	900–1.1 KHz	The sound of the tone reverberating through our sinuses
Bass harshness	2.5–4 KHz	Harshness and brightness of the overtones
Bass air	10 KHz and up	The sound of the air moving out of our mouth

All the other voice parts in an a cappella group will have the same four upper elements, with different frequency ranges but not the thump. So, what does that mean for the engineer mixing an a cappella performance? If there are ten people in the group and one of them sings bass, then the engineer is setting the EQ and adjusting for forty-one total sonic elements. Using the elements to adjust each voice to sound sonically balanced across each individual singer's sonic elements makes the entire performance sound better. Play around with this until you get quick at adjusting different voices. Turn up the volume on each sonic element frequency, and listen to how it sounds. Learn what different frequencies sound like. It is truly the way to great-sounding concerts.

OVERVIEW OF THE JOB OF THE SOUND ENGINEER

As sound engineer, you must take care of the technical needs of the show during sound check in order, from the basic through the complex. First, you will adjust for the room acoustics with an EQ on the mains and adjust speaker placement and the crossover between the subwoofers and mains. Second, you will adjust and dial in the gain structure of your artist's inputs. Third, you will adjust the mix with volume and channel EQ. And last, you will add in effects for a more pleasing sound. Don't move on to the sound check until you have addressed each issue, in order. Skipping to channel EQ when your room hasn't yet been treated is a recipe for a bad mix.

During the show, the needs of your mix will change slightly and the situation is more creative in nature. But just as with sound check, skipping steps will only create a bad mix. First, handle any overall EQ or volume issues. The artist will perform at a different level than at sound check. You will possibly have to make quick adjustments to the main and subwoofer EQ now that the room is full of people. Or as I always say, a room filled with a thousand sacks of water. Second, ride your mix into balance by adjusting fader level and possibly compression due to the artist's increased energy. Third, and only then, can you move to the most fun part, the effects and creative mixing ideas. The talent level of your artists will usually dictate how much time you have for creativity. Are you just riding faders to balance and blend the artist? If so, you might not have the time to get creative.

A CAPPELLA–SPECIFIC TECHNIQUES, ROOM EQUALIZATION, AND EQUIPMENT

Now, let's get into the specifics. A cappella performances may be held in a variety of venues, so the space itself will have characteristics to consider that can affect the sound—the type of venue, the size, the surfaces, and the furnishings. If you establish room equalization properly, any instrument or artist performing in that space will sound better. First, you must start by listening to the room with a flat EQ, with no technical adjustment. Use familiar songs that you have heard on multiple sound systems and stereos.

Listen for frequencies that stick out, focusing especially on the low end and low midrange between 50 and 630 Hz, which covers the range of most singers. Insert a thirty-one-band stereo EQ or four-band parametric equalization on the main L+R send off the mixer. Put the subwoofers on a separate auxiliary send. Don't forget to also insert an EQ on the infills, balcony fills, or other zones or matrix at the venue. If you choose to use pink noise or software that adjusts the EQ to flatten the room characteristics, do so sparingly. Use your ears more than the technology. Although the room is technically flat using that equipment, the human ear will always perceive the room as not pleasing. Once your standard music in the room sounds good, it's time to consider specific mix ideas for a cappella sound.

The vocal percussionist (VP) or beatboxer is a good place to start. Split the VP input out to three faders using a Whirlwind three-way splitter or internal soft patching on a digital mixer. This creates the opportunity to equalize and place effects on the upper drum parts without affecting the kick channel and vice versa. The three channels are as follows: the kick; the snare and overhead channel; and a vocal channel, in case the performer sings on the same microphone. This gives you the ability to effect and equalize each channel differently for swift midsong changes from VP to singing. Just mute and unmute the channels. Also, don't forget to route the kick channel to the separate subwoofer send.

As for microphone choice, dynamic microphones that can handle high sound pressure levels (SPLs) work best for VP, such as the Shure Beta 58 or the Sennheiser brand with the 945 super-cardioid capsule. Try each microphone without the capsule being "cupped" by the performer's hand. Different capsules may react well or poorly based on how the microphone is held.

Next, ask the group to sing a vamp or a repeating section of a song. Build your mix from the bottom to the top by bringing up the bass microphone first. Equalize the microphone, and then bring up the next microphone and voice part, usually the baritone. Do this until you have all the microphones up and working with a basic EQ on each. Make sure and send only the bass microphone to the subwoofer auxiliary send. Balance the low end with high EQ. Brighten the channel at around 4.0 and 12 kHz. The goal is to make the bass clear without being muddy at 100 or 200 Hz through 400 Hz. Never put a high pass filter on a vocal bass. The human voice is very dynamic. Even though most basses can't sing notes down to 50 Hz, they have natural subharmonics that will sound and ring down there. Let it thump and be sonically low. Good microphones to use on vocal basses are Shure's Beta 58, Beyer Dynamic 88, or Sennheiser 945, because of their large proximity effect.

Once I've worked through each part and have the whole group singing individually, I bring up all the parts to hear them together. It will be apparent if you need to remove some of the lo-mid frequencies (between 200 and 400 Hz) to clear up the mix. Then add in the VP to fill out the mix.

Now, add the effects. But take note, if the balance and blend is not correct, reverb and effects will not fix it. Basic effects will suffice until you become more advanced and creative. Usually two good reverbs will be sufficient. Use a short, warm hall reverb set between 1.8 and 2.8 seconds' decay, and a second bright hall reverb set between 4.0 and 5.0 seconds' decay. Blend the two depending on the song and the venue. For more advanced engineers, use one delay as a timed three-bounce delay that goes with the tempo of the song, used only as a special effect on certain parts of songs. Lastly, you could use a subharmonic bass doubling effect, otherwise known as an "octavizer," to thicken up the bass. Make sure the octave effect is only sent to the subwoofer send.

THE THREE COMPONENTS OF A GREAT A CAPPELLA ENGINEER

There is a symbiotic relationship among professionals in the music business. Each role makes money and needs the other roles to sustain its business. For instance, an arranger, singer, or writer lives in the creative realm but to earn a living must be a good businessperson. A promoter lives by running a business but must choose creative projects to be successful. An engineer lives by the technical but must also be creative to do a good job and be able to run a business to make a living. An audio engineer is one of the most difficult jobs in music because it incorporates skills in all three areas—technical, creative, and business. Success as an audio engineer is determined by a balance of skills in each area that tie together in such a way to turn opportunities into success stories.

Technical Skill

An audio engineer needs to learn the equipment and theory behind sound. There is no better way to learn than to have to learn it on the fly. Personally, I was thrown into several situations where I needed to learn mixing consoles or outboard gear correctly before mixing shows. I challenge you to put yourself into uncomfortable situations specifically to gain knowledge of the equipment. You will need to be able to use and understand the equipment well enough to make it transparent to the audience. Of course, you need basic sound engineering knowledge to even start.

If you are beginner, start self-teaching and researching to understand all you can about sound. Start with signal flow. How do sound equipment components all hook together to produce sound from a source to the final product? Second, start to understand sonic qualities of instruments and how to adjust a graphic equalizer and parametric equalizer. Third, start learning different mixing consoles that are on the market, both analog and digital. The first consoles I used were small Mackie analog consoles. But what really put my career over the edge was learning the Midas Heritage 3000 analog mixing console, and I'm glad I was forced to learn it! Download the owner's manual of the Midas Heritage 3K, and read it until you fully understand the signal flow and features of the console. If you are serious about being an a cappella engineer, you must learn that console. You will forever understand and be able to operate any and all mixing consoles in the world. Next, expand to learning digital consoles.

Some engineers believe that technical skill is all you need to be successful in the business. Yes, that's part of being a good engineer but not totally true. Let's look at the creative side of engineering a concert.

Creative Skill

Have you ever been to a concert where artists introduce their engineer during the show? Have they ever said their engineer is the fifth, sixth, or seventh member of the group? If so, they have an engineer that is a creative force behind them as they perform onstage. This is one of the most important keys to being successful and getting hired by artists. More importantly, it's how to keep the gig. Creativity on the mixing console can give you your first "big" break. Now you can't just go throwing reverb and delays, creating octave effects, and panning into the show and expect the artists to like it. You *must* listen to their music, all of it, so you can understand where they are as artists and creative individuals that make up a music group. It is a deep thing to understand, but it is a must if you plan on being their "sixth member."

Always try to emulate the effects in a live mix that you hear on the artists' recording studio projects. Also try to stay within the bounds of their creative choices. For instance, I found out that I was going to mix Sonos, now known as Arora, a very effect-driven a cappella group that used a lot of effect pedals to enhance their sound. I listened to every piece of material I could find to wrap my head around their creative mix choices, even as I flew to the show. When I mixed them for the first time at the 2010 SoJam Festival, the audience reacted and loved what they did. And Sonos loved what I did. Here's a piece of advice: always remember that you, as the engineer, are there to enhance and support the creative choices of the artist onstage. You are there to make the artist shine while you remain invisible to the audience. Effect choices and creative mixing behind the board should always be bound by those rules. As I will explain later, you never want to give the audience a reason to turn around and look at you! Overreaching effect choices do exactly that.

Technical skills are imperative to understand and use effects and the mixing console in a creative way. It's equally critical that the equipment doesn't hinder your creative choices. Learn the equipment!

Business Skill

There are many business skills needed to effectively run a sound engineering business. Of course, there's marketing, whether that's social media marketing, person-to-person, or advertising and producing media to show off the business, and more. But the focus here is the most important skill of great sound engineers: people skills! I've been the benefactor of many engineers who were fired or lost their clients due to some very simple person-to-person issues. You might think this is not very important, but it is. You must be pleasant and enjoyable to work with—from your personality to your demeanor and from how calm you are under pressure to how you smell.

First, and very important, is personal hygiene! I know of an engineer who showed up for a five-week European tour with one pair of pants and three T-shirts. And he didn't do laundry the whole tour. Not only that, he didn't brush his teeth and then said, "check one, two" into the artists' mics every day. Needless to say, the artists called their management halfway through the tour and made sure he never worked with them again. It's a sad but true story.

Second, you must be nice—as in friendly, courteous, helpful, and humble. That's hard for some people, but if you are going to travel on tour or fly to other countries, you will be spending a lot of time with the artists. They must like you or you will be replaced. See it as the customer service side of being an engineer. If they ask you for something during sound check, don't question it based on your technical prowess. Give them what they asked for, and do it with a smile and a genuine service attitude. Also, you will be working with a lot of other technical people at each venue. You are going to be walking into different venues and will need a lot of help. Building a rapport with them quickly is the key. Here's a tip: when walking into a theater or venue, don't start talking shop and asking for everything you need right away. Nobody wants to work with someone that comes into his or her turf and starts barking orders. Introduce yourself to everyone, get their names, shake their hand, look them in the eye, and smile. Then just take some time to hang out, ask questions about the area or town, and allow them to get comfortable with you. Make sure to get them laughing with a joke or two; then after about fifteen minutes, turn the conversation to the technical needs that day.

Set up all your equipment and get ready for sound check. And here is one more trick to use for the artist: make sure that everything technical is totally set up and checked ahead of time. You know, that technical skill you need? Here is where it blends in with business skill. Make sure everything is perfect and in working order before the artists even come to the venue. And when they arrive, be sitting in their green room or dressing room eating their food or having a soda. Why do I do this? Because it instills confidence in the artists that there is nothing to worry about as far as sound. They immediately relax. This small gesture is an important business skill because it ensures that the artists only worry about their performance and creativity, and not the sound. It also sets them up to realize that if I'm not there in their dressing room, there is a big issue that I'm handling and I won't let them sound check until everything is checked and fully functional.

Now that we have defined the main three skills needed to be a successful audio engineer, how does it all apply to *you*? First, you must identify your own personal tendencies and your strengths. Are you creative first and foremost, not technical, but have great people skills? Are you mainly technical, have good people skills, but find creativity more challenging? Identify your strengths; then focus on improving your deficiencies. If I were a very creative-type person who had good people skills, I'd focus on learning all the equipment—and focus on it hard. You will need to be good technically to mix a creative show without technical difficulties. Who cares if you have an awesome set of reverbs and delays on your artist if you have constant feedback and failing microphones?

If you are a technical-minded person who loves and easily understands the gear, can you relate to your artist person to person? Can you slide away from being technical once the show starts and add effects that enhance the artist, being the "sixth member"?

This is the ultimate career where left- or right-brained people need to become left *and* right brained. It's an exercise in training your brain to work on both sides equally and respond to the needs of the situation. Besides the three skills we've discussed, your ability to mix a great sounding show comes down to genetics. We are all human. We all hear things differently.

KEYS TO SUCCESS AS A SOUND ENGINEER

Success Key 1: Invisibility

Always remain transparent to the audience, as mentioned previously. A good live engineer must possess the ability to remain invisible to the audience. All the glory goes to the talented individuals onstage. No matter what you do, you must never take the focus off the artist and put it onto you. From your effects, EQ, mixing, and technical aspects, the audience perception should always be that the artist holds the key to the great sound.

Success Key 2: Exceptional Customer Service

As a performer, there is nothing worse that showing up for a gig and having an engineer with a bad attitude and a closed mind. If the engineer is too bold, argumentative, or just in a bad mood, the artist will lose trust in that individual's engineering abilities, taking focus and energy from the show. The artists should have nothing to worry about onstage except their own performance!

It's simple but essential: greet the artist with a smile and respect. Handling an intense situation such as a concert will only get worse if you show your emotions. Hide behind a smile and a good attitude. Have a "whatever you want" attitude. *They* are the hired artists, and they were hired for a reason—not because their sound engineer is great but because they generally know what they are doing in creating their own music. Listen to the artists and do what they say. Don't argue. Just work with them and do what they want. Of course, if the artists are new to the business, they will most likely look to you for suggestions. Even then, don't step on their toes. Offer suggestions, not demands.

Don't be late, be early. Don't smell bad. Keep your mouth closed more than open. Be efficient but courteous under stress. And most important, be patient. You are not in charge of running the show; you are just in charge of being invisible once the show starts.

Success Key 3: Listen and Trust

The gear is not the most important aspect of your job. Believe it or not, the settings, the numbers, the knobs, and the equipment are not the most important part of your job. Your job is to create a mix and an experience that the majority of the audience will perceive as pleasurable. Since you are mixing for humans, who are all different and unique, each person will perceive your mix in a unique way. Focus on what sounds good regardless of the setting. The audience will never see your settings and won't care.

Although I've stressed how critical it is to know your equipment, once you are in the performance, let go of the technical side. It's hard when just starting out, but you must be comfortable in your abilities to control the gear without it controlling you. To some degree, most engineers got into sound because they were attracted to the detailed and complex technical side of the job, right? We like to twist knobs, look at numbers, and see what a different setting does to a sound. Now, *throw all that out the window!* For the sound check and show, focus on what you hear, not the numbers or settings, but how your mix feels in the space and how the audience reacts to it. Blend your talents of technical skill and creative skill. Practice closing your eyes and dialing in the mix to create the ideal sound experience. Then when you have it sounding right, don't look at the numbers or dials. They don't matter.

IN CLOSING

I'll leave you with one final thought: the definition of a *great* sound engineer is one that pleases the largest percentage of the audience, and it's never 100 percent. The question that you cannot answer until you get out there and start mixing shows is this: Will your mix please the largest percentage of the audience and your clients?

So, get out there, find a new group to mix, and be their sixth member! Grow with them and help make them famous. Put yourself in situations that make you learn on the job, and prepare for your next opportunity. Mark Kibble of Take 6 told me, "Success is when preparation meets opportunity." Start preparing.

WHEN

Sing for Your Life: A Cappella Ensembles for All Ages

II

SCHOLASTIC A CAPPELLA

Schools are generally a place of learning in which students are educated about many aspects of the world so they can find their place in it and hopefully one day add to the body of knowledge that is studied by the next generations. Rarely are schools the birthplace of something new, but in the case of a cappella it can be argued that collegiate a cappella is a significant driving force in the current contemporary a cappella movement.

In this overview of scholastic a cappella, I'll work backward, starting with the collegiate community, then high school, and finally middle school, as that's the way in which the style has spread, in part because of the birth of a new sound and style in the collegiate world, and in part because only recently have younger singers begun to learn the techniques of contemporary a cappella, thanks to their directors, many of whom sang in collegiate a cappella groups themselves before becoming educators.

COLLEGIATE A CAPPELLA

When one speaks of the collegiate a cappella community in the United States, they're almost always referencing the common style of music that was born at Yale University in 1909 when the Whiffenpoofs were formed; then spread through Ivy League schools and similar universities, almost all on the East Coast of the United States; and finally when the style changed to incorporate vocal percussion and a more complex, modern style and exploded from two hundred groups in 1990 to more than three thousand in 2017. Almost to the last these groups are student directed and student organized with very little official oversight from their college, excepting perhaps an annual stipend from the student activities fund and a listing on the college web page.

Collegiate a cappella groups usually range from about twelve to twenty members in size, most hovering around fifteen members, as that's both the size of a fifteen-passenger van (that was the maximum size by necessity when I was in the Tufts Beelzebubs) and because more than that number begins to become challenging if you want a group to sing on individual microphones, be they wired (mic cord tangling is an issue, also known as "spaghetti") or wireless (increased number of frequencies and interference, plus increased cost).

There is also an experiential benefit to a group that size, in that they're not so large as to need risers (standing in a two-row arc works well), and they're not so numerous as to appear as a sea of faces. In a typical thirty- to sixty-minute collegiate a cappella set, you can get a chance to hear and know most if not all of the members, as a result of a variety of solos, duets, and spoken interludes, be they more standard spoken introductions or comedic skits.

Collegiate a cappella groups are completely student organized and directed, which means every rehearsal, meeting, and concert is managed by a student. Groups generally have a single music director, whose job it is to run rehearsals (including preparing and distributing learning recordings), choose repertoire, decide which songs will be sung during a concert, run auditions, and so forth. An assistant music director isn't uncommon, in case there's value in breaking the group up into sections to run difficult passages, and to help prime someone to take over the position in the future, as music director is the one job that requires a skill set that your average college student likely doesn't possess unless the group is a part of a conservatory or has a strong music program.

Alongside the music director is almost always a business manager who handles all the concert bookings, finances, group business meetings, and logistics. It's not uncommon to have a separate person who organizes a specific major annual tour, which usually happens over spring break (except in the case of the oldest groups, such as the Yale Whiffenpoofs who tour all year long, requiring most of their members to take the year off of school—people are in the group for only one year—and the Harvard Krokodiloes who take an annual summer tour).

Filling out the officer corps for most groups is the role of president, who serves as the group's figurehead and liaison with the school administration (always important to have a good relationship as much money and opportunity flows from here) as well as alumni and admissions departments (both very likely to hire the group for school outreach). The president also handles internal group issues, from members who need to be shushed from talking too much during music rehearsal to members who miss too many rehearsals or otherwise require discipline. Having a third officer also helps ensure there are three people at the helm of the group, so there are never ties that require breaking when major decisions arise.

Other officer positions can include historian (which I highly recommend—keeping track of the group's photos, recordings, posters, and such during the year as well as introducing the newer members to past stories and such), social media manager/publicist (an increasingly important role), videographer, choreographer, and so on.

The school year usually begins in the fall with the returning members coming back to campus before the rest of their cohorts so they are prepared to sing for the incoming freshmen, which is every college group's greatest recruitment tool. Arrangements are usually chosen that favor a smaller group (especially if many members graduated), and school orientation committees are almost always very excited to have the school's a cappella groups perform during orientation week to have some entertainment to break up all the meetings and logistics.

Once everyone else returns to campus, be it August or September, the next order of business is auditions. Every group on campus sets a time, puts up posters, and spreads the word, most on their own, but in a few cases, such as Harvard and Stanford, auditions happen all at once. Universities with several a cappella groups sometimes have an a cappella group board or council made up of members of the various ensembles who agree on the annual schedule (so major end-of-year concerts don't overlap), work out audition protocol (so groups who want the same member can have an equal chance), settle disputes, and sometimes even have a song registry so no two groups are singing the same song at the same time.

An audition usually starts with the auditionee singing a solo, followed by some brief vocalizations up and down (to check vocal range and tessitura) and perhaps a bit of sight singing. If at any point members of a group are not impressed (often indicated by some undetectable signal), the singer is usually dismissed before going through the entire process. If all goes well, the auditionee is usually invited back to a callback in which a complete song is taught and sung with the group to see how the individual fits in. Speaking of fitting in, the group usually schedules some time to get to know the person as well (when I was in the Beelzebubs I made sure one current member was always a little late, so we had some time to casually chat).

Group members then have the difficult task of deciding whom to take, which in many groups requires unanimous agreement (a wise move, as it eliminates any "I never voted for him" comments down the road), which can stretch late into the night. Also, groups sometimes struggle when a great singer is available but doesn't sing the voice part needed (the highest and lowest voice parts are usually the most in demand as inner voices are easier to find). Sometimes internal shuffling occurs to make room for great members, and sometimes people aren't accepted but are urged to return to the next audition when there will be room.

Those who are chosen often find themselves involved in some ritual, be it a midnight serenade outside the new member's window or an elaborate ruse to bring everyone together to a special spot on campus under the guise of it being a second callback. Schools with coordinated auditions sometimes have a coordinated time when all groups are released at once en masse in a mad rush to go "tap" their favorite singers in hopes of having them accept before other groups get to them. For those who don't make the group, there are sometimes auditions again in the winter or at the end of the school year if there is space in the group. In fact, the Harvard Callbacks were formed by singers who all met waiting in the communal room during callbacks, after none of them made their respective groups. Just like many farm teams that eventually make it to the major league, the group is now thirty years old and has won many awards, placing them among the elite groups at Harvard.

Once a group begins rehearsals (usually twice or three times a week, varying based on the current group's various class schedules), members will find themselves auditioning again, this time for a specific desirable solo. Music directors assign parts, but the assignment of solos is usually too emotionally charged for any one person to handle in perpetuity. One process that works well is to wait until a song is learned (the music director might not learn a part so he or she can cover whoever ends up singing the solo) and then have the group sing the song over and over again, in a circle, giving each potential auditionee one pass at singing the song. Then those who auditioned leave the room and the remaining people decide. If the song is one in which most people audition, those remaining in the room can decide on their top few choices and invite the others to return, so the decision can come from a majority of the group. As is always the case, the calculus regarding the best person for the song as well as which members need a solo or already have many solos will differ for different group members, but in the end the majority usually makes a good choice.

In addition to the orientation concert, most groups usually have a major home concert on their own campus around homecoming (midfall), the end of first semester (just before the holidays), mid-second semester (February or March), and the end of the school year. They will also perform at a variety of school events for the faculty, parents, and the like as well as sing the anthem at local sporting events (on and off campus), perform for local business, perform and perhaps do an educational workshop at local schools, and so forth.

The importance of high school performances cannot be overstated. It is a good source of income throughout the school year, a very enthusiastic captive audience, a chance to sell your album and make fans for your upcoming full-length concerts, an opportunity for members to teach some skills to the choir in a workshop, and a chance to encourage more students to sing and inspire some to come to your school and audition in future years. Plus, with the contacts you make it's possible that graduating music majors will find themselves employed in a school district at which they performed a couple of years earlier.

The most enjoyable concert for any college group is when it is invited to sing at another college, resulting in a college road trip. Road trip gigs usually happen on the weekend, sometimes on a Friday night (resulting in missing some Friday classes) and more often on a Saturday night. Singers pile in a couple of cars or a single large van (which is always more fun) and arrive in time for sound check (which may or may not involve amplification). Dinner is usually provided by the host group (pizza is the default), and once the concert is over the host group usually throws a party, which is the source of many a cappella singers' greatest stories and memories. Unless the group is within an hour's drive, groups usually stay the night, with sleeping accommodations varying (dorm common rooms and fraternity/sorority basements often become overrun with sleeping bags). The next morning, the touring group stumbles back into the van and make their way home, unless they have another gig the following night.

Most collegiate groups are student directed, organized, and run, but there are a handful across the United States that are a part of the school's curriculum, result in college ensemble credit, and are directed by an experienced faculty member. Mix from the University of Colorado Denver, directed by Dr. Erin Hackel, has won several awards (including the Pentatonix Macy's Challenge and the A Cappella Educators

Association [AEA] competition) and are now venturing out as a professional group. Brody McDonald's Ethos at Wright State University is another example. This kind of official collegiate ensemble singing popular music is the latest iteration of a long tradition of collegiate vocal jazz ensembles, such as Gold Company at Western Michigan University (directed by Greg Jasperse), and larger ensembles that sing a variety of popular music (such as the Singing Hoosiers at Indiana University, directed by Ly Wilder).

When it comes to competitions for collegiate groups, the biggest is undoubtedly the International Championship of Collegiate A Cappella (ICCA), which now has over three hundred groups involved annually (comprehensive information can be found at http://www.varsityvocals .com). Although that seems like a staggeringly high number, it's only around 10 percent of the collegiate a cappella community, meaning the vast majority of collegiate a cappella groups don't compete (lest you believed the entire community existed primarily for competitions, along the lines of *Pitch Perfect*). There are a few regional festivals that have competitions around the United States, including major hubs such as Boston (BOSS [Boston Sings]) and Los Angeles (LAAF [Los Angeles A Cappella Festival]) as well as smaller towns such as Bentonville, Arkansas (Voice Jam).[1]

In addition to live performances on and off campus, many collegiate groups like to preserve their performances in the form of audio recordings and videos. Twenty-five years ago collegiate a cappella albums were primarily archival, the equivalent of an auditory yearbook of the year's songs, but now these albums are incredibly professional, thanks to digital recording and editing software. True music videos were too expensive to make a generation ago, but now everyone carries a video camera in their pocket as a part of their smartphone, and the result is a steady stream of performance videos, rehearsal videos, and high-production videos that would have cost six figures to produce just twenty years ago.

Social media plays a significant role in collegiate a cappella nowadays, as most groups find guest groups for their home shows and find potential hosts for tours online. Music videos remain a group's best publicity tool and are the most effective method of advertising their sound and quality to potential fans and bookers. Group members change each year (sometimes even each semester), but Facebook pages and Twitter accounts remain constant, allowing students, community members, and past members of the group to remain in touch with and follow a group's development.

Speaking of alumni, there is no stronger foundation upon which a collegiate a cappella group can be built than a strong alumni association. Graduates of the group can and will eagerly provide advice, arrangements, performance opportunities, meals, and floors to sleep on during tours, as they would like to see their group grow. Not much is needed from the current group to make this happen, as most of the work should be done by graduates (forming a simple organization, keeping a database of names, sharing information periodically, and organizing annual alum-only events, plus major weekend reunions every five years), but the undergrads should keep the graduates engaged by inviting them to rehearsals, making sure they have great reserved seats for homecoming shows, and the like. Every collegiate group will have good years and less good years (be it the result of inexperienced leadership, less talented members, bad decisions, etc.), but with an involved alumni organization a group will never fall apart or disband, and the rough patches will be considerably less rough while the best years will be made even better.

HIGH SCHOOL A CAPPELLA

There are close to forty thousand high schools in the United States, and almost all have at least one choir. Although the specific numbers of groups singing contemporary a cappella is almost impossible to know, the number has been increasing steadily for the past decade, as many programs have been embracing singing popular music in complex vocal arrangements. Additionally, some programs that used to focus entirely on vocal jazz or show choir repertoire have expanded to include a cappella. Moreover, with three thousand collegiate a cappella groups graduating a third of their membership each year (on average), we have two decades of music educators who sang in collegiate a cappella ensembles as undergrads and are eager to teach the style to a new generation of students.

The differences between high school and collegiate a cappella are few, with the biggest singular difference being that at least half of all high school groups are a part of the music or choral department, overseen and usually directed by an experienced faculty member. Although high school groups are composed of younger singers, the best ensembles rank with the finest collegiate a cappella groups as the value of a great leader cannot be underestimated. In fact this year (2017) had a high school ensemble (Forte, directed by Ben Spalding) beating not only collegiate but also professional a cappella groups to win the coveted Contemporary A Cappella Recording Award for Best Pop/Rock Album (previous winners include Pentatonix, the House Jacks, and Sonos/ Arora, and a collegiate group has never won it). Oakland School for the Arts' Vocal Rush placed third in the *Sing-Off* season four, placing above many professional groups. Do not underestimate the potential of a great high school a cappella group!

Competitions exist for high school groups just as they do for collegiate, with the International Championship of High School A Cappella (ICHSA) being the largest (and like the ICCA, also organized by Varsity Vocals). There are also single-event competitions specific to high school groups (such as the AEA's annual National A Cappella Convention) as well as "open" competitions, such as VoiceJam, which invite all levels of groups. Adjudicated festivals, such as heritage festivals and music in the parks, are another way for a group to gain recognition and perhaps a trophy, as a trio of music educators will both offer performance comments (written or voice recorded) and work with the group immediately after the performance. Note that these adjudicated festivals are primarily organized for classical choirs, and although they often have a judging sheet for vocal jazz or show choir, they have yet to fully embrace contemporary a cappella. As a result you may get some confusing or confused comments, but there is value in all feedback, even when given by an educator not experienced in this particular style.

When it comes to performing opportunities, recording albums, making videos, using social media, and just about every other aspect of running a group, there is no significant difference between high school, collegiate, or even professional. Learn from other groups, see what works, and build your own list of great ideas and best practices to build a fan base in your region and eventually worldwide (yes, the biggest high school groups sell albums everywhere and get invited to festivals around the globe).

MIDDLE SCHOOL A CAPPELLA/CHILDREN'S CHOIRS/ BOY CHOIRS

A decade ago the idea of having a middle school group sing contemporary a cappella was with rare exception unreasonable. The repertoire is too hard, the experience of singing without instruments or percussion would result in the pitch center and groove unraveling, and the overall density of harmony just too difficult for their inexperienced ears to follow. This is no longer the case, as a cappella can be heard everywhere, and now we have a generation being raised on the sound of complex, dense harmony.

Middle schoolers, with the right director and repertoire choices, can indeed begin to sing three- and four-part arrangements. The challenge of changing voices indeed exists, but this is no surprise to middle school educators who learn to move certain individuals from one voice part to another. In addition, contemporary a cappella has one option that other styles don't: the ability to take a boy with a rapidly changing voice and put him on vocal percussion until his vocal chords settle. No one needs to sit out; members can perform throughout their middle school years without fear of cracking.

No major competitions yet exist specifically for middle school groups, but there weren't any for high school groups either a generation ago, so as the field grows and the number of groups expands there will no doubt be opportunities.

NOTE

1. A comprehensive list of a cappella festivals is included at the end of this book.

12

PROFESSIONAL A CAPPELLA

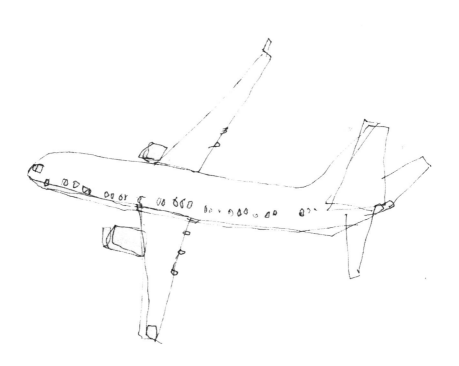

The definition of "professional" has long been a matter of debate in the contemporary a cappella community. For many, if your group is making money from performances, you are a professional. In others' minds, a truly professional group is one that is making a full-time or at least part-time career of a cappella. Either way, once you have graduated from school, if you're planning to make money in a performing group, you should consider yourself a professional.

A group's infrastructure is something to figure out early on, as the organization is an important aspect for conducting business. Is the group a nonprofit with a board of directors, an LLC with all members as equal partners, or owned by a couple members and the other singers are employees? There are no absolutes when it comes to making these decisions. Look at what other groups have done, ask advice, and see what fits your circumstances best. You can make changes down the road, but it becomes increasingly difficult as more money and people's livelihoods are involved.

It is of course a good idea to take your group's agreements (When will you all be paid? What constitutes a reasonable group expense?) and write it down in the form of a simple contract. You can spend weeks discussing every possible scenario (I speak from experience), and yet in the end most won't come to pass. Instead a simple page or two as to your intents, how members will leave (Will they continue to be paid? Do they get bought out? How much notice do they need to give to leave in good standing?), and how conflicts will be resolved (mediation? arbitration?) should be enough, with local and state laws governing (and overriding) most scenarios you might consider. Thankfully, most people who are drawn to a cappella know how to work together and are reasonable, so although conflicts do arise, most can be handled amicably.

Gigs are the lifeblood of any professional group, with only a trickle of income nowadays from audio recordings and videos (unless or until a group becomes extremely successful). Start with free performances (busking in heavily touristed areas with business cards in hand and singing at private parties and farmers' markets); sing at open mic nights; work your way up to small local performances for your early fans (local theaters often have Monday and Tuesday nights open); contact performing arts centers to perform as an opening act for headliners that don't have their own opener; contact sports arenas to sing the anthem; see if you can perform for local radio and television stations (especially morning shows); and look for any other opportunity to build a fan base. In time you'll have your own full-length show, at which point you can reach out to local colleges and high schools (especially if you have an educational component, which makes you much more compelling to high school as well as elementary schools) and book your own shows further afield as word of mouth spreads. Whenever possible look to get agents to represent you, especially in specific markets (such as a college agent for NACA [National Association of Campus Activities]); see if you can create a show for cruise ships (multiple groups make a majority of their annual income on ships); and make sure you have a great website so you'll start getting contacted for corporate events (which pay well but aren't something you can actively create). Foster relationships within the a cappella community, which will lead to invitations to perform at festivals and other community events. Leave no stone unturned, and remember that it's the business of music: you need to spend at least as much time on the business as you do the music. You're likely not singing more than ten hours a week, so be sure to spend the other thirty to forty hours on everything else that will make more singing increasingly lucrative.

Audio and video recordings, although not initially a profit center, are very much needed to help promote a group. You don't need to spend a great deal of money, as simple videos of great performances can generate their own interest. Pentatonix's early videos—five members sitting and singing in front of a white wall—are a perfect example of compelling simplicity. A great idea, arrangement, and performance will trump high production value in almost any situation. It is worth investing some time learning how to record and videotape your own group, as you likely have more time than you have money in the early stages, and the investment up front can save you tens or even hundreds of thousands of dollars down the road; plus you can always use professional editors and mixers to make your performances shine. Patreon and other online platforms through which fans directly support groups can help defray the hard costs of audio and video production, and in rare cases (such as the group Home Free) when a fan base grows large enough, it can result in a profit.

Making the move to full-time status or even part-time status from being "weekend warriors" can create stress in a group. Will we make

enough money to sustain ourselves? Unlike a single individual entrepre-
neur, a group is composed of individuals with different spending habits
and different levels of risk tolerance. As a result not everyone is likely
ready to make the jump at the same time. The best way to navigate this
impending step in your careers is to keep expenses low; stockpile as
much of a financial cushion as you can before making the leap; see if you
can find some investors in your friends and family (pay them back with
interest, of course); and aim for a date in the future where you can try
to book as many gigs in a specific window as possible, justifying a leave
of absence from work. Eventually the leaves will become too much and
everyone will need to either shift to part-time status if their employers
will allow, or find additional sources of income (check the careers section of this book for ideas).

The biggest a cappella competition for nonscholastic groups is the
Harmony Sweepstakes, with regionals across the United States and the
finals in Marin County (just north of San Francisco). This event is over
thirty years old and has been an important step in gaining national and
even international recognition for young groups (former national winners include Northshore A Cappella, m-pact, the Idea of North, Toxic
Audio, and Naturally 7). In addition, there are many festivals around the
world that welcome new a cappella groups as participants and performers (a comprehensive list can be found at the end of this book).

An entire book could be written about the best way to steward a
professional a cappella group from founding to final concert, and yet as
soon as it was written it would likely be at least somewhat out of date,
as technology and the music industry have been rapidly changing and
show no signs of stasis. As such, no book could hold all of the options
and best practices, particularly for such a new player in such a rapidly
changing music business. To get you started, several if not most of the
career interviews in this book's careers chapters (14–17) directly address
different aspects of professional a cappella, from starting an ensemble
to touring and recording. Once those are digested, the best next step is
to do some research into the specific career paths of groups you would
like yours to emulate. Contact groups, ask industry leaders, and stay
engaged. This is the way bands have always found success.

Thankfully the a cappella community at large is widespread and extremely supportive, but don't just reach out when you need help or you'll

rapidly gain a reputation as self-interested. Engage with fans, go see other groups' concerts when they're in town, stay active in social media watering holes (such as the Contemporary A Cappella Society [CASA] Facebook group), offer support and advice when you are able, and most importantly make friends of your cohorts across the region, country, and world. There is no more supportive artistic community anywhere.

⑬

RECREATIONAL A CAPPELLA

Not everyone wants to make a career of a cappella. Just as a majority of collegiate a cappella singers aren't music majors, many people want to keep singing while pursuing their careers in a wide range of fields. They still want the connection, the community, and the joy that a cappella brings; they just don't want to make it a source of income.

Much of what was written above about professional groups applies to recreational groups as well. One important difference is the size of a group. Professional groups need to stay as small as possible so the members can support themselves, which is why most have (on average) five members. Recreational groups, on the other hand, can't be counted on to always be at rehearsals or a concert, so every voice part needs to have multiple members (and every solo should be double-cast for the same reason). However, there's a dynamic in an a cappella group that gets lost when there are so many members that you need risers to see them all onstage. The ideal size appears to be between twelve and twenty members, which is in keeping with the average size of collegiate a cappella groups.

No one is getting paid, so a group's infrastructure wants to be as hassle-free as possible, which means spreading around responsibility between many members so the necessary tasks don't become overwhelming.

Each group needs a music director (multiple MDs works as well, with different people directing different songs), someone to handle logistics (a president), someone to handle performance opportunities (a business manager), a social media guru, and so on. The more you spread around the responsibilities, the less any one person will get burned out.

With members busy in their day jobs, few have the time or energy to create their own custom arrangements. Thankfully, nowadays there is a good deal of published contemporary a cappella repertoire available online. (At the risk of sounding like a commercial in the middle of my own book, as of this book's publication I have 613 contemporary a cappella arrangements in print. Sheetmusicplus.com is the easiest way to find them all.) In addition, setting up social media accounts is easy (and free); simple, free website templates abound online; a group logo can be designed via bid; and so on. There is a free or inexpensive option for almost every aspect of your new group other than rehearsal space (you can look for a local community center or church, if you outgrow your living room) and snacks. Don't forget snacks. Snacks are very important to recreational groups. An a cappella army marches on its stomach.

How does one find a recreational group? The first place to start is by reaching out to major organizations: the Contemporary A Cappella League, the Barbershop Harmony Society, Sweet Adelines International, Harmony Incorporated, and Chorus America. Each of these organizations maintains lists of groups across the United States and around the world, making them the best place to start. Beyond them, you can reach out in major online watering holes, such as the Contemporary A Cappella Society (CASA) Facebook group, which is open to all, and ask if anyone knows of a group in your area. There are also many smaller a cappella Facebook groups for the major urban areas and more populated regions that have fewer members, but those people have a more in-depth knowledge of the area. Finally, you can reach out to existing groups you know of in the area, particularly those that aren't full-time touring ensembles. If you happen to have a Harmony Sweepstakes regional near you, scroll through the page that features the past few years' participants to see if any are near you. You may find there is a group but it isn't exactly what you'd been hoping for (a larger chorus rather than a small ensemble, older repertoire rather than the latest hits, etc.). Before deciding against it, drop by a rehearsal, as you may find the people and the sound are worth your while.

If a recreational group cannot be found in your area, it is time to start a group. Before you panic, know that many before you have successfully started groups and that a cappella couldn't be more popular so you will most likely be able to find interested people in your area who have been waiting for such an opportunity. There are several chapters on how to start a group, run auditions, run your first rehearsal, and so forth in my book *A Cappella* (written with Brody McDonald and Ben Spalding). There is too much information to repeat here, but I will leave you with a clear directive: don't do it alone. If you're going to be music directing the group, find someone who can help you with the business side so you can focus on the various musical tasks. If you're not a music whiz, then find someone who is, so you can take care of logistics. More than one person is great, but be sure there is at least one. There is strength is numbers, and you will be much less likely to burn out or give up if you're carrying only half (or a third, or a quarter) of the burden.[1]

The a cappella community is very welcoming toward recreational groups. Casual adult groups are most certainly welcome at all of the festivals and competitions open to professional groups as well. If your group is interested in networking with other like-minded singers, join the Contemporary A Cappella League (CAL), a nonprofit organization that exists to help foster and promote recreational groups like yours. Bottom line: you're not alone; everything you're trying to do has been done, so reach out and find the easy solution so you can focus on singing, camaraderie, and fun. And snacks. Did I mention snacks?

NOTE

1. My wife started an a cappella group this month in San Francisco, after twenty years away from a cappella (she sang in college—that's how we met—and then she had a postcollegiate group for a few years before becoming too busy in grad school). She had to cap the group at twenty members after just two weeks, and the phone is still ringing.

WHERE

Careers: Opportunities for Full- and
Part-Time Employment in A Cappella

14

IN THE THEATER

When you look back at the history of a cappella, you realize it has been a music of the people. From prehistoric singing to summer campfire sing-alongs, from field hollers to gospel choirs, and from barbershop rhapsodies to street-corner serenades, the people singing a cappella have been doing it for fun, not for profit. The past twenty-five years have changed this, such that more people are making a career of popular a cappella music than perhaps ever before. Yes, the professional classical choirs and paid church singers have long existed, but now there's a new class of vocal harmony worker, thanks to the surge of interest in contemporary a cappella.

But how does one enter this marketplace? And is there enough work within it for everyone who is interested? As with any desirable field, the jobs go to those who not only show talent but also back it up with responsibility, approachability, timeliness, and professionalism. I had several production assistants work for me on *The Sing-Off*, both in the United States and abroad (Netherlands, China, and South Africa), and although they all very much wanted a career in music, they varied wildly in their ability to get the job done, whatever the job happened to be.

To this end, I urge you as someone looking to enter the workforce to realize that talent isn't enough, and in many cases talent will take a backseat to responsibility. If you were someone who had a difficult time handing in school assignments on time, if you're someone who needed a lot of hand holding to complete projects, and a teacher or parent hovering over you to ensure you would work rather than spend all your time on social media, you may be better suited for a more traditional desk job with clear responsibilities. A cappella is a new field, and one in which most people are self-employed, which means you need to hustle new work, get current jobs done on time and under budget, and work harder and faster and more efficiently than the competition. Vocal harmony is a field that is still growing, but that won't necessarily happen forever, and in the end clients will return to the people who produced great work for a fair price within their timeline.

One other consideration when looking at the following list and descriptions of careers is that most people find themselves doing a variety of different things, either because one pursuit won't support them fully or because the job at hand requires it. In my earliest days, after graduating and starting the Contemporary A Cappella Society (CASA), I did whatever a cappella work I could find, knowing it would all lead to other work. I would arrange, coach, produce events, publish the newsletter, produce albums and create compilation albums, tour with the House Jacks, and so on. Since everything I did was within the field of a cappella, it would often lead to additional work, such as a group asking me to come coach them as they worked on an arrangement of mine, or have me produce the track in the recording studio.

Later on, this experience proved invaluable, as I found myself arranging, directing/coaching, and producing for Disneyland and Disney World, *The Sing-Off*, on Broadway (*In Transit*), and so on. A cappella has many things about it that make it unique, and the more you know about it technically, logistically, and creatively, the more you'll be able to work in a variety of capacities.

The analogy I like to use is that of a water strider (I called them "water skeeters" growing up; others call them pond skaters or Jesus bugs, from the family Gerridae): a bug is able to walk on water by never putting too much weight on any one leg. So it was with my career, never putting too many eggs in one basket; instead, I balanced myself carefully between different jobs based on demand: Late summer brought a deluge of back-to-school arrangements, followed by a fall House Jacks tour, and then holiday work. Spring was full of coaching and events as well as groups wanting to record albums. Summer was all about festivals, and when there were holes in my schedule I'd plan for the future: writing blogs, building new companies, and working on music for publication (which could happen anytime).

However, I'm just one person, and my path was a unique one, perhaps unreproducible, and now, twenty-five years later, the field has grown in depth and breadth, with a variety of experts who know more than I do in their craft. As such, rather than give you my own perspective on the variety of careers in a cappella, I thought I'd reach out to some of the best and brightest in the field to get their perspective and insight on what they do. Some of them are part-time; some are full-time. Some do only what they're discussing in the interviews below; others span a variety of other fields as well, both within and without a cappella.

Note: the following careers are by no means exhaustive. For instance, there are individuals who perform as solo artists, either as beatboxers or with a live-looping device. Also, people such as Mike Tompkins, Sam Tsui, and Peter Hollens make a good living as solo a cappella performers by releasing videos in which they sing all the parts (their income comes from ad revenue from their performances as well as paid downloads of their recordings). No doubt with each passing year new careers will arise, reflecting the almost limitless versatility of the human voice.

First, let's look at the most traditional of a cappella careers: performing. As much as many advances in audio and video technology have brought a cappella into homes worldwide, it is still always best heard live, and as a result the majority of people making a career of a cappella make the majority of their money on the road. If you like airplanes, adventures, and the roar of a crowd, this is the place to start.

LOCAL AND REGIONAL PERFORMING—JON RYAN

If you're regularly making money in a particular industry, you're a professional. Such is the case in a cappella as well, although many "weekend warriors" might not consider themselves professional musicians because they're not full-time. The fact is many of the great musicians throughout history have not relied entirely upon income from their performing and recording. Just as there are countless local rock groups, DJs, wedding bands, and the like, peppered across America, so are there many a cappella groups who are beloved in their region, performing for tens and even hundreds of thousands of locals each year.

One of the best is Boston-based Ball in the House, who for over twenty years have performed in the greater New England area. They sing anywhere and everywhere, and are frequently seen performing one of their educational shows by elementary and high school students, both private and public, throughout the school year. Jon Ryan, arranger and beatboxer extraordinaire, has been with the group since their founding just after he graduated from Skidmore and the Bandersnatchers.

What drew you to this field of a cappella?
I sang in college and loved it. As president of the Skidmore Bandersnatchers, I got some experience booking performances, working with student government and other organizations on budgets, and leading a

group of guys with varied levels of interest—all things that helped immensely in my next steps. I didn't exactly know what that would be at the time, but I know I wanted it to be in music. After graduation, I sang in the Vineyard Sound (a semipro a cappella group based on Martha's Vineyard, working full-time over the summer) for four summers, and had my first real taste of being a full-time performer, rehearsing and gigging all the time, even if just for two and a half months a year. That experience of making money performing and wanting to do it full-time year-round and not just over the summer was what led me to start Ball in the House. The fact that we were a cappella was purposely chosen because I loved the sound of harmony combined with vocal drums and saw that this sound was something that people seemed to love listening to. It was a way to be unique and differentiate ourselves from the many instrumental bands out there.

What experiences and education do you find have been most useful? What skills and knowledge do people need coming into this kind of work?

Musical education is great—it allows you to use a shared language with other musicians, and we find ourselves using our vocal technique, sight-reading, and solfège every day. However, I would say that in making a full-time career in music, business and interpersonal skills have been the most useful. They are skills you'll use within your group but even far more outside of the group.

In general, there are two areas of focus for a career in music: recording and performing. In recording, you'll be dealing with budgeting the project, working with engineers and producers in the studio, communicating your artistic goals with them, and promoting the final product (CD, MP3, video, etc.), just to name a few. In performing, you'll be dealing with a presenter to book the show (talking fees or ticketing, expenses, set length, etc.), working with your contact to advance the show to cover all the details (load time, overall details for event, selling merchandise, etc.); going over sound, lighting, and staging with the tech contact; and working with the promoter to advertise the show, again, just to name a few. It's these details of planning and working with others that really contribute to the success of a show or project. The artistic side of things is something you can practice and hone inside your group, but to do what you really want/need to do—get your music in front of other people through performances or recordings—you'll need to work closely with many others in a business relationship.

Of course, you may have someone in your group who has the technical know-how to engineer and mix your own music and the knowledge and creativity to produce yourselves, but you'll still at some point have to deal with people, organizations, and systems outside your group. Even on the opposite end, where you may have an agent to book you shows, a promoter to take care of publicity, and a manager to take care of all the details, you'll still need to communicate clearly with your team and have a basic understanding of everything going on. I can't think of a single case of a band that purely focused on the artistic side of things and let their team take 100 percent care of the business side of things that didn't eventually devolve into mistrust, lawsuits, and even breakups.

I will say that 100 percent of my own business and interpersonal skills have come from experience and learning on the job and not from the classroom (for better or worse). But these were both things that I paid careful attention to in the early stages of our career—watching, questioning, and learning from other groups and team members we worked with.

How has the field changed since you started?

It's definitely a much more crowded field now. When we started out, there were very few groups that were performing in schools and showcasing for performing arts centers, so it was easier to get work. Now we have to work much harder to stand out among the many a cappella groups working in those markets.

On the other hand, because there are so many more groups and because of a cappella's greater visibility in general, many agencies, showcases, and performing arts series actually have a separate a cappella category, ensuring that some part of these opportunities are going to a cappella groups.

What are the technical aspects of your work that most people don't understand or know about?

I touched on these briefly above in talking about some of the things you'll be dealing with in booking, advancing, promoting, and actually performing your shows. There is so much that goes into each performance, from long before the show is booked to after the show is completed. I think it's easy to imagine all the aspects that go into arranging, learning, and performing music because it's something most of us have done but much more difficult to be aware of and to actually be successful at all the details that go into making a performance happen at a professional level.

For example, sound and tech are a super important aspect of a cappella. It's very easy for a group to be mixed poorly and sound terrible because of that. Imagine a sound engineer who isn't 100 percent sure of who is singing each part and has the background baritone part standing out in the mix—even for a great, perfectly in-tune performance, that's going to really negatively impact the sound the audience hears. To prevent that (or more accurately, lessen the chance of that happening), you'll want a good solid sound check.

What are the chances that'll happen if you just walk into the venue an hour before your set time and tell them you need six mics and that one is going to sound like a drum, another like a bass, and that four more mics are all singers but will be switching off between background and leads, often within the same song? Will you need wireless mics, and will it affect your staging/choreography if you don't have them? What if they don't have enough mics for everyone? What about the size of the stage? Are there other acts performing as well, limiting your sound check time and leaving you with just a few feet of space in front of the curtain while a full instrumental band is setting up behind it? What will you do if the sound engineer boasts of his or her own expertise in mixing a cappella and insists that you won't need a sound check? We travel with our own wireless mics, in-ear monitors, and even PA but multiple times have come across sound engineers who insist that we use the theater's own equipment. Another frequent issue is a tech crew that has no idea how to integrate our gear into their theater's system (and sometime no idea how to properly use their own gear!).

There's enough to worry about when it comes to actually performing—tuning, blend, staging, and lyrics—that the last thing you want to be worrying about onstage is numerous tech issues (not being able to hear yourself, feedback, effects not working, etc.). Now imagine dealing with all these variables a hundred plus times a year in a different venue every time. You can't just leave these details, gear, schedule, and so forth, up to chance—you'll need to communicate your needs and expectations in advance and do everything possible to give yourself the best chance of success.

What is the scope and range of what you do?

In order to make a full-time career out of this and to be able to deal with the ebb and flow of the economy and other external factors, we have a pretty broad scope of performances (with 85–90 percent of our income coming from performances)—arts-in-ed work, workshops and master classes, school family night/fund-raisers, colleges, performing arts centers and music series, fairs and festivals, and private and corporate work. Then of course we have recordings and merchandise to sell, with occasional licensing and commercial work that can contribute to income as well. Many of these are separate fields, in that they have their own agents, clients, and ways to get the work (showcasing, advertising, auditions, etc.). They weren't all developed at the same time, but all took serious work and cultivation to build up.

What does a typical day or week look like for you?

There's actually very little that's typical for us, as there's always something new and different. When we're not touring, it's great to have a lot of flexibility in our schedule, especially for those of us with families. If there's a week when we're not touring, we'll typically take weekends off and then meet in person or over Skype to go over business one to two days per week, and meet up to rehearse, record, make videos, and so forth, two days a week.

For a sample week, here's a tour we had recently:

Sunday: Meet up at the band van, and drive together from Boston to Syosset, New York (approximately four hours).
Monday: Up at 6:30 a.m.; load in at a middle school at 8:00 a.m. for a 9:00 a.m. show. 10:30 a.m.: Drive to Maryland (approximately four hours), rehearse for about forty-five minutes, and crash.
Tuesday: Up at 4:30 a.m. for 7:15 a.m. load-in (D.C.-area traffic!). Shows at middle school 8:15 and 9:15 a.m. Back to hotel 11:30 a.m. Time to chill and then two-hour business meeting. Relax at night.

Wednesday: Up at 5:30 a.m. for an 8:00 a.m. load; perform 9:00 and 10:00 a.m. shows at school. 11:30 a.m.: Drive to next school and grab lunch before loading in at noon. Show at 1:00 p.m. On the road again by 2:30 for drive to Georgia. Arrive at hotel at 3:00 a.m.

Thursday: Up at 8:00 a.m. for a 10:00 a.m. workshop with a local high school choir; teach them a song they'll perform with us that night. Quick lunch; then load in gear for a 1:00 p.m. assembly. 2:30–4:30 p.m.: Rest back at hotel before another sound check, load in and set up merchandise, sound check with the high school choir, quick dinner, and go over set for the night show. 7:00–9:00 p.m.: Concert. Meet and greet, pack and load out gear, grab some late-night ice cream to soothe our tired throats, and then head to bed.

Friday: Up at 6:30 a.m. to drive to South Carolina for 10:30 a.m. promo at a high school. Lunch there; then visit the chorus for forty-five minutes, load in gear, and then workshop with another choir for a performance the following night. 3:30 p.m.: Back to hotel to catch up on business work. Go to local bar to see friend's band perform at night.

Saturday: Free time during the day. 4:30 p.m.: Load in merchandise, re-sound check, have dinner, go over set for 7:00 p.m. show. 7:00–9:00 p.m.: Concert. Similar to Thursday night, we'll meet and greet, pack up and load out gear, grab a treat, and then crash.

Sunday: Day off! (before five shows in next two days and then driving from North Carolina back to Boston).

How many people would you guess are doing this professionally?

I really have no idea—three hundred? My guess is there are 30–50 percent in production and 50–70 percent in performance. But I really have no idea. Many groups I know shift from having periods of being full-time to just being part-time (sometimes a very busy part-time). A couple groups have gone from full-time to part-time and then actually back to full-time!

What percentage of your income comes from this?

One hundred percent. For us, we have everyone on salary to make sure everyone can devote themselves to this full-time and be available for any shows and tours.

What advice do you have for someone starting in this field?

Plan performances as soon as you can find something—don't rehearse till you're "perfect"—nothing will whip you into performance shape than actually having one scheduled and actually doing it. Think about what you're trying to do (your goals) beyond "just being in a band" or "singing for your living." Try to find something unique about what you do or how you do it. Have patience and be willing to drudge through some bad or free gigs. Pay your members, but also put money back into the band (e.g., you make a hundred dollars and there are six of you, so give each person ten dollars and invest the remaining forty back in the group). Look for professional help on certain needs (demo recording, photos, videos, website, etc.). It's okay to search for bargains, but also be willing to pay for things that will be a good investment in the group's future.

For gigs—use freebies to get your voice out there, ask friends (a cappella and otherwise) to open for their bands or to get connections, look for open mic nights and street performing. Don't focus exclusively in the a cappella community either—as great and knowledgeable as it is, it's still only a small percent of the general population of music lovers. The general public might not fully appreciate your twelve-part original with all those perfectly tuned thirteenths, but they definitely like and appreciate harmony in general.

At our last a cappella festival where we spoke about being a full-time band and offered advice to groups just starting out, I wrote up a "but" list that encapsulated many of the points above:

1. Reinvest in group, *but* pay yourself too.
2. Find your identity and hone that; play to its strengths, *but* also be flexible for certain audiences.
3. Make sure your group is clear on your style, what you want to do, and what your goals are, *but* don't be afraid to adjust slightly to the strengths of new members that come in.
4. Don't be afraid to turn down gigs, *but* don't automatically turn down gigs you think might suck.
   Side point—"exposure" almost never works—it's typically an excuse to not pay you anything—*but* in certain situations, it can be okay when you know exactly who you'll be performing for and feel it would be worth your time.

5. Don't be afraid to invite friends and family, and help them spread word about what you do, share social media, and so forth, *but* don't be that jerk that posts ten times a day and makes people feel guilty or annoyed.
6. Be strong in what you feel your strengths are, *but* always look for something you can learn from critiques.
7. Don't be averse to spending money on an expert or for help (graphic design, lawyers, agents, etc.), *but* don't be afraid to try new things yourself; talk to and get advice from other people in the community.

In what ways do you see this field growing or changing in the future?

I think it'll be interesting to see the long-term effect of the growth of YouTube and video on live music performances, but in general, there is always a need for live music in one way or another, and with much more general awareness of a cappella as a medium, there seem to be more and more desire and opportunities for a cappella performances. As the community grows and grows, there are more chances to collaborate and perform with that other college group, that other semipro group in your town, that pro group that's stopping close to you on their tour, and so on. I also think the Internet will continue to give visibility to just what's possible without instruments, pushing more and more groups to not only be better but also experiment with unique ways to present a cappella, fill gaps in musical genres, and to reach a wider general audience.

NATIONAL AND INTERNATIONAL TOURING— WALTER CHASE

Sometimes a regional a cappella group will make a big enough splash that their group takes it to the next level and becomes a nationally and internationally recognized touring act. In the past, this was almost always a by-product of success touring on the regional level as well as a successful album, but since the rise of YouTube, it's possible for a group to be vaulted to the upper echelons of professional a cappella without leaving the house. Of course, online ad income isn't sufficient to feed an entire a cappella group and their families, so they take to the road to capitalize on their success, selling tickets, albums, T-shirts, and the like, while entertaining their fan base and making new converts in person.

No one knows the a cappella touring scene better than Straight No Chaser, and their music director Walter Chase, who have been one of the hardest working groups in a cappella since their viral "12 Days of Christmas" video. Their busiest time of the year is the holidays, as it is for many a cappella groups. They tour nonstop from October through December, selling out large performing arts centers, a feat that most rock groups with a song on the radio can't duplicate.

What drew you to this field of a cappella?

There is no other job I feel more qualified to do than arrange and perform for a professional a cappella group. I started arranging for a cappella the summer before my senior year in high school. In college my degree was music education, but my life at school for four years including summers was arranging, performing, and producing a cappella music. I had coproduced five albums with my two groups Delusions of Grandeur and Straight No Chaser by the time I was twenty-one. I spent the good part of the next eight years writing charts for other groups, engineering albums, and performing/producing a cappella for cruise ships. And then the "12 Days of Christmas" went viral. . . .

The specific answer of "what drew me to a cappella" professionally and once and for all would be the CEO of Atlantic Records, Craig Kallman. Being signed to a record deal took me from moonlighting to "fulltiming." That was my break. I had done the work to prepare myself to be on that stage, to be in that studio behind that board, and to be ready to arrange specifically for this type of ensemble: ten-part male a cappella. There were zero promises of financial success. There was no clear path of how a ten-man a cappella group could survive as a full-time entity. Regardless, what drew me to take the plunge and dive without a net into professional a cappella was that I had spent more time and passion crafting my skills to one day do this for a living.

What experiences and education do you find have been most useful?

My high school marching band experience taught me more about discipline and focus on a common goal than anything I've experienced. Our marching band was three hundred plus members. I am still in awe of the organization it took for our band director to get us, hundreds of teenagers, on the same page (shout out to Carol Lutte). It taught me at an early age to bury my ego and realize that greater satisfaction for me came at the success of the group.

In high school, I also was blessed with a choral director that taught me the value of music theory. I was able to test out of four semesters of theory and ear training in college from what I learned at my public school in Easton, Pennsylvania (shout out to Ed Milisits). He made music theory understandable, helped draw the line of how to use it as an arranger, and even made it fun! The other major education Mr. Milisits gave me was how to use Finale music notation software. Having a strong understanding of a music software interface before going to college was a tremendous advantage when it came time to transcribe charts for my groups. Having a mastery of it after twenty plus years, now that I am known in the world of a cappella, allows me to share my work efficiently with the world.

There has been no experience or education that could prepare me for directing an a cappella group more than standing in the horseshoe itself and just doing it. With every group that I have led as a peer or produced as a consultant, from my six-man group in high school to quartets that I was brought in to direct, nothing teaches like being thrown into the fire. Need to learn how to call an audible from the stage for a set list that you notice is too "risky" for a more conservative audience? Need to learn when doubling a vocal versus tripling a vocal in the studio is better? Need to learn how to give a tough music note to another member of your group who is also your best friend of twenty years? All of the books in the world won't teach you like experience itself.

What skills and knowledge do people need coming into this kind of work?
Many professional musicians have zero formal training. This is also possible in a cappella, but the deck is stacked in an environment where knowing how to blend, sight-reading music, singing straight tone, and "turning on the performance" for any type of audience is necessary. Every member of Straight No Chaser sang in the undergraduate group. Although the stakes were lowered, there was our chance to learn the rhythm of teaching, learning, and performing a set of music for the stage and studio.

Ear training is incredibly useful in just about every stage of a cappella. From sight-reading a major third to being able to hear the best way to imitate a drum loop for vocal percussion, there is heightened need to listen in our profession. There is also a level of ear training involved in how to stand and sing in a group with only vocals. Accuracy and precision is in greater demand when the lack of louder instruments such as bass and drums are absent, and adjusting one's ears to respond accordingly is a very important skill.

Having worked with some of the best producers in the vocal world, you learn quickly who really knows how to maneuver in the world of a cappella. There is a nuance with what syllables work for a particular harmony line without sounding too cheesy—which would be like learning a new language for someone outside of the a cappella world. You also need to have the knowledge that an a cappella group is, in most cases, a tight-knit group of people first, performers second. The bonds created singing such a vulnerable art form should not be taken lightly by an outsider voice.

How has the field changed since you started?

Before Straight No Chaser signed with Atlantic Records, there was no *Pitch Perfect* franchise. There was no *Sing-Off* or Pentatonix. We've seen interest in a cappella explode in high schools. Personally, I've met more and more a cappella–educated fans visiting our postshow's signing lines.

Social media has become the central advertising focus for most every performing ensemble since SNC was signed back in 2008. YouTube has given life to so many vocal artists with that Brady Bunch–style multibox format becoming synonymous with a cappella. The growth of a cappella forums, conventions, and academies born via social networking in the past five years has been inspiring.

What are the technical aspects of your work that most people don't understand or know about?

In order for a ten-man a cappella group to exist, we need to tour a lot. SNC performs somewhere between 120 and 150 shows a year. We live mainly on two tour buses, traveling back and forth across the country and abroad. There is a technical mind-set that exists with this lifestyle.

Living dressing room to dressing room with a small family of fourteen other people requires walking a personal tightrope of acceptance and patience for others. Knowing how to travel and perform at your highest level is an art, especially considering international time zones and sleep. Crafting a set list on a European run of shows where comedic lyrics and English-as-a-second-language audiences are involved is always a challenge. Finding your footing on the road in this world is essential and always challenging.

The human body has its limits. The most technical challenge of my job might be the ability to sing full voice at every show. Aside from our grueling schedule where we might have eight shows a week with four shows happening in two days' time, a cappella requires singing for the entire show. Where a vocalist in a band might have guitar solos to rest, I might be singing nonstop (sans song introductions) for two one-hour sets a show. Add to that the postshow signing lines we do after every show (thirty to sixty minutes); that's a lot of strain on the voice. Our schedule is also most chaotic during the holidays when flu season is in full swing.

I may be listed as a tenor on our group's website, but during a show as a "swing voice," I may be covering several different voice parts in the course of a single song. This phenomenon is more likely to occur on a song that I arranged where I may be more comfortable covering a part than teaching it to someone else. For example, I may be singing a tenor two part for the majority of the song. At the bridge section there is a super-high falsetto part that I feel I can cover best: I'm jumping off my tenor two part to cover basically a soprano line. That same song might have a breakdown section where the vocal percussionist can't cover all of the auxiliary drum sounds we arranged; now I'm covering a percussion line for my third-voice part in the same song. Now envision transitioning between those sections and the vocal exercise that entails. That's live a cappella in a nutshell.

What is the scope and range of what you do?
    As a member of Straight No Chaser, there are many hats that I wear. From performer to arranger, and from producer to project manager and basic staging choreographer, there are a lot of roles the group takes on that a more lucrative outfit might outsource. We have a member of

the group that is our business manager. We have a featured soloist that doubles as our stylist. We have a few guys that write scripts and direct our video content. It is a small business grossing millions of dollars run with a high level of internal delegation.

The creative content is not directed to us by our record label, management, or any outside source (apart from the demands of our fans!). During the time at home, I will block out hours to flush out needs in our set list and upcoming projects. If our first act closer seems it has reached its limit of use, I will brainstorm for as long as it takes to find a list of songs to consider arranging. Once a song is determined, it is not enough to just write a "cover" of a song. An experienced arranger will find a new twist in style, meter, or vibe to make the song their own. Once that is determined, I'll need to figure out how to make that song work for less than a dozen male voices.

Trial and error over years of arranging for ensembles with instruments (big band, orchestra, and piano accompaniment) helps me to understand voicing in order to then adapt it best for vocals. I will record myself singing all of the parts using computer software (Logic or Pro Tools). This allows me to demo exactly what the arrangement will sound like. Then it's time to pitch the demo to the group. If it passes "the democracy," I will then transcribe what I arranged creating sheet music (using Finale music software). At our next rehearsal or sound check, I will teach the song to the guys, taking note of any challenges or errors I might have made during the process. After a few rehearsals, I'll coordinate with our choreographer for staging and, if she's not available, teach the blocking myself to the group. Once it is ready to perform, I'll record our sound check, listening back for any errors and spots where the performance can be enhanced. If this song is being first recorded for a project, the process is exactly the same but done on microphones in a studio.

This process of arranging or in some cases being the project manager for an upcoming live show performance, recording, or one-off television or promotional event is complicated but manageable when organizing occurs during the half of the year I am touring with Straight No Chaser. Our group has a mobile recording studio that we purchased and travel with domestically. I have portable recording equipment and MIDI keyboards that can fit into a backpack. Our tour buses have a front and back lounge that can easily convert into a "home" studio. The knowledge of how to create on the road when in a group like SNC has become a great strength to continuing to produce new content.

What does a typical day or week look like for you?
I have two very different lives for my time in Straight No Chaser: home and away. Both involve work on my part, but let's focus on my time away from home. Around 80 percent of my time with the group happens with us living on two tour buses traveling the country (or abroad) and performing a "one-off" (or one show per city and then moving on to the next). These buses are well equipped for everyday living. Drivers are provided to take us through the night as we sleep. A typical fall tour for Straight No Chaser will last eleven weeks totaling around seventy shows where six nights a week will be lived on these buses (with a usual day off staying at a hotel that night).

A typical day: I wake up on our tour bus in my bunk sometime in the early morning. The venue we will be performing at that day will grant access at 9:00 or 10:00 a.m. I'll make some coffee in the front lounge, eat something small, and begin to coordinate my day. I will be looking to see if there is a gym available nearby, sometimes provided for free access by the promoter of the concert. If it's laundry day, some venues have washer and dryers. Wi-Fi is generally available in each venue for work. I'll head to the gym either before or just after lunch, which is provided by the venue at our scheduled time of noon. Showers are located in the dressing rooms of the venue. There is now a free chunk of time until dinner is served at the venue at 5:00 p.m. I might watch a soccer match on the tour bus (if the satellite isn't blocked by a building that day). If I'm working on an arrangement, I will set up shop in the front lounge. If I'm not feeling well, I might try to nap in our bunk area of the bus, which is isolated from daylight and quiet. Our group sound check is 5:30 p.m. If we are rehearsing a song, our sound check may go as long as thirty minutes. We will talk through any musical or staging notes we have from the previous shows. After testing the mics for our sound engineer, we will disperse until our scheduled meet and greet with any local fans or press that is set seventy-five minutes prior to showtime. A half an hour before the show, I will start warming up and getting dressed. Ten minutes before the show, I will locate my lavalier microphone (used for giving starting pitches to the band via an electronic pitch pipe) and my in-ear monitor pack (used for listening to my group mix). Five minutes before the show I will circle up with the band to discuss any notes, say a prayer as a band, and then head to the stage. Each set is a bit over forty-five minutes with a fifteen-minute intermission. Following the last song, I will head to my dressing room to drop off my in-ears and pitch pipe, maybe mix myself a drink, and then head to our group meeting area before heading together for our signing line. Our signing line occurs in the lobby of the venue with all of us sitting at a long receiving table where we will say hello, shake hands, and sign whatever folks bring. After a few group pictures, it's back to the dressing room to change. Making sure not to leave anything behind, I'll board the bus and relax before the drivers arrive to take us to the next show's location. Once the adrenaline settles, I will head to my bunk, watch a TV show or listen to a podcast, and then fall asleep.

How many people would you guess are doing this professionally?
Professional a cappella seemed like a dream to me ten years ago. I knew of pro groups that were able to sustain themselves through touring, album sales, and publishing alone before we were signed. These groups were the cream of the crop: Take 6, The Real Group, Rockapella, the Swingle Singers, the House Jacks, the Bobs, the King's Singers, and Chanticleer, to name *the* few. If you added solo performers like Bobby McFerrin, counted arrangers and producers like you (Deke Sharon), plus the few industry organizers such as the folks at CASA, you were talking about maybe a hundred full-time a cappella professionals. That number has expanded in the past ten years with more groups able to sustain the public interest, some major engineers now specializing with a cappella–only studios, and more arrangers, sound engineers, and teachers seeing full-time work with the exploding high school and collegiate scene.

As for strictly full-time touring a cappella groups that make the majority of their income hitting the road and not with album sales or publishing, there may be only a dozen. SNC is one of these bands, having been listed as an overall top forty act for the last three years in *Pollstar Magazine* (the main trade publication for the touring industry). Granted, we have ten guys splitting album profits after we settle expenses and commissions. We record cover songs (so we don't have any songwriting income), and don't have songs playing on the radio, so without a massive touring presence we would not be a full-time music ensemble.

What advice do you have for someone starting in this field?
The running joke for me about "how to get a record deal in a cappella" is simple: start a college a cappella group, video your group doing a performance, wait seven years to post it on YouTube, and eighteen months later the CEO of Atlantic Records will call. SNC caught lightning in a bottle, and anyone that thinks starting a career in this field is anything but that needs to understand that reality.

Regardless, there is a reason I feel SNC has succeeded and I have thrived once given the opportunity. We/I may have lucked out, but the work we/I did before, during, and after the group was signed is what allowed us not to fizzle out. Before I found SNC, I was rehearsing my own quartets for fun. SNC's work ethic in school, which included spending summers together gigging, rehearsing, and living on our own dime, was ingrained in us and maintained once we went pro. After college, when there was no reason to arrange a song, I would work with groups to continue to hone my skills. It may take a miracle to get a shot at doing this for a living, but what I always could control is how hard I worked to prepare for that shot.

In what ways do you see this field growing or changing in the future?
A cappella groups touring professionally, fighting for the same dollars as Broadway shows, comedy acts, or similar niche music ensembles, have an expected uphill climb. TV is king. The most successful touring acts in our field have been products of *The Sing-Off*. The more chances a cappella can penetrate popular television, the more groups will have the public's eye, which could fast-track a touring fan base. Content is king. Netflix, Amazon, Hulu, and the like, are producing shows and specials at an unprecedented pace. The need for unique content will certainly lead to opportunities for the music industry—and with luck, a cappella.

I can speak only from what I see, and what I see in our signing lines after shows since our professional inception is more and more young adults. These kids are craving a cappella. When I ask them where they heard of us, it's always new media: YouTube, Pandora specifically. Many are part of their own a cappella choir at school. It's easier for youngsters to start a group on their own than it was for me twenty years ago. Every recording and ready-to-teach sheet music is a click away. This accessibility will lead to more young adults buying tickets for concerts.

I've gotten to watch the evolution of our live show change from a traditional stand-and-sing horseshoe with wired microphones and a couple moving lights to a full-on production that rivals any touring outfit. We've gone from star drop to pixel flex LED screens and full video wall. We've added comedic intro videos to the start of both sets, directed and produced by the group. I can see the next wave of a cappella performers being even more theatrical. The model is there with Broadway, where simple pop-up scenic design has become portably complex with new technology. With all the visual bells and whistles, our live sound is quite traditional. We don't use Auto-Tune or try to affect our sound beyond a "believable" vocal replication. This practice will be the new frontier for touring acts as there is so much ground to sonically explore in a live setting.

THEME PARK PERFORMING—TIFFANY COBURN

Believe it or not, the world's largest full-time employer of contemporary a cappella singers are theme parks. There are currently five a cappella groups in Orlando, Florida, alone: Disney has the Voices of Liberty and the American Sound Machine at Epcot as well as the Dapper Dans at the Magic Kingdom, and Universal has the Hogwarts Frog Choir and Sing It. For young singers who are looking for a reliable paycheck and the opportunity to perform thirty sets a week, or older singers who continue to want a life of performing full-time but without all the travel, theme parks are your best bet.

Tiffany Coburn has been singing in the Voices of Liberty since 1989, an impressive run in a single job for any employee in any company, let alone a vocalist. Her flawless soaring soprano voice can also be heard in viral video sensation Voctave.

What drew you to this field of a cappella?
I actually got into a cappella by accident. I was working at Disneyland and heard there was a group in Florida at Disney's Epcot Center called

the Voices of Liberty and they were holding auditions. I thought, a job where you get actually get paid to sing; I'm all about it! I flew down to Orlando and was overwhelmed when I heard the group sing; they blew me away. I auditioned, and after a long two months, they called and said I was hired.

What experiences and education do you find most useful? What skills and knowledge do people need coming into this kind of work?

I've always said that Voices of Liberty was my college. I sang in church and school choirs growing up but had not had any formal training. I took piano lessons in junior high so I knew how to read music a little bit. Over the years I have gotten better at reading just by doing it. If there is one skill I would tell someone to concentrate on, it would be knowing how to read music.

Vocal training, of course, is an asset in this business, but I've been around some singers that are completely "mechanical" in their singing. I think that if you can "feel" the music when you are singing, have fluidity and passion, that takes all the training in the world to the next level!

How has the field changed since you started?

When I started with the Voices of Liberty in 1989, a cappella was not as mainstream popular as it is now. I think that the Voices of Liberty was more of a novelty of beautiful music that people had never heard before. The popularity of the group now seems to be enjoyed by people that really understand and appreciate the complexity of what we do.

What are the technical aspects of your work that most people don't understand or know about?

You must listen, listen, listen! The inner workings of an a cappella group is much more difficult than it appears. In the Voices of Liberty, we tune "up" to our lead soprano. She leads our train in pitch and tempo. In general, blending, vowel matching, staggered breathing, and control of vibrato are the essential components of our sound.

In a cappella singing, the pitch may drift at times sharp or flat; you need to be aware and flexible enough to go with it as a group. This seems to be especially hard for people with perfect pitch because, when the group tends to go sharp or flat, someone with perfect pitch has trouble going with them. I have a friend that told me that he literally has to transpose in his head while he's singing to compensate for the change of pitch.

What is the scope and range of what you do?

With Disney, I am expected to know my music, to be a representative of their standards of excellence, and to interact with guests and help make their experience "magical." Whether I am singing for a convention on property, singing the "Star Spangled Banner" for an event, or singing on a track that is played in the park, I am expected to be the best that I can be at all times. I love the fact that I'm in a show where the audience is sitting on the floor surrounding us and I get to meet and talk with them after each performance. It's special when you receive a letter from a guest that talks about how you helped make their vacation special. My grandfather asked me once, "What other job would allow you to have applause everyday for what you do?" How can I not love what I do?

What does a typical day or week look like for you?

Where I used to roll out of bed with my high notes, I now find that I need to take time to warm up before my day begins (this is where the training probably would have been good for me to have learned earlier in life!). My day at Disney begins with a quick rehearsal three times a week at the beginning of the shift, and I then perform seven fifteen-minute shows with thirty minutes in between each performance. When I'm not at Disney, I travel with my own solo performances, am a session singer, and also am a part of another a cappella group called Voctave. As you can tell, I do not have a typical day or week; each one is different when you are a performer.

How many people would you guess are doing this professionally?

That is hard to say, but I would venture to say that there are more professional opportunities today than ever before. With the popularity of shows like *Glee, The Voice, The Sing-Off*, and so forth, plus the accessibility of YouTube and the Internet, the opportunities for a singer to be heard are endless. I'm fortunate to be a part of a great company where I have a job singing music I love, a regular paycheck coming in, health insurance, and many other benefits.

What percentage of your income comes from this?

One hundred percent of my income comes from singing.

What advice do you have for someone starting in this field?

Let passion be your guide. I know singers who may not be the best but are passionate with what they do and they have a successful career. Know what you're good at, but don't be afraid to try new things. Listen to all types of music so that you are a well-rounded singer. Don't burn any bridges if you can help it. Be professional, be respectful, and above all else, just be nice.

In what ways do you see this field growing or changing in the future?

Music, over the years, went from radio stations playing a limited variety of music and was driven by what the stations wanted you to hear. Now with Internet, the types of music have exploded. A good example of this is the number of categories of the Grammy Awards thirty years ago and now. A cappella has found a niche in the music field, and the popularity keeps growing. The fact that a group like Pentatonix dominated the holiday music charts over all other types of music is incredible. The quality of talent that is emerging at such young ages of singers today and the resources to learn online is beyond comprehension. To me, the future of a cappella continues to grow each year, and it's exciting to be a part, no matter how small, of encouraging a new generation of singers that are a part of this music we call a cappella.

PROFESSIONAL HOLIDAY CAROLING—RENE RUIZ

Most major cities have companies that hire singers annually and train them to sing in group configurations to fill client requests for holiday carolers at office/home parties, businesses, hospitals and nursing homes, shopping malls, theme parks, and even film and television or commercial appearances. Although this is seasonal work, it is a full-time job for many from Thanksgiving to New Year's Day.

Rene Ruiz is no stranger to the stage, having cut his teeth at Disney World with Toxic Audio (now performing as Vox Audio), whose fame grew outside the theme park and eventually grew into an off-Broadway show (*Loudmouth*). As a journeyman singer, arranger, director, and coach, he works on a variety of projects, without a doubt as to how he'll be spending his December.

What drew you to this field of a cappella?

The work is flexible and offers singers the opportunity to make some extra income during the gift-buying season. On many occasions, it's also possible to actually bring joy, nostalgia, and welcome entertainment to grateful audiences through vocal harmonies.

What experiences and education do you find have been most useful? What skills and knowledge do people need coming into this kind of work?

The image of Victorian-era "Dickens" carolers in their top hats and fur stoles is pretty iconic, and most companies put together costumed quartets to sing everything from traditional sacred Christmas carols to secular holiday songs and children's classics. It's important to find out if the company you're auditioning for supplies you with a costume for the season or if you're expected to have your own. A custom-made or bought costume can easily cost anywhere from one to five hundred dollars depending on the complexity, but that money can be made back easily within the first season.

Sight-reading skills are always an important asset to any a cappella singer, but most companies provide rehearsal tracks to learn from at home or schedule group rehearsals in the months prior to gigs being assigned. The ability to blend and tune is incredibly important since the people you're generally sent out to sing with change from event to event. You're almost never singing with the same quartet twice in a season so the ability to adapt to the singers around you is important.

Memorization skills are important as many companies require you to perform "off-book." This could mean anywhere from fifty to eighty arrangements ready to be sung at a moment's request. If you're ambitious enough to sing with more than one company in a season, the number of arrangements you'll have floating in your head at any one time can double or triple! Knowing your music determines how many gigs you'll be assigned and whether or not you're asked back in subsequent years.

The ability to adapt to an environment is important as well. Gigs can happen indoors or outdoors, on-mic or off-mic, in loud noisy parties or quiet somber worship services. Knowing your voice well enough to know how to project or pull back can protect you from oversinging or burning yourself out for the season.

How has the field changed since you started?
As a cappella becomes more mainstream, the demand for "contemporary" groups has been increasing. This means more modern song lists and more complex arrangements are being added to repertoires. It also means that an additional costume possibility can enter the picture. Some groups have added a vocal percussionist to the traditional quartet.

What are the technical aspects of your work that most people don't understand or know about?
Caroling work is a great way to practice "reading" audiences in live performance situations: knowing when to add an up-tempo "sleigh ride" song after too many lullaby carols, or feeling out if your audience wants to sing along or listen respectfully. Performances like these are usually a form of environmental theater and can benefit from or strengthen basic audience skills.

What does a typical day or week look like for you?
This all depends on the types of contracts a company might get during a season. They might get a full-time daily contract at a shopping mall or theme park. This means regular daily work with consistent daily call times and span of day at a set performing space with regular set times. Most often, it's a series of individual gigs assigned with varying call times during the daytime or evening throughout the season. The more open your availability determines how many gigs you might get assigned.

How many people would you guess are doing this professionally?
A single company in any one city can hire anywhere from twenty to sixty singers depending on the amount of work they expect to be offered in a season. Most of the cities I've lived in (Orlando, New York, and Los Angeles) have anywhere from five to six companies supplying singers to clients.

What percentage of your income comes from this?
I work primarily as a freelance performer so I like to pack my schedule in December. I could usually make enough in thirty days to take my vacation time January to March.

What advice do you have for someone starting in this field?
Remember that the time to start researching the companies that hire singers in your city is at the beginning of summer. Most of these companies start holding their auditions somewhere around July to August. Familiarize yourself with holiday music of all kinds. Being able to sing (even solo!) someone's particular favorite or obscure Christmas/Hanukkah/Kwanzaa song could mean a generous tip for an industrious caroler!

LIVE SOUND ENGINEERING—TONY HUERTA

No matter how well a group sings, if the person behind the audio board doesn't know what he's doing, the group will sound terrible. Equalization (EQ), balance, feedback, reverb, effects . . . so very many things can go wrong, and yet when they go right, the audience is swept up in the sound of perfect harmony.

There are but a few truly elite live audio engineers for contemporary a cappella, and Tony Huerta is in that pantheon, mixing the likes of Take 6, The Real Group, Pentatonix, *The Sing-Off* tour, Vocalosity, and dozens of others. Chapter 10 is written by him and is about running live sound, but here is some insight into his career as an engineer.

What drew you to this field of a cappella?
I started listening to doo-wop music in high school and got hooked. I got a few guys together from the school choir and taught them parts. Little did I know those were my first arrangements. We entered into several talent shows and won! I was hooked. I was drawn by the raw vocals and a performance directly from the body. When I got to college, I started three more groups. One was called Exact Change. We shared the stage with the House Jacks in 1993 at Acappella's Restaurant, a local Denver music venue. That's where I met Deke Sharon. We've stayed in touch off and on for all these years!

What experiences and education do you find have been most useful?

What skills and knowledge do people need coming into this kind of work? When I look back and reflect on what experiences helped me gain the skills necessary to be successful, it's a varied set of circumstance and learning opportunities. Let's look at the knowledge you will need. First, I went to college for music at the University of North Colorado and gained knowledge of chord structure by singing in the vocal jazz groups. Then arranging and performing my own arrangements in different groups gave me voicing techniques and style. I taught myself to beatbox for the 17th Avenue Allstars, a pro a cappella group, and learned feel and groove. Each situation gave me tools I use every day in my career. But most importantly, I learned early on that people skills are most important. Who cares how talented you are as a singer, beatboxer, sound engineer, studio engineer, or production manager if you are not enjoyable to work with? Be the most likable person in any and all situations. But you better have the knowledge and confidence in those skills to back it up! So, when I say be likable, that means personal hygiene, that means easygoing, and that means calm and cool under pressure. That's the skill that cannot be taught.

Now, let's talk about technical skill. If you want to be successful as a sound engineer, you must learn the equipment of the trade. I was thrown into live engineering because I had the knowledge of chord structure, beatbox, and EQ qualities of beatbox, and because I was easy to work with. Mark Kibble of Take 6 recognized I had the basic knowledge to mix and work with them. I met him as he worked with the Colorado All-State Jazz Choir. He got my e-mail address, and two weeks later, I got a call from their management and was asked if I would mix them and if I had my passport. I said yes and that I was available. Then I received an e-mail with the airline tickets so I could get my passport expedited. They were first-class tickets to Ecuador! I fell off my chair. That moment changed my life.

Now, here is where the skills necessary to be successful come in. I didn't have them, and I knew it. I knew what Take 6 should sound like because I was their biggest fan. But I didn't know how to get the equipment they use to make that happen. I got their equipment rider and didn't know any of the equipment on it. So, with that monumental task in front of me, I got to work and put myself through a learning regimen.

I downloaded every owner's manual of every piece of gear on the rider, and I spent day and night reading, taking notes, visualizing, and learning every function. If you'd like to know what I learned first, get the owner's manual for the Midas Heritage 3000. I flew to Ecuador and conquered the sound and equipment, and had the time of my life doing it. I've been with them ever since.

The second part of this story is what made my career last. First, I was easy and enjoyable to work with. Second, I was forced to use the house mixing consoles for every Take 6 show for nine years. I would download and learn different consoles and equipment for every show I mixed. I can now say that I can walk into any situation, know how to use the gear, even if I've never used it before, and have a successful concert. So, never stop learning the tools in your trade!

How has the field changed since you started?

The field has changed in the last twelve years. First of all, the industry has moved from analog to mostly digital processing and mixing consoles. That was a huge shift in how audio is processed. First of all, most new engineers have tools at their fingertips that only seasoned engineers had before. That's good and bad. Just because you have it doesn't mean that you should use it. New engineers don't take the time to fully learn the processes of the different audio-processing tools. Second, a cappella music has exploded on the world music scene. There are way more mixing opportunities than there were twelve years ago.

What are the technical aspects of your work that most people don't understand or know about?

Being an audio engineer is a widely misunderstood career. Most people think I'm a DJ! When they attend a concert, they have no idea that there is one single person between the artist and the audience. And depending on that person, their experience at that concert can vary widely, in a negative or positive way. I always say, "An audio engineer has the opportunity to screw up any good concert, regardless of how good the artist is." And it's true. An audio engineer can make any good singer sound bad. But a good engineer can make a great artist sound incredible. That's the goal.

What is the scope and range of what you do?

The scope and range of my career changes daily. That's what I love about it. No concert is ever the same. It's constantly changing and requires constant technical changes and constant creative changes. Even if I'm mixing the same artist every night, the venue, the crowd, and the sound is different and uses a different set of skills. I mix big band concerts, a cappella concerts, musical theater concerts, symphony shows, and rock and roll, in theaters, jazz clubs, or giant churches, outside music festivals, on the beach, in the mountains, on a cruise ship, and all around the world. That's the best part of the job; it's never the same!

What does a typical day or week look like for you?

I probably work about twenty to thirty hours per week. But that's deceiving because I travel quite a bit, about one-third of my time.

Monday: Usually my day off.

Tuesday: The e-mails roll in from my clients. Some clients want suggestions on what equipment they should buy. Some clients want help running Pro Tools or audio equipment. I've realized that I'm the virtual help desk for anything audio for live shows or studio in a cappella music. I usually spend my entire Tuesday answering e-mail, posting marketing on social media, or keeping my business finances in order.

Wednesday: Studio workday. I have a lot of live concerts that I record and promise mixes for my clients. It takes about eight hours a week to remix those concerts for my clients.

Thursday: I usually take most of the day off and sometimes fly out to a different city for the Friday concert.

Friday: I'm usually traveling to a city. The day usually starts at 4:00 a.m. Fly until 1:00 p.m. Go directly to the venue. Set up for two hours making sure that the sound is in perfect working order. Sound check for Take 6 at 5:00 p.m. for about thirty to forty-five minutes. Dinner at 6:00. Show at 7:00 p.m. Show over at 9:00 p.m. Break down my equipment and get to the hotel at about 11:00 p.m. Answer e-mails and check my social media; post on social media about the show I just mixed or some cool moment that happened. Sleep!

Saturday: Wake up at 5:00 a.m. and travel to another city. Setup, sound check, dinner, show, pack up, social media, and sleep.

Sunday: I wake up around 10:00 a.m. and go catch my flight home. Sunday night, relax and recharge to start it all over again.

How many people would you guess are doing this professionally?

It's a small community of a cappella engineers. I know of only three engineers that tour and mix professionally full-time. There are probably ten more that I know of that mix part-time. We used to have more pros, but they have been offered other careers that take precedence. One guy used to mix for Pentatonix but now sings with the Manhattan Transfer. Others have become artists' management for the artists they used to mix for.

What percentage of your income comes from this?

I make about 40 percent of my income from live sound engineering, 25 percent from studio engineering and mixing, 20 percent from equipment sales, and 15 percent from teaching and clinics for groups, schools, and engineers.

What advice do you have for someone starting in this field?

How do you get into this field you ask. Jump in and start engineering for a new a cappella group or band. Take them to the top and help them have a consistent product. Take it upon yourself to learn the tools and equipment of your trade, and attend an a cappella engineering course by me! Learn every piece of equipment you can find. Be chill, not over-eager, not annoying, not smelly, and in calm control always. Make them want to work with you again because you have the skill and the social skills to succeed. Ask for help and advice from other engineers in the field. I've learned something from every engineer I've met and worked with. Ask them questions! A four-year degree is not needed. What is needed is the drive and work ethic to learn on your own and then apply it when the opportunity arises. Mark Kibble, of Take 6, explains my success in the business. He said, "Success is when preparation meets the opportunity!"

You will never be able to capitalize on opportunities if you are not prepared for them. And no one can fully prepare you for the opportunity except you.

In what ways do you see this field growing or changing in the future?

A cappella music is growing at an incredible rate. There is a shortage of good a cappella engineers now. Technically, the industry has hit a plateau. The digital change has happened and will be here for a long time.

What are the most important keys to success in your career?

During the show, it's the ability to blend technical skills with creative music skill. And to never give the audience a reason to look at you for a technical issue or mix choice.

Before the show, it's having the technical knowledge to set up and use any sound system.

For sound check, it's having all technical issues worked out so that the artists have no worries or even a thought of the technical side. They are free to focus only on their performance.

Be the one they want to work with again!

Here's something to always keep in your mind as an engineer. A good engineer is one that pleases the largest percentage of the audience, but it's never 100 percent. Work hard to blend your technical knowledge and creative musical talents into a cohesive and consistent product from your clients to their fans. It's not about you; it's all about the artist!

15

IN THE RECORDING STUDIO

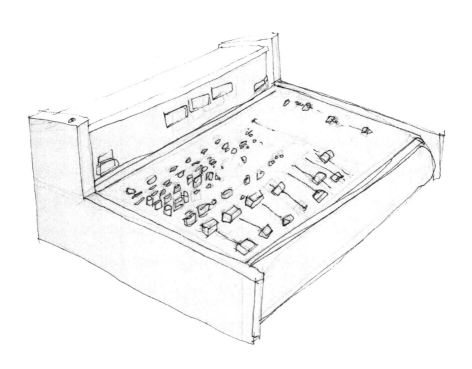

Not everyone who loves a cappella enjoys travel. Some want to sleep in their own bed at night and work day after day at the studio downtown . . . or at home in their pajamas. As modern recording technology developed, most major recording studios closed, and in their place has risen an army of laptops and portable recording rigs that can make a professional-quality album in any basement or closet. If you want to stay close to home yet still immerse yourself in a cappella every day, read on:

SESSION SINGING—FLETCHER SHERIDAN

The idea of walking into a studio and singing for a living while you sleep in your own bed at night is a dream for many singers who tire of the road. However, the job is more challenging than it seems: breaking into the business is tough; it's really only a full-time job if you live in major film, television, and commercial cities like New York or Los Angeles, and the skill set required—reading music flawlessly, singing in different styles, and infusing each line with the right emotional intensity—is beyond many singers.

Fletcher Sheridan beat the odds. In dozens of films and television he has been behind the scenes as a solo singer (e.g., as the solo voice of Zach Galifianakis in *The Hangover Part III*) and part of a choir for soundtracks or music scenes (*Harry Potter and the Deathly Hallows* and *Family Guy*), and even on-screen (*About a Boy*, *The Office*, and *American Pie*). Sometimes he's singing a cappella, sometimes not, as the job is always different.

What drew you to this field of singing?
Even before I could understand why, I've always loved the versatility of the human voice and singing harmony. I think my first introduction to it was barbershop! The high school I went to had the Far Western District Champion Quartet, and I got in as tenor 1. I was a sophomore, and my voice hadn't changed yet, so I was the high guy who could belt it all! Listening to four guys lock a chord and ring it out was otherworldly to me. Flash-forward fourteen years, and I'm MD'ing a world-class a cappella group and still giggle with joy every time we lock a chord perfectly. Recording a cappella is fun because you're chasing after that

giggly joy with every moment you record. That, along with the ability to digitally manipulate wave forms, gives you a vast creative playground at your disposal. You really can do anything your mind can come up with, especially with an instrument as versatile as the human voice.

What experiences and education do you find have been most useful?

All of it! I've been obsessed with vocal pedagogy and music theory since high school. Being a session singer calls on you to work quickly. In order to do that you need both the ear *and* the brain to get you there. Beef up on theory but also learn things by ear. Transcribe the parts off an a cappella record as best you can but also analyze the chords. There is a technical language to music and an instinctual one—mastering both will make you an asset in any recording session. Experience-wise, I find the things that forced me to grow are the things that have served me well in my career. Growth requires you to face your demons, both internal and external. You can deal with them from a place of fear, or a place of freedom, and I think both are valid ways to grow. Singing lead soprano in m-pact was one of the most valuable experiences of my career but one of the most challenging. In the beginning I was a mess of fearful nerves, crying before shows and taking beta-blockers to get through it. But I came out of it a stronger singer than I ever could have imagined. A different example would be my time working with the film composer John Powell. I would go to his studio and workshop music and characters for animated films he was working on. We would arrange on the fly and use every ounce of our vocal ability. Being in a studio situation where there were no wrong notes or mistakes was so liberating. That freedom gave me the ability to do things I'd never thought I was capable of doing.

What skills and knowledge do people need coming into this kind of work?

As much of both as possible! Most people start out singing on larger choral sessions, so coming in with a good amount of choral experience under your belt is a good start. On top of that,

- Be a good reader—no, you don't need to be able to cold-read Schoenberg, but be able to read with minimal bobbles. The scoring stage at Sony costs several *thousand* dollars per hour to use, and the longer you take to get it right, the more you are costing the composer/production.

- Be able to sing in other languages—you don't need to be fluent, but understand the rules of Latin, Spanish, and German (extra credit for French!) enough to sing them properly. Understand pure Latin vowels and how to execute them—they will come in handy more than you know.
- Be able to blend—you'd be surprised how few people truly get this one. It's something that typically takes months to achieve, but in the studio you've got to blend and find your ensemble within minutes. One great way to work on this is to join a caroling company. You are put in a quartet with three random singers with varied musical backgrounds and vocal approaches, and your mission is to sound like a group that has been singing together for years. Every gig is typically with a different lineup, so the process is always new.
- Network your tail off—be able to look someone in the eye and have a real conversation with them. People don't hire you based solely on your skill. They also hire you because they like you, and you're the type of person they can stand being stuck in a small recording booth for eight hours with! Don't feel like you have to have that stereotypical LA discussion that starts with, "What projects are you working on?" People see through that. Talk about your cat, talk about your favorite season of *Breaking Bad* or your recent vacation. When you talk, always end what you're saying with a question. When networking, always strive to make real, true professional connections that extend beyond the superficial.

How many people would you guess are doing this professionally?
I'd say a couple hundred people do session singing professionally, with less than half of them making their living at it.

What percentage of your income comes from this?
I am proud to say all of my income comes from being a professional musician.

How has the field changed since you started?
I think the overall career choice of being a musician has changed. Gone are the days of just doing one thing. Nowadays, it's all about diver-

sification, always reassessing your skills and what you can do with them. Yes, I make a vast majority of my living from session singing, but I also arrange, compose, and do voice-over work. You spin as many plates as you can, and the only way you get enough plates to make ends meet is if you are expanding on your gifts. The people in my field that I see with the longest careers are the ones that understand this and continue to diversify their skill set.

In what ways do you see this field growing or changing in the future?

I think networking will change. As film and TV have evolved over the decades, the need for larger groups of singers has diminished. Session singers traditionally focused on networking with other singers to get work. I think it will shift to building relationships directly with the composers.

What advice do you have for someone starting in this field?

Mission statement of the session singer is to be quick, calm, and joyful amidst the chaos of creativity.

To be an effective session singer, you have to enjoy the notion of walking into a gig with little to no idea what you will be doing. Composers may have sheet music, or they may not. They may have a clear idea of what they want you to do, or they may have you there to help them find their way. Will you be a pop tenor today, belting your guts out, or a light, floaty, baroque countertenor? Perhaps they'll want characters! With session singing, nothing is known, and you have to get from zero to a pristine performance as quickly as possible. This means you need an extensive toolbox of skills available to help you. You can only amass that through experience, and you can only amass experience through doing things that musically kick your butt.

When I began down this career path, I was singing boy soprano in film choirs. They still recorded everything together at the same time— the adult choir, children's choir, and orchestra all in the same room doing full cues. As recording technology has evolved, along with the recording process itself, those elements are recorded separately. Now, it's all about isolating each element in the music so it can be controlled in postproduction. This means the composer can take the time and get every minute detail exactly the way they want it. That minutia leads me to the three pitfalls to avoid as a session singer:

1. Lost in translation. When you sing live, you're engaging all five senses. When you go into the studio, you have to rez all five of those senses down to one. That means there has to be a shift in how you convey the emotion of what you're singing. The listener can't see you singing your heart out, so you've got to make them hear it. Many singers don't respect the sensory downshift, and their performance in the booth suffers for it.

2. Death by a thousand cuts. Being in the studio is like being under magnifying glass. You have to be comfortable with this. Let's use the example of singing the word "love" for six beats. Seems pretty simple, right? Not so fast! They may not like your vowel when you sing the word "love." Maybe your diction isn't clear, and they can't understand you singing the word "love." They may want that held note to be straight tone for the first four beats and then with a little vibrato added in for the final two beats. They may want you to darken or brighten your tone. God's in the details, and those who ignore the minutia are done in by it.

3. Focus, Daniel-san! Mistakes happen. I have a simple standard I try to hold myself to in the studio: never make the same mistake twice. Whether that is a performance error or a reading error, try to maintain focus, and never make that mistake again. After an eight-hour session, this can be easier said than done.

Finally, be patient, keep your eyes on your own paper, and allow your dream to grow up with you:

- Be patient. Getting onto a show like *The Voice* grants its contestants instant celebrity. Some are able to take that flash of an opportunity and do something with it, others not so much. Building a career takes years, which means you must be patient. There will be times you doubt the path you're on, get burned out, or feel stuck. If you're doing the stuff I've mentioned above, then you're doing a pretty darn good job. Just be patient, trust yourself, and continue looking for opportunities to sing. Opportunities beget more opportunities, and that can take time.

- Keep your eyes on your own paper. With social media being what it is, it will be really easy to see a bunch of your peers doing things you'd like to be doing. Don't consider their success your failure. Keep your focus on what you're doing and what you've done.

- Allow your dream to grow up with you. How many times have you heard it? "I've wanted to be a [dream occupation] since I was a toddler!" If a toddler walked up to you and told you what to do with your life, how much credence would you give him or her? Probably not a lot. Yet so many people grow up chasing a toddler's dream. I'm not, in any way, telling you to give up on a dream you have. I *am* saying that you shouldn't be afraid to ask if it's a dream you still have. If it truly is, keep on going! If not, allow yourself to find other dreams to follow.

SINGING AND PRODUCING PARTS RECORDINGS— TIM WAURICK

It is not necessary to read music to sing in a choir, vocal group, or a cappella ensemble. Those who don't read music need a way to practice their part until they have it memorized, and the most effective way to do this is to use a "parts recording": one part (your part) is in the left channel or ear, and all the others are on the right. This way you can listen to the whole arrangement as a unit, then listen to just one ear to practice your part, then listen with both ears to practice your part, and finally when you have your part learned, remove the left ear and sing along with the other parts (a la "music minus one"). This is how we teach the Barden Bellas their parts on *Pitch Perfect*, how an increasing number of music educators are speeding up the "note plunking" process in their a cappella groups (allowing for notes to be learned outside rehearsals and precious class time to be used focusing on crafting the music), and how many barbershop singers learn. It's the norm for many barbershop choruses to use learning recordings (aka "multitracks"), so that anyone in the community, even those who don't read music, can fully participate in the ensemble.

If the goal of previous generations was to create the perfect barbershop singer, Tim Waurick is it. He can sing all voice parts, understands the phrasing, theory, and practice backward and forward, and can breathe life into a bunch of notes on a page, which is why it isn't a stretch to call him barbershop's most-in-demand parts-recording creator, which by extension makes him the most prolific parts-recording specialist in the world.

What drew you to this field of a cappella?

I began singing barbershop music in middle school because it was the select ensemble. Unlike many, my initial draw to barbershop music and a cappella was the camaraderie. Eventually, I heard some of the top barbershop quartets, namely, the Gas House Gang, Keepsake, and Acoustix. I was drawn to their music, more specifically, their explosive and dynamic tags.

What experiences and education do you find have been most useful? What skills and knowledge do people need coming into this kind of work?

Barbershop music requires a great ear and the ability to ring chords with great expression. Multitracking and creating learning tracks takes a great degree of patience and skill. Professional learning tracks require good vocal production, an extensive range, and some degree of expression as well as the ability to sight-read. Beyond that, you have to be able to sing well with yourself.

How has the field changed since you started?

Learning tracks used to be produced by a four-track recorder or even four people standing in a square and each holding a tape recorder to their mouths. I started recording multitracks with a four-track recorder and eventually graduated to using a computer. The main goal of starting my TimTracks business was to create something that people would enjoy listening to. I remember using learning tracks when I was in high school and always felt like it was a chore. I wanted people to enjoy the learning process by having something fun to sing along with.

What are the technical aspects of your work that most people don't understand or know about?

The increasing selection of pitch-correction products, such as Melodyne, has allowed people of various singing levels to produce a product that is at least in tune and accurate. Most people wouldn't believe the number of hours that I spend recording to ensure the product is as natural and well produced as possible. The thing that I work on the most in the studio is expression and interpretation. I believe that you can't take shortcuts. I use as little pitch editing as possible and take great pride in the hard work I put into each learning track. I am not a factory and do my best to approach each song as an artist.

What is the scope and range of what you do?

I've created learning tracks for over fifteen International Barbershop Quartet champions and for every International Championship chorus that has won in the past fifty years! I've recorded learning tracks for the Barbershop Harmony Society since 2005. Over 33 percent of my business comes from outside of the United States. I'm honored that so many people would have so much confidence in me.

What does a typical day or week look like for you?

I'll record three to four songs in a typical week. I will start with a lead part on Sunday and will then record bass, baritone, and tenor on Monday. I'll then record lead for the next song. Following that, I will mix the first song—usually on Monday night. A typical day looks like this:

Monday:
8:00 a.m.–9:30 a.m.: Bass, song 1
9:30 a.m.–10:30 a.m.: Workout
10:30 a.m.–11:00 a.m.: Breakfast break
11:00 a.m.–12:30 p.m.: E-mails, business, and warm-up
12:30 p.m.–1:30 p.m.: Baritone, song 1
1:30 p.m.–2:30 p.m.: Tenor, song 1
2:30 p.m.–4:00 p.m.: Lead, song 2
4:00 p.m.–4:30 p.m.: Break/snack/late lunch
4:30 p.m.–7:00 p.m.: Edit/mix, song 1
7:00 p.m.: Dinner, finish day

I repeat that process on Tuesday, Wednesday, and Thursday. I generally take Friday and mostly Sunday off, especially when I have out-of-town shows with my quartet, Vocal Spectrum. Friday is usually spent working on e-mails, the website, and mixing and mixing.

How many people would you guess are doing this professionally?

There are about three or four people recording barbershop learning tracks on a full-time basis. Another ten to fifteen have a part-time learning track business.

What percentage of your income comes from this?

Ninety-nine percent of my income comes from creating barbershop learning tracks.

What advice do you have for someone starting in this field?

Creating learning tracks takes more time and can be more difficult than you think. It requires a lot of "voice use" in extreme ranges and can be quite tedious. Sometimes your day depends on how your voice feels and how good the arrangement is. My advice is to never overbook yourself, be smart with your voice, don't overuse pitch editing, and build a large catalog of songs that can sustain you when you are in need of time off.

In what ways do you see this field growing or changing in the future?

More and more people are creating learning tracks. With home studios becoming more and more affordable, many people are creating learning tracks for their own chorus/quartet. Although there are more people creating learning tracks for their groups, the market is still in need of professional learning tracks. Most barbershop choruses use learning tracks, and I offer a catalog of over a thousand songs for them to choose from instantly. I predict less need for custom learning tracks but a continued need for the quick-fix catalog songs. Personally, I plan to continue in this profession for the rest of my life and look forward to recording many more thousands of songs!

EDITING—ALEX GREEN

As digital recording technology has risen to prominence, new tools have arisen to help polish vocals. Although Auto-Tune is the best known by name, Melodyne is the more powerful and ubiquitous program within a cappella circles, as you can use it to correct tuning, move notes and rhythms, and so on. Singers, both a cappella and not, no longer need to sing perfectly, a boon to amateur collegiate and high school groups whose albums over the past twenty years have gone from sounding like an audio yearbook to Grammy-Award quality.

Editing recorded a cappella tracks is a great way to get into the general field of recording, as busy engineers and producers often farm out their editing work to young, reliable cohorts, which allows them to bring a recording project in on time and on budget. An editor will open previously recorded tracks, tune pitches (but not perfectly—knowing how much is the right amount is key), align rhythms where needed, "fly" (copy and paste) vocal passages when needed, and sometimes even build a vocal percussion part out of a sloppy performance or a few solo sounds. It's not the most glamorous aspect of recording, but knowing how it works and being able to do it well is an essential step in being a modern a cappella recording specialist.

Alex Green graduated from the Tufts Amalgamates just as this technology became ubiquitous and started his career, which he continues to do to this day. As is the case with others in the a cappella recording field, editing is not his only role on many albums, although it is where many engineers in a cappella make much of their money, especially when first starting out.

What drew you to this field of a cappella?
It all happened very organically. I started messing around with recording music while I was in high school; I was in a couple of bands playing guitar and singing, and my (in hindsight, pretty bad) songwriting led me to want to record everything I wrote instead of just trying to remember what I did after writing down lyrics. Meanwhile, as soon as I found out I was accepted to Tufts University, my choir director immediately started talking to me about a cappella there—she had gone to UNC and was involved pretty heavily with the a cappella scene there in the midnineties. Once I got to Tufts and was accepted into the Amalgamates, all the recorded aspects of what we did kept sort of poking at the back of my mind, saying, "Hey, you might want to do this."

When the Mates started recording our next album, I was sort of thrust into the process; I was sitting in at the console, producing takes, and pressing buttons. For some silly reason, I fought the compulsion to pursue music as a career for a bit, mostly because I had, at the time, already committed to a different major—archaeology—but as soon as the production process for that album was finished, I was elected music director; we immediately started talking about the next album, and then it clicked. I was fully hands-on for the next album, doing most of the recording, a good portion of the editing, and a bit of mixing. By the time we finished that album at the end of 2010, I had graduated and was singing in, recording with, and otherwise marinating with Overboard outside of Boston. I soon realized that performing wasn't my forte nor my real passion and that my place was on the other side of a console at a desk, making music happen as opposed to making it come out of my mouth. So, along with Alexander Koutzoukis (yes, two Alexes; yes, it's silly; yes, it's fun), I formed Plaid Productions in February 2011, and it was off to the races. Now, I get to help other people make music and express their artistic vision, which interestingly enough, affords me way more opportunity to be creative and express my artistic vision than I would as a performer myself.

What experiences and education do you find have been most useful? What skills and knowledge do people need coming into this kind of work?

"Knowing the right people" sounds immensely clichéd, but for various reasons it's the most important knowledge you'll gain. Of course the connections you acquire can get you work, clients, referrals, and so forth, but more important is the exchange of ideas and some of the technical skills you're unlikely to either acquire or prioritize otherwise. For example, there's a significant chance that, unless you speak with the right people beforehand, your strategy as an engineer will focus exclusively on recording singing that's in tune rather than singing that's compelling. You'll end up with impeccably tuned tracks that sound more boring than an unbuttered piece of toast.

As for more specific skills, being able to read people both musically and personality-wise is crucial. As I just said, getting compelling and emotive performances is arguably the most important part of recording a cappella, and figuring out how to get those out of people requires some amount of rapport and back-and-forth; you can't just look at someone or hear them sing once and have them figured out.

In addition, some very basic but essential skills in this field are attention to detail, punctuality, and a committed work ethic. Most albums are both on tight deadlines and require immense amounts of tedious post-production work to get them across the finish line, and one mistake or oversight can turn into a cascading failure down the line. For example, setting a tempo incorrectly can make a song feel as if it's either dragging or rushing, even if everything is sung "correctly." Enunciation can either be overdone or become impossible, groove can disappear, and then instead of a cohesive song you have a bunch of people singing roughly the same thing with no connection to one another.

More than anything else though, being in a group for four years and being music director was really the most useful experience. All of those skills—analyzing people's learning styles, attention to detail, and so forth—plus others such as selective listening, envisioning the end point and figuring out creative steps to get there, and others, are all developed by being in a collaborative group and being the director thereof.

How has the field changed since you started?

Interestingly, not much. If anything, it's grown in size and recognition, but the actual work taking place hasn't changed appreciably. If anything, it feels somewhat as if it's all catching up to how I was working when I started—providing a comfortable experience when recording in order to make being a dynamic and compelling singer feel easy and effortless, and then highlighting as much of those performances as possible in postproduction without sacrificing listenability for a perceived organic quality.

I know that's a bit of a mouthful, so let me sum it up a different way. My goal is always for people to hear their album back and think, "Wow, I had no idea we could sound like that, and it's really us sounding like that!" When I started doing work, there was still a big focus on bells and whistles, laser beams, and other "what can we do to a voice" effects. Now, it's more about "what can we do with our voices," a subtle but important difference that places focus on the instrument on the front end rather than what can be done to it afterward.

What are the technical aspects of your work that most people don't understand or know about?

I think people may underestimate the tedium of some of what we do. Sure, there's the outward-facing recording, which always has us in front of people, talking to and singing at them, but a good portion of my week is spent clicking on and nudging orange blobs on a screen that represent words and notes, and lining them up with one another. This pitch and time correction is what we call "editing."

When you're editing, the goal is always to be as transparent as possible. If someone can tell that a voice is edited, it'd better be intentional. No performance is perfect, and sometimes the things we ask of singers to make their singing more compelling or more interesting can, by design, make the pitch and rhythm of a note or phrase demonstrably worse. The idea there, though, is that this out-of-tune, scratchy, maybe a little behind the beat phrase is imparting a new texture on the song, and we always make sure we record singing that we know we can edit later. No matter what you record, the idea behind editing is to remove any outright distractions that would take a listener out of a performance, while leaving enough flaws still there—slight fluctuations in pitch, push and pull of timing within measures, and so forth—that make a performance uniquely human. While no one wants to hear blatantly out-of-tune singing, no one wants to hear human laser beams either.

Something a little more obvious that might make sense to more people though is the constant "make it louder" argument. There's the loudness war in the wider music production field, but that's not what I'm talking about. Depending on the group, arranger, and director, we get a lot of notes asking for individual things to be turned up in a mix all the time, at different places, on a micromanagerial level. Occasionally, we'll get to the point where either at a certain section or even as a mix overall, we're asked—accidentally, but asked nonetheless—to turn multiple competing parts or even everything up. Obviously we can't do that, since the end result is just a more squished, just-as-loud version of the previous mix. So instead, we ask people to figure out instead what needs to be turned down, since figuring out what doesn't need to be heard forces people to think more critically about what the important parts of a song and arrangement are.

What is the scope and range of what you do?

I think I've answered most of this above, but just to get specific—on a particular project, my role can include any and all of the following: arranging for performance or studio, producing and coaching vocal performances, recording, editing mixing, playing group therapist, being a conceptual sounding board, and being a chef.

All of those have happened at one time or another, and on occasion, all of them have happened at once for one album.

What does a typical day or week look like for you?

It's hard to say what sort of day or week is typical, but let's work with one during which I'm at home at my studio. I try to get up at a reasonable hour in the morning, usually around seven or eight, have my breakfast, and get right to work. At the moment, I'm just finishing up an album for which we did all of the recording and editing, and just did some last tweaks to a couple of mixes this morning. Later today I'll be jumping onto another project we just started with another group, as well as a corporate gig that I was subcontracted out for earlier this week. Sometimes I'll spend mornings sending and answering e-mails from current or prospective clients; other times I'll have my nose to the grindstone trying to mix two or three songs in a day for an upcoming deadline that may or may not have been pushed up or dropped on us with little notice and a plea for help. Any number of things can come in at any time.

How many people would you guess are doing this professionally?

Certainly more than when I started. In 2011, I could comfortably name all of the roughly dozen people doing work on albums in the United States and abroad; now I'd have trouble naming even half on the Eastern Seaboard. Granted, not all of those people now are working on albums you'd consider "major" or even "well known," but the point is that there are tons more people now both doing and interested in doing this work.

What percentage of your income comes from this?

One hundred percent—this is my full-time job and I treat it as such.

What advice do you have for someone starting in this field?

Other than all of the advice that I've given above—practice. Start early, talk to people already in the field, acquire knowledge from them, and just start recording yourself. You know your own voice best, so figure out what your voice can do and how you can start cataloging all of the various tones, sounds, and vocal acrobatics you could ask of other people. Figure out how microphones react to your voice, and likewise with software and plug-ins. The more you know about the technical stuff and the back end before you even start thinking about charging for your time, the better you can focus on the artistic and the creative when the time comes.

In what ways do you see this field growing or changing in the future?

I can't be sure, but I think the medium by which we distribute music is going to change. I have absolutely zero skill in working with video, but more and more groups are moving toward it. So, I'm mentally back in networking mode a lot of the time whenever something audiovisual comes up.

As for the music itself, I think we're seeing oversaturation in some styles of singing, and some styles of production again. Gigantic, washy soundscapes were all the rage several years ago, and we've reached peak reverb right around now. We tried to stay away from that trend as much as possible, since I've always found throwing everything in a cave to be a bit of a cop-out the same way that recording a group singing in a church or stairwell makes them sound deceptively good. Pick the right huge-hall emulation and slap it at 50 percent mix across all of your background vocals and any group can sound instantly better, no matter how mediocre their blending or emotion is. It's a cop-out, and I'm glad to see it disappearing.

Appropriate space, texture, and extreme contrast are the next wave of what people are going to be interested in, and I fully plan on being ahead of the curve on this one again.

MIXING—BILL HARE

Of all the stages involved in recorded a cappella, mixing is the one that is most challenging, as it requires a nexus of artistry, taste, engineering, technical knowledge, musicality, and the willingness to sit in a chair for long hours twisting knobs until every little moment sounds exactly right.

There are many great a cappella engineers, but as our community was just getting started there was really only one: Bill Hare. The sound of contemporary recorded a cappella owes more to his technique, style, and pioneering than any other person, in part because many of today's great engineers either studied his work from afar or worked with him directly.

What drew you to this field of a cappella?
    I wasn't drawn to a cappella, a cappella was drawn to me! I owned a professional recording studio in the San Francisco Bay Area starting in the early 1980s, and at that time there were few options for any kind of musical artist to make a decent recording outside of looking through the Yellow Pages and finding a studio. Back then, most studios didn't specialize in certain genres or instrumentation as they do today and were prepared to figure out how to record anything that made a sound. I would record a punk band, a string quartet, and an opera singer all in the same day. One day I recorded someone's motorcycle engine.
    Vocal harmony was definitely not something that was new to me the first time a collegiate a cappella group (the Stanford Mendicants) first came to my studio in 1988. What *was* new was that they were singing rock, pop, and R&B songs that were current on the radio at that time— but they were a glee club of sorts, without even the courtesy of having at least a piano to accompany them. I was amused but not impressed.

What changed your attitude toward a cappella then?
    I like to think I changed it to fit me, rather than the other way around. The other groups at Stanford started calling on my studio, and even though their music (and sometimes musicianship) seemed a little silly to me, I was enjoying working with them personally; [they were] smart young people rather than some of the burned-out ex-hippie guitarists I was accustomed to working with. Since I had a background in music theory from my own college days, and most of the Stanford a cappella kids were studying something besides music, I was able to help them correct some of their arrangements, coach them musically, and gain their trust as a fellow artist.
    I never thought this "vocal elevator Muzak" would go anywhere, but I started having a lot of fun experimenting with these groups (with their blessing) and adding new levels of production with each project. Without an Internet to turn to yet, I had no idea that this was a "scene," or that any other of these groups existed outside of the ones at Stanford.

How did you find out that it was bigger than just Stanford and that your "experiments" held any value?

I got a letter from a college kid named Deke Sharon at Tufts University in Boston. He had started an organization called CASA [Contemporary A Cappella Society], with its own newsletter and awards. We were getting some award for the follow-up album I had done for the Mendicants in 1990, and they were gushing about the sound of it. Wow . . . someone all the way in Boston heard the album—that enough was impressive to me as most local music in those days *stayed* local.

Each album I did after that would also get attention from this organization in Boston, and in 1993 an album I produced for Stanford's Fleet Street Singers won Best Male Collegiate Album, with the last part of CASA's description saying, "The best engineering we've ever heard on any collegiate album. Ever." I was personally given a CARA for Best Engineering and Mixing, the first time I was ever officially recognized as an audio engineer. Okay, then, maybe I've found a niche . . . where are these other groups?

When did you know that this might become a full-time gig?

The seven groups at Stanford were keeping me quite busy, with ever-increasing time spent and budgets per album. In 1996, I moved from the much larger commercial studio to a new space in my home built specifically for recording vocals. I gave up recording instrumental bands to concentrate on the Stanford groups, as well as other vocal-oriented projects (mostly barbershop groups and solo vocal demos). Not having the financial overhead of a commercial building combined with the changing recording technology at the time freed me to become even more experimental. Around this time I met Deke Sharon in person for the first time, and we talked about maybe one day collaborating on a project.

How did you go from just working with one school to working around the world?

Many things came together at once. Deke and I did end up working together on projects for his professional vocal band, the House Jacks. This group was already internationally known, and of course, the talent and creativity jump from collegiate was immense. With original songs and amazing arrangements, as well as a mature flexibility on the band's part, I felt I was making "real" records again. The 2002 *Unbroken* album by the House Jacks was the door that led to everything that followed. Groups from around the world heard this album, creating a lot of buzz for not only the House Jacks but also my production work. From there, I collaborated with Deke on albums by the Danish group Basix, as well as his own group from his college days, the Tufts Beelzebubs. These albums established new markets for me in Europe as well as the wider collegiate scene, and the Internet making the world much smaller and immediately accessible was a completely new concept and was fortunate timing. The original momentum from these albums continued through thousands of others and still sustains today.

What advice do you have for someone starting in this field?

Obviously, my path was kind of unique as I myself was unaware that I was starting a new career until some years into my journey, but the concept is the same: you won't have any idea what you are doing at first, and your first project (maybe first fifty projects), most likely won't win many accolades. But if you can stick with it, and keep finding clients (even if it means working for very cheap or even free), you will develop your own sound eventually. Just a few decent successes can open doors to new veins of the a cappella markets, as well as repeat business that can sustain for many years—for example, that very first group I mentioned, the Stanford Mendicants; I am currently working on my sixteenth album with them in twenty-eight years.

What do you see for the future of a cappella?

This journey has already surpassed my wildest dreams, so I am as excited as anyone else to see where it goes from here!

MASTERING—DAVE SPERANDIO

An album isn't finished once it's mixed, if you want it to sound great in every environment: on computer speakers, in earbuds, in headphones, in your car, and on a big stereo system. Mastering is the final process in the making of a great album, as (ideally) a separate set of ears is able to space songs properly, make sure songs aren't too loud or quiet, and gently shape the overall equalization (EQ) such that it sounds great everywhere.

Dave Sperandio ("Dio" to his friends) was one of a cappella's first great engineers and recognized the need for a cappella albums to be properly mastered (most weren't). As a result his name appears on perhaps more a cappella albums than anyone else on the planet, with good reason.

What drew you to this field of a cappella?

I grew up singing and sang with several a cappella groups in high school, college, and after (semiprofessionally). One of the semipro groups I sang with after college had recorded an album we were pretty happy with, but we decided we wanted to try something different for the next record. We'd heard some of the new contemporary all-vocal music that was being released at the time (circa 1999), and we decided to hire an outside producer (Jeff Thacher of Rockapella) to help us create an album that was a bit closer to a "radio" sound.

I'd been a part of other recording projects, and I'd done a good bit of recording on my own with an old four-track and a Roland VS-880, but watching Jeff work in the studio was when I really realized that music production was something that interested me. I also realized that the "sound" we were pushing for—and indeed the entire idea of treating vocal recording more like a "real" contemporary pop/rock music process—was part of the future. I hoped I might be able to be a part of that future and also accomplish a goal of entering the music business (and incidentally leaving corporate America, IBM, where I was working after college to put food on the table).

At that time, there were only a few other producers who were beginning to treat a cappella recording and mixing in a similar fashion as you would with a rock, pop, or R&B band: voice parts as instruments, or instrumentation. Besides Jeff, I think I knew of Bill Hare, Jon Clark, and Darren Rust (of the Blenders). I listened to a lot of their work and tried to figure out how they did what they did. I had a full-time job at the time, but I began dabbling on my own at home with Pro Tools (and later Melodyne, in its first incarnation). I also began to formulate plans for what would eventually become my a cappella music production companies (diovoce and VocalSource), as well as dreaming up the

SoJam a cappella festival and the *Sing* compilation album. I approached my college a cappella group and offered to help them produce their next album, and they took me up on my offer, as did a handful of other groups in the Southeast.

As it turns out, that was the start of an explosion of growth in the entire contemporary vocal music movement, especially with regard to the use of production in recording. Groups started hearing the music their peers were putting out and they wanted to push themselves to try new things. Within a couple of years I had enough business to take the risk of quitting my day job so I could pursue music production as a full-time career. It turned out to be a good gamble. Looking back, for me it was a case of having a few epiphanies at just the right time and place, and being willing to invest in my future.

Eventually others started to enter the field of vocal music production and it became more saturated. At the same time, I had been mastering "on the side" for several years and felt that I had an opportunity to do more good work there, for myself and for the vocal music community. The combination of these factors inspired me to form Vocal Mastering to provide a needed service and to help educate producers and musicians about what mastering was, why it is needed, and what it could do for their music. That was 2012; since then books, TV shows, and movies such as *The Sing-Off* and *Pitch Perfect*, and of course groups such as Pentatonix have thrust the art form much more broadly into the public eye. One result of this has been more groups, making more art, and creating more recordings. Business has grown every year since I started doing this.

What experiences and education do you find have been most useful? What skills and knowledge do people need coming into this kind of work?

I acted primarily as a producer in the first few years of my career in music production, working alongside an engineer (back when there were budgets for both roles!), so I had plenty of time to just sit back and watch, trying to soak in as much as possible. I'm fortunate to have had a few talented and generous engineers who were willing to patiently explain to me what they were doing while they were working on projects I brought them to record or mix. I also read a lot of books about audio production, though I never took any formal classes on the topic. Eventually YouTube came along, and of course there are quite a few tutorials online now.

Importantly, when I first started out I listened to a *lot* of music with a critical ear, trying to think about not only how they were doing the things they did but also why they made the decisions that shaped the sound they created. [I listened to] a lot of a cappella music (*BOCA, The Hot Lips Sampler*, Spiralmouth's album, and whatever else was new at the time, along with standards like Take 6) but also plenty of non–a cappella music too. I was always listening to music and picking it apart.

All of that said, most of what I have learned has been via trial and error and iteration. I didn't have YouTube for the first several years, so if there was a specific sound I heard in my head or in another song that I wanted to try to create, I just sort of had to try different things until I found something that got me close to where I wanted to be, then tweak, iterate, and iterate again. I can't stress enough the importance of iteration. I'm still iterating today, every day.

I think one of the main things that separates producers—aside things from creativity, vision, style, personality, work ethic, and so forth—is the number of mistakes they've made. You want to make many mistakes, early and often. Sometimes your mistakes can teach you so much, and in an actionably useful way; experience is absolutely the best teacher here.

How has the field changed since you started?

My first experiences as a performer with recording a cappella music were on two-inch magnetic tape. If you made a mistake, you sang it again until you got it right. There wasn't really "punching in" to grab a single note like there is now; if you wanted to make a really precise edit, you used a razor blade to literally cut and splice the tape. Since then the media has changed a few times (DA-88, ADAT, and finally DAW—digital audio workstations), each time allowing for more flexibility and options. Where before the barrier to entry cost might have been a hundred thousand dollars, now you can get good results with a laptop and maybe five hundred to a thousand dollars of equipment, along with plenty of patience.

Specific to mastering and how it has changed, when I started out the loudness wars—an ever-escalating push to make the loudest record— were just getting really rolling, but we weren't anywhere near where we are now in terms of reduced dynamic content. If you listen to an album from 2000 and compare it to one from 2017, you'll probably be shocked at the difference in volume and dynamic contrast. You'll probably also notice differences in timbre; in 2000 a lot of stuff was being mastered to tape, which tends to give a softer, rounder sound, especially in the higher frequencies, and a fuller sound in the lows. This comes with added distortion/noise, but many people found that distortion/noise to be pleasing.

Today magnetic tape is still being used to master records around the world, but not so much in the a cappella music space. I'd say probably 95 percent of a cappella records that I know about are mastering either through an analog chain connected to a DAW, or just a DAW. Mastering using only a DAW or "in the box" allows for instant recall of projects in the cases where revisions are needed, and enables the use of limitless copies of plug-ins designed to emulate analog hardware, instead of just the one hardware compressor, EQ, or tone box.

There's been a growing desire in recent years to move away from the super-clean digital sound to a gentler, warmer sound. Plug-in manufacturers have done a great job creating virtual emulations of many of the multi-thousand-dollar hardware boxes that are used in mastering, and this helps a lot. I don't think it quite compares (yet) to analog, so I use a hybrid setup of analog hardware and software. It's a little less flexible in terms of recall, but in mastering I don't have many revisions and I really love the way analog gear affects the sound of vocal music, especially when it's been completely in the digital realm up to the point it gets to mastering.

Another way things have changed is that almost everything is now done on a "just-in-time" basis. And when I say just in time, I mean sometimes within hours of album pressing or upload. I'll get an "emergency" request for a single (or an album) one morning out of the blue, master it and send it off, and by the afternoon it's on YouTube or Buzzfeed has picked it up. It's crazy, but it keeps you on your toes.

What are the technical aspects of your work that most people don't understand or know about?

Probably 90 percent of what I do is listening. That isn't technical per se, but knowing what to listen for is. And that just comes with targeted, specific experience: sitting in the same chair, in the same room, with the same speakers, and listening to tens of thousands of songs. It gives you the perspective you need to make decisions confidently, and quickly.

Before you can get to that point though, you need to make sure you have confidence in the accuracy of your listening environment. Using acoustic measurement software and a microphone, you can measure the frequency response of the room you're working in and identify any problem areas—frequencies that are being boosted or attenuated because of the way the room itself is constructed (or potentially because of your monitors). Once you know what your room "sounds like" you can use a combination of room modification/treatment and software to help "tune" the room such that you can consistently know—and aren't guessing at—what you're hearing. This is critical to make sure that what you do translates in the real world, on any system.

During the mastering process itself, once I have listened to the track, gotten a feel for it, and identified any areas of focus, I start to dial in any adjustments I think are called for. While I'm doing this I'm constantly referencing the original (unmastered) track, making sure to compensate for the loudness I'm adding in the mastering process so that I'm not being fooled by the ear's natural tendency to perceive louder as better. Each time I make a change, I flip back to the volume-compensated raw mix to ask myself, Is this better? Would it be better without it? If the clients have asked me to reference a specific track or album, or perhaps a "fake master" they did themselves, I'll flip back and forth between that reference and the track I'm working on. I'll also try different combinations of tools, and try them in different sequences—always asking the crucial question, Is this better, or just different?

Sometimes a track may have been poorly recorded, or have sonic issues that weren't picked up earlier in the process. Oftentimes I'll be able to clean up noise, hum, clicks/pops, rumble, things like that, using something like a spectral editor (which visualizes frequencies/gain across time) or EQ. It can be tricky to do this without leaving fingerprints, as it were—there's always a sonic cost when you alter a track in this way, but when done right sometimes you're able to help get rid of some elements that might otherwise have distracted from what the artist was trying to do with the piece.

What is the scope and range of what you do?

I do still record and mix a handful of curated groups, but most of what I do now is mastering and consulting. In mastering, I work with quite a bit of vocal music, but also country, rock, hip-hop, EDM, video game soundtracks, bluegrass—you name it.

As far as the mastering process itself, there are three main parts:

- Correction of sonic issues
- Creative enhancement
- Creation of media for distribution

At its core, mastering is the final stage of audio production. It's the final opportunity for quality control and corrective measures, as well as the last opportunity for creative input—importantly, from an objective ear, unattached to any previous sonic decisions and able to assess the recording from a fresh and informed perspective.

Mastering is also the last chance to make sure a project sounds as good as possible—and sounds good on as many systems as possible—before its release. I try to make sure the mastered files, or "masters," are optimized for playback on multiple systems and environments.

Logistically, here's what goes into each mastering project:

- Setup: Complete download and import source material, sample-rate conversion (if applicable), and labeling of tracks.
- Auditioning: The source material is listened to, to evaluate and identify needed areas of focus.
- Processing: The source material is processed as needed. This can include equalization, compression, noise reduction, or other processes. When this is completed, the masters are printed in real time (sixty minutes of material = sixty minutes to print mastered files).
- Sequencing: The mastered files are put in order and spaced appropriately.
- Media creation: The mastered files are exported/assembled as WAV files, a DDP fileset, or a CD.
- Verification (aka "QC," for quality control): The final mastered project (aka "premaster") is auditioned in real time, sometimes by a separate engineer, to verify no errors exist.
- Distribution: The final, QC'd premaster is uploaded or sent via post to client or distributor, label, and/or replicator.

- Archival: The mastered project is backed up, and all settings stored for future recall.

In addition to recording, mixing, and mastering, I also consult for a few dozen clients around the world, helping them improve their work as well as providing advice when I'm asked to do so. I feel it's a "win-win-win" scenario: I am successful only because I help others be successful, and they in turn are successful because their clients are successful and happy.

The relationships and interactions I have with other doers—getting to help them, learn from them, and watching them learn and grow—these are the best parts of my job, and often of my days. I'm fortunate to have been witness to a number of remarkable people doing great and bold things for the music community and also for the professions of "a cappella audio engineer," "a cappella–centric fine arts director," "a cappella event coordinator," and others. I try to do my part to hold up my end of the bargain too and pay it forward whenever possible.

What does a typical day or week look like for you?

In the morning I'll review the projects for that day (the ones I know about; often others will come across my desk later in the day), download any media I've been sent, set up the sessions, and start listening. When I've got a good handle on the project and what needs to be done, I'll start making whatever changes are needed and print the mastered track when I'm satisfied with it. If it's an album, I'll repeat this process, working sequentially as a listener would hear the album.

Once this is done, I'll export the media/assemble the mastered media in the desired format (usually either WAV or DDP; I haven't made a CD in about four years) and verify/QC it or have another engineer QC it for me, to make sure I haven't missed anything. When we're happy, the project is sent electronically to the client to audition. If any revisions are requested, I'll make them and repeat the process. A typical day might mean I'm working on two full albums, or one full album and three EPs, or a bunch of singles. I may also have a call scheduled with a producer to chat about a project, or I may spend time listening to mixes before they are ready for mastering, providing notes to the producer so that he or she can make the changes before it's time to have the project mastered.

How many people would you guess are doing this professionally?

Mastering specifically, focusing primarily on vocal music? Maybe three or four. Mastering engineers in general? A rough guess would be in the low thousands.

What percentage of your income comes from this?

About 75 percent of my income comes from mastering. The rest is from recording and mixing that I do for longtime clients or for new projects that I'm really excited about (and that have a budget), and from consulting or teaching.

What advice do you have for someone starting in this field?

Mastering all-vocal music—especially in the style of modern pop/rock/hip-hop and at louder levels—is extremely challenging. Much more so than with non–a cappella music, in my opinion. The way sustained voices behave under limiting and compression is unique and re-quires a careful, delicate touch—as well as a very specific set of tools—to deliver maximum clarity and loudness while maintaining dynamics and musicality without causing added distortion, smearing, or artifacts. It's not hard to make something relatively loud and bright, but it's hard to do so transparently. It's hardest still perhaps to know when to not do anything at all. But it can be done.

Start by setting up a listening and work space. As I mentioned earlier, it needn't be a $100K room, or even a $10K room, but if it's not well tuned you will need to do a *lot* of trial and error to know what your room is doing to what you are hearing so that you can compensate for it. Make physical modifications when possible. Use room-correction software when not. Get the best monitors you can afford (you should make sure the frequency response of your monitors/headphones is at least 30 Hz to 20 kHz), or better yet if you're working in a bedroom or similar, the best headphones you can afford. Note that best doesn't mean the ones that sound the best but rather the ones that are transparent and that you can be confident in using. Spend the time needed to tune and become familiar with your room and monitors before you do anything else.

Read *Mastering Audio: The Art and the Science* by Bob Katz. Listen to as much music as you can. Find albums you feel have a great sound, and find out who mastered them. Approach those mastering engineers directly (we won't bite), and buy an hour of their time over Skype. But have respect for their time: only do this *after* you have scoured YouTube, read every blog and mastering form you can (Gearslutz.com, DigiDo.com, and Groove3.com are good starting points, along with whatever you can find on YouTube), and put in your time listening. Finally, start hacking around on your own. Make mistakes and learn from them. Iterate, iterate, iterate. And keep up to date on changing standards and tools.

As far as finding work, start with your own music. Find someone who doesn't have a budget for mastering (and as such wouldn't have their album mastered at all if not for you) who is willing to let you use your growing skill set to master their project, in exchange for you doing it at no cost. Redo it as many times as you need to until you're comfortable with it being released. As you get better, people will start to find you, and you can branch out by leveraging past work to secure future work.

In what ways do you see this field growing or changing in the future?
The album seems to be dying, or at least being shortened. We've gone from eighteen-track a cappella albums to twelve-, ten-, or eight-track albums. We're seeing a lot more EPs too, and quite a lot of singles and music videos. This doesn't really affect the mastering process, but it does often mean working with the same clients more frequently, on shorter projects.

There are a few services out there now that offer "online mastering." What they are doing isn't really mastering as much as it is sweetening—juicing the highs, bumping the lows, and making it louder—and there's quite a bit more to the mastering process than that. They can sometimes do a pretty good job of getting a song up to commercial levels and can help smooth things out; other times they can do more harm than good. As the algorithms improve I think we'll see these services being used more for low-budget recordings that would have otherwise gone unmastered. They can also provide a useful reference while mixing, of what a song might end up sounding like after it's been mastered.

Right now clients still usually (though not always) want their masters to be pretty loud. I think the main reason for that is that CDs are still around, even though most people don't listen to CDs. People will rip a CD, pop it into their music player, and play it next to their favorite albums (often ones whose budget was five hundred times higher than theirs), and if it doesn't feel as loud, or hit as hard, they get upset.

That said, I think most people listen to music at some point via a streaming service like Spotify, Apple Music, or YouTube. These services have now all started using loudness normalization to ensure that everything measures at the same standardized average loudness level: they will bring up the loudness of more dynamic tracks that fall below this average loudness level and reduce the loudness of less dynamic tracks that fall above this average loudness level. If a track is louder than their given standard, it will potentially be turned down. This is known in the mastering world, but clients haven't really caught on. Since many are still releasing on CD and are already on a tight budget, generally only one master is created, at CD-loudness levels. I think mastering engineers need to start working to educate both producers and their clients about this change, and about the benefits of also creating a master for streaming (or for MFiT—Mastered for iTunes). Again, if CDs ever die completely, I think you'll see more and more dynamic records being released, and our ears will thank us for it.

PRODUCING RECORDINGS—ED BOYER

No two recording producers are the same, each having arrived at their position through their own unique set of experiences and circumstances. What they all share is an understanding of the technical and logistical as well as interpersonal and emotional aspects of making a great record.

With Pentatonix, *Glee*, *Pitch Perfect*, and *The Sing-Off* on his resume, Ed Boyer is one of a cappella's most experienced and in-demand producers. He consults, arranges, records, edits, mixes, and masters—whatever it takes to make a great recording.

What drew you to this field of a cappella? What experiences and education do you find have been most useful? What skills and knowledge do people need coming into this kind of work?

Because production is usually a convergence of many other skills, and because the path to becoming a producer is relatively less vocational (though it's changing, the educational journey toward becoming a producer is much less structured/predictable than, say, that of a civil engineer), producers tend to evolve from other occupations.

I, for example, was a vocal performance major in college who sang with an a cappella group on the side, mainly for something social to do. When the director graduated, I was, by default, the logical replacement (the only remaining music major in the group). This led to arranging and teaching/coaching singers, and, once the group had decided to record an album, familiarizing myself with the recording process. Eventually, without having ever decided it was something I wanted to do, I'd gathered enough know-how that producing the recordings myself became the natural, logical next step.

Through word of mouth, and because the first few recordings I did were recognized in the newly burgeoning a cappella world (thanks Internet!), producing recordings for my own group evolved into producing a handful of recordings for other groups. It was enough to help pay bills while I was gigging as a singer, interning at studios, and splitting rent with my future wife. Over time, the projects became more frequent. Ultimately, it became my full-time job.

What are the technical aspects of your work that most people don't understand or know about? What is the scope and range of what you do?

So, what do you do?

I produce a cappella music.

That's a job?

It's always been a strange conversation. Even now that there are reference points—pieces of pop culture I can point to and say "I helped make that"—it's still far from a normal exchange, mostly because a cappella is still on the fringes of mainstream culture but also because people don't really know what a music producer *actually* does.

Is it George Martin arranging strings for a Beatles record, or is it Christopher Walken's SNL character storming in to demand more cowbell? Is it Imogen Heap programming sounds with a musical glove, or is it Berry Gordy constructing an assembly line of writers, engineers, and musicians? In short, producing is *all* of these things. It's doing whatever's necessary to deliver a completed work.

Most times, this means getting hands-on with the music in some form or another: writing, arranging, coaching/coaxing performances, maybe even performing. It also often means—and this is increasingly true as smaller recording budgets mean more vertical integration—being comfortable with the more technical aspects: engineering, programming, editing, mixing, and so forth.

Other times it's about group dynamics. A producer's job may simply be to get the right musicians in the right room and let their good "chemistry" take over. Conversely, a producer could be tasked with mediating between members of a group whose personalities clash or whose creative visions don't align.

How many people would you guess are doing this professionally?
There are many full-time producers who do the occasional a cappella recording and many a cappella engineers who record or mix groups and occasionally oversee the entire project, hence producing. That makes the number difficult to judge. Dozens?

What percentage of your income comes from this?
For over a decade, I've been booked solid—sometimes as a producer, other times as an engineer, an arranger, a singer, and so on—tapping whatever production skill is needed for a given project.

What advice do you have for someone starting in this field?
The takeaway (if I've told the story correctly) is that the path to becoming a music producer isn't conventional. It's not a specifically obtainable skill so much as a wide set of skills that all need cultivation. If you want to be a producer, become a performer, become an engineer, become an arranger/writer, become a director . . . get involved in music creation in as many ways as possible and with as many different people as possible. Then, when the opportunity to produce presents itself, your skill set will be ready to go.

In what ways do you see this field growing or changing in the future?
So long as there are recordings, there will be producers, and producers will need to do whatever it takes to get the job done. That won't change, even as music styles and tastes do.

16

IN THE REHEARSAL ROOM

If you want to create a cappella but not spend a lot of time on the road or in front of a computer screen, the scholastic world awaits. Every high school has a choir (or should), and nowadays almost every one of those choral singers yearns to be in his or her own a cappella group. School districts are increasingly embracing a cappella as they see enrollment in vocal music surge, as resources and repertoire increase year after year. In addition to directors, arrangers and coaches make the lion's share of their money from all levels of scholastic groups. If you like the sound of the school bell, and more importantly like changing lives, read on.

SCHOLASTIC GROUP DIRECTING—BRODY McDONALD

Most of the careers listed in this section require a measure of risk and entrepreneurship that doesn't necessarily come naturally to some people. For those of you who would like a steady paycheck, regular hours, health care, and the like, the safest and most reliable career option for you may be directing a school group. Most contemporary a cappella directors oversee high school ensembles, but there are a growing number of middle school groups, and even some collegiate groups, that are faculty directed as opposed to student directed.

Brody McDonald is one of a kind. With a strong education and lots of experience in both choral and barbershop idioms, he stuck a toe in the waters of contemporary a cappella with his high school group, and before you know it he's neck deep, with a group on *The Sing-Off*, which led to us writing a book together (*A Cappella*, with Ben Spalding) and another on his own (*A Cappella Pop*), and starting Camp A Cappella together. Plus now he directs a collegiate group at Wright State University, all of this having happened in just a few years.

What drew you to this field of a cappella?

If I'm being completely honest, I blundered into a cappella by accident. I graduated with the intent of being a "traditional" concert choir director and thought I would supplement my program with the same small groups I experienced in college—barbershop quartets. Ironically, my first high school job could not have been further from that scenario. I inherited a choir program with a large competition show choir, and unfortunately that was the only thing about which students cared. They hadn't been exposed to other genres, so I began passing around my CD case on the bus. It was full of barbershop and had a few a cappella CDs, including a sampler that contained a Rockapella song, "Bed of Nails." One of the students tried to find the sheet music to that song to audition with a small group for the school variety show. While he never found that chart, he did find another a cappella song, and their group was very entertaining. Around the same time, we were cold-called by a college a cappella group that offered a free concert. The kids went wild. I realized this would be a great ensemble to handle all the gig requests we received where a forty-person show choir just didn't fit. At that point, I just dove in and started learning, trying to stay one step ahead of my students.

What experiences and education do you find have been most useful? What skills and knowledge do people need coming into this kind of work?

I have found that the greatest education has been simply to seek out those who are involved in the a cappella community and to learn from them. I had gone through college and got very involved in barbershop singing, so I knew the value of learning about a genre through immersion, trial and error, and seeking the advice of multiple mentors. I asked questions upon questions. Thankfully, people were very kind. Now that I am in the position of knowing something, I'm happy to pay it forward and share that knowledge. Having said that, a solid foundation in vocal technique, music theory, and ensemble singing go a long way. A cappella isn't radically different from other forms of vocal music, despite the fact that many think it is so.

How has the field changed since you started?

I believe that a cappella has evolved in the same way that other genres have in the past: jazz, barbershop, and so forth. It started as a social form of music, but over time, more and more trained musicians and educators have gotten involved. This has helped increase both the amount of ensembles and the overall quality of those ensembles immensely. The increase in academic demand has thus driven publishers to produce more sheet music, more books, and more resources as a whole. A decade ago, a cappella at a NAfME [National Association for Music Education] state convention was unheard of. Now, convention performances and presentations are regular, even ranging up to ACDA [American Choral Directors Association] National Conference.

What are the technical aspects of your work that most people don't understand or know about?

The biggest learning curve for me (and for many) was how to properly select and use a sound system to enhance the performance level of the group. I didn't have experiences in college that taught me the ins and outs of microphone technique, let alone which microphones to purchase, how to run a sound board, basics of equalization, and so forth. There's a lot that goes into good sound for amplified groups. Of course, a cappella doesn't have to be amplified, but the groups I direct are.

Another area of directing that mystifies the uninitiated is how to handle vocal percussion. Vocal percussion (VP) is difficult to understand for most directors because (a) they never did it, (b) they don't know how to do it, and (c) it is typically not notated in arrangements. Therefore, directors often feel they are flying completely blind! One thing new directors should remember is that VP is not *that* difficult to wrangle. We all listen to pop and rock groups regularly, so we know the function of a drummer. That is essentially what VP is. If we can steer vocal percussionists in the direction of the right style and help them to keep good time, the rest will work out. There are numerous online resources to help vocal percussionists craft their sounds, and most of them need permission to explore more than direct guidance. They need an "editor" to help filter their attempts rather than hard-and-fast instruction.

What does a typical day or week look like for you?

My full-time job is a choir director for a public school. I teach choirs from grades 7–12, leading two middle school and two high school choirs each day. I assist with a third high school choir as well. I direct two a cappella groups: Eleventh Hour at Kettering Fairmont High School and ETHOS at Wright State University. I work with Eleventh Hour after school one night a week. ETHOS is an adjunct position at WSU, and that's another night of the week. A cappella accounts for two of seven groups I direct each week. I also run Camp A Cappella and manage that throughout the year, so I am thinking about or working on that project daily.

What is the scope and range of what you do?

In terms of the two groups with whom I work (Eleventh Hour and ETHOS), I serve as their artistic director. That is to say, I shape their overall artistic vision and rehearse them. We hire out arrangements, choreography, and recording services, all of which I facilitate. I must also manage their respective budgets.

In terms of Camp A Cappella, I am a cofounder (along with my partner, Deke Sharon) and general manager. I oversee an executive team of six that, in turn, oversees a complete staff of roughly sixty. I am involved in all big-picture decisions throughout the year, including marketing, curriculum, facilities, housing, guest artists, production, and more. We have a fantastic crew to do the heavy lifting, so Deke and I are blessed in that regard.

How many people would you guess are doing this professionally?

I'm hard pressed to even guess. I would say as semiprofessionals (a cappella being one of a few jobs) in the thousands. I would guess full-timers would be the hundreds.

What percentage of your income comes from this?

Roughly 25 percent of my total income comes from a cappella at this point. My full-time job is director of choirs for Kettering City Schools. Eleventh Hour is a small supplemental; ETHOS is a part-time adjunct positions for Wright State. Camp A Cappella is a for-profit company, but like most start-ups under five years old, most of its resources are tied up in growing the business. I also receive royalties on the books I have published, paid annually.

What advice do you have for someone starting in this field?

Anyone who is interested in being a choir director who also does a cappella should concentrate on being a solid "standard" choir director first. In the educational world, a cappella is the tail, not the dog. It would be difficult to find an all–a cappella directing position. I would encourage anyone who wishes to become a choir director to do the following:

1. Teach as early and often as you can, even in college and/or high school. Do not wait for student teaching to start the process. Face

time is everything. Offer sectional help to local schools. Work with a church choir. Volunteer anywhere you can. You'll never be "ready" to teach, so the sooner you jump in the figurative deep end, the better.

2. Play piano. You can be a choir director without playing piano, but your life will be easier if you can play. Piano proficiency also bolsters theory, which will help you with arranging should you decide to do so.

3. Study voice. Directing vocal groups of any style requires technical ability with the voice. A solid chunk of directing is essentially helping your singers build technique—like a group voice lesson. Better ensembles are made of better singers.

4. Listen, listen, listen. Listen to recordings and live performances of as many genres of vocal music as you can. If you want to specialize in a cappella, get heavily involved in that community. There is no substitute for "soaking in" a culture.

In what ways do you see this field growing or changing in the future?
     I think a cappella will evolve in a few key areas as we move into the future. The biggest change will be the reduction of change. That is to say, we are seeing the "standardization" of a cappella into a few key "formulas." The proliferation of a cappella competition is producing a "winning formula," which is a phenomenon we have seen before in the world of show choir. Also, the increased output of published arrangements spurs new groups in the direction of specific voicings. As these factors continue to grow, more future directors will become more and more familiar with the "model" of a cappella as it becomes culturally and educationally institutionalized.
     As this happens, the a cappella ecosystem will grow and divide. On one hand, there will be more products and services that are aimed at the masses—published arrangements, books, instructional DVDs, and so forth. On the other hand, there will be an increased number of "boutique" vendors, aimed at custom arrangements, coaching, choreography, recording, and so on, as groups seek to find ways to "gain the edge" and separate themselves from the masses.

ARRANGING—TOM ANDERSON

Back in the early days of collegiate a cappella, few music directors arranged, and groups happily traded and sang arrangements of the fifty
or so classic songs for decades. Then once the style allowed for pretty
much any song to be sung, directors began to see the value in having
their own unique repertoire and had to learn to arrange their own music. With over three thousand collegiate groups graduating somewhere
in the range of fifteen thousand seniors each year, and assuming 10 percent of them arrange, that's 1,500 arrangers unleashed into the ranks of
adulthood each year. Not to mention all of the existing arrangers, high
school directors, and the like, there are more contemporary a cappella
arrangers than ever before in history. How can one ever hope to make
money at this?

Tom Anderson has the special sauce. As a collegiate a cappella singer
and arranger turned pro, he honed his skills . . . and then threw in the
towel as he got a law degree and joined a practice. A few years later,
longing for the creative life, he left the legal profession right around the
time Peter Hollens (for whom he does all the arranging) exploded in
popularity, and he has never looked back.

What drew you to this field of a cappella?
In hindsight, it's now clear that I'd been drawn to vocal harmony from
a very, very young age, going back to my dad getting the Beach Boys'
Made in U.S.A. compilation tape when I was in first or second grade,
though I certainly wouldn't have thought about it in those terms at the
time. The real lightning bolt, unequivocally, was when I got Boyz II
Men's first album, *Cooleyhighharmony*, the summer I turned thirteen.
I was immediately head over heels in love with that sound of pure vocal
harmony, both on the a cappella parts and elsewhere. Shortly afterward,
a friend I played jazz with introduced me to Take 6 (and, inadvertently,
a bevy of other terrific groups like Rockapella, the Persuasions, and
Ladysmith Black Mambazo, as the medium he chose to introduce me
to T6 was the Spike Lee *Do It A Cappella* album). Fueled by a couple
of years in top-forty radio at the time (around 1992–1993) when vocal
harmony, and even a cappella, were enjoying a moment very much in
the sun, I was off to the races.

As for what drew me to arranging in particular, I started doing a cappella arrangements, at age thirteen, because I was nuts enough about the stuff to have put together a quartet of guys at school to sing it and we had to come up with music somehow (if you relied on published contemporary a cappella scores at the time, you could choose from, to paraphrase the Blues Brothers, both kinds: "For the Longest Time" or "Kiss Him Goodbye"). We practiced exactly once and went our separate ways, but I kept arranging at every opportunity ("opportunity" here meaning, e.g., trigonometry class), so by the time I got to college and joined a new group that had just formed and needed an arranger, I had the (at the time, rare) advantage of having been at it for five years already.

I kept arranging through college but tapered off when I started law school. I would arrange a handful of pieces a year for two groups at the University of Oregon, On the Rocks and Divisi, for whom I was doing regular work because Peter Hollens and I had met and become friends around that time, but for the most part I was focused on a "grown-up" career. Later, however, after three years of law school and five of active practice, I found myself deeply unhappy and walked away from the constant stress and conflict of litigation. I wasn't even planning on pivoting to arranging full-time; I just knew I couldn't keep doing what I had been doing, and, probably irresponsibly, I didn't really know what was next. But as fortune and coincidence would have it, that transition took place just as Peter was ramping up the first few months of his solo career after *The Sing-Off* (I left law practice the same month we released "Poor Wayfaring Stranger" with the Swingle Singers); thanks to the increased visibility afforded by my work with him, within a couple of months I had enough work coming in that I was arranging a cappella full-time, and I have been ever since.

What experiences and education do you find have been most useful?

In terms of the fundamentals, I took piano lessons (fourteen years of classical and eight of jazz), and I sang in choirs and played in (curricular) bands all the way through middle school, high school, and college. Because I come from an instrumental jazz background and because my undergrad degree is in music composition (a course of study that, at least for me, was 99 percent focused on instrumental work), while my performing experience is overwhelmingly vocal, my actual training and formal education are overwhelmingly instrumental, and in a wide spectrum of idioms to boot—that knowledge of the instrumental side of things is absolutely invaluable, even when writing solely for voices. I think it's pretty widely accepted, however—and certainly I subscribe to this viewpoint—that the best teacher, by far, is experience. In this case, that means arrange, arrange, arrange. Try everything. Fail. Fail a *lot*. Ask absolutely all of the questions. As much as humanly possible, have your stuff sung, even if it's just a single informal reading section with some friends, and adjust what you do based on what you hear. When you're not arranging, transcribe arrangements you've heard elsewhere. To use a mechanical analogy: take the watch apart, study the role of each little wheel and spring, and figure out how to put it all back together again. Learn from everything you hear that generates a reaction in you, whether positive or negative—try to understand why it made you feel that way. And when you finish all that, arrange some more.

What skills and knowledge do people need coming into this kind of work?
   Certainly there's much to be said for, for example, curiosity, passion, and drive—all the typical stuff that's important to success in pretty much any field. In terms of specific skills and knowledge, I certainly recommend people be as fluent as possible in as many different musical concepts as possible—theory, of course, but also music history and literature, for darn sure orchestration, every possible style and idiom you can think of (grunge! salsa! Stravinsky! ragas and talas!) . . . whatever information you can arm yourself with regarding how music, or a particular kind of music, functions or is structured; be endlessly thirsty for that. There's always some pooh-poohing of this sort of knowledge—"Paul McCartney can't read music!" or whatever—but I'm always reminded of a favorite comedian of mine holding forth on the advisability of doing X without customary prerequisite Y: "You could do it—that don't mean it's to be done! You can drive a car with your feet if you want to; that don't make it a good [expletive] idea!"
   Also crucially important, yet not actually related to music in any way, are skills in networking, entrepreneurship, and above all, time management. I learned these on the fly, out of necessity; indeed, as with any skill I care about, I'm still working on them, and I don't expect to finish anytime soon. I know they can seem amorphous and "corporate," but

they are absolutely, vitally important, and I wish that I had understood that fact many years sooner.

With regard to any of the above, whether the musical skills or the more general, you don't need to have these skills to get started, but unless you can develop them along the way, you're putting a huge and unnecessary obstacle in your own path, and one that indeed may be insurmountable. Also, and this should go without saying, be nice to people. Be respectful. Be generous. Do unto others, and so forth.

How has the field changed since you started?

There are way, *way* more of us now—not just arrangers but also producers and, especially, a cappella singers. So that's a tremendously positive development. As is the proliferation of high school (and even younger) groups. And of course the fact that there's just a much, much bigger market for contemporary a cappella music than ever before (and, selfishly, that we no longer have to explain to people what "a cappella" means).

Arranging, in particular, has changed in that there is an entire world of new possibilities realized by technology. When Boyz II Men and Shai were dropping a cappella radio singles in the early nineties, they . . . sang their arrangements. Into microphones. And that, at least from an arranging perspective, was that. (Todd Rundgren had done incredible pioneering work in this regard on his 1985 album *A Cappella*, but few, if any, picked up the torch for many years afterward.) By the late nineties, experimentation with digital manipulation of the voice was becoming more and more prevalent, though it was still predominantly a "gimmick" in many/most instances. In recent years, however, arrangers with a thorough understanding of the possibilities afforded by such manipulation have made a regular practice of arranging with the entire process in mind, rather than thinking only as far as the live vocals themselves, and while my first love in a cappella is still (and ever) the essentially unadulterated human voice, I'd absolutely argue that our art form has benefited greatly as a result.

One thing that I think has perhaps changed for the worse is the sense of individuality that, in my observation, seemed to be more prevalent when there was less money/fame involved. When everyone was just making a cappella music at subsistence level out of sheer love for the art form (because no one was really offering any other compensation of real, life-changing significance), there was a lot more impetus to create groups like the Bobs, the House Jacks, Spiralmouth, and ARORA— groups of truly original, often broke, weirdos putting out into the world all this incredible art that was/is comprehensively and unmistakably theirs and, indeed, them. But now there's a much different end game for many, and as a result, there's a lot more imitation and a lot less originality. Hopefully the pendulum swings back the other way before long, not in terms of a cappella's place in the Zeitgeist, but in terms of people's desire/need to have an identity of their own and to have that identity inform their creative process at every step.

What are the technical aspects of your work that most people don't understand or know about?

As far as gear, I don't think there's anything that would catch people off guard. I work almost exclusively in Finale, my computers are off-the-rack Macs, I work on either the ubiquitous AKG K240s (if in the studio) or Apple earbuds (if elsewhere), and I have a variety of M-Audio keyboards that I use depending on my circumstances (88-key in the studio, spare 61-key in the studio closet, 49-key in the car, 37-key when I fly, 25-key when I fly with just a carry-on . . .), and all my work is saved to Dropbox and backed up on an external HD for redundancy, but that's about as exotic as it gets.

To use a slightly different meaning of "technical," I've learned over the years not to ever cut corners in terms of how my scores appear on the page. Whatever I have to do to convey my intentions 100 percent accurately to those reading the score is always, always worth the additional effort. I've been using Finale for almost twenty years, and I have my own macros and shortcuts programmed to a custom array that dramatically streamlines my notation entry process. I spend time thinking about staves, brackets, stems, spacing, margins, font size, and any engraving issue whatsoever that I can think of that might make a difference to the reader. And I always do what I think will make my score easiest for that person to read. I didn't always do that—most notably, for many years I didn't write in the melody line ("it takes forever to put in, and they can just learn it from the original anyway") or bass syllables ("it's a bass line; just sing dm's and bm's; it's not rocket science"). I've since learned better: the arrangement exists to serve the needs of the client (and the song!), not to serve mine.

What does a typical day or week look like for you?
I typically work from my home studio. Most days start with catching up on correspondence, which can take a few minutes or a couple of hours, but for most of the day I'm generally just here with my headphones on, crafting arrangements. It varies widely depending on what the piece calls for and what the client wants, but a single "typical" arrangement generally takes between six and eight hours, and I generally do between 100 and 120 arrangements a year (or a little over two per week, if you're the prorating type). When I first went full-time with arranging, I used to work in long, irregular, insane, first-year-medical-resident-type shifts punctuated by cursory attempts at sleep, but I've learned that long-term productivity is far better served (at least for me) by a regular (and somewhat human) schedule, so I'm generally up at seven something, at work around nine, and work until somewhere between seven and midnight (albeit not straight through—partly because it's important to spend time with my wife in the evenings when she's home from work, and partly because I'm easily distracted by the fact that *Wikipedia*, YouTube, Sporcle, and MLB.TV exist—and so I end up putting in a seven- to ten-hour workday, but it might be spread over fifteen or more hours). I also serve on the board of directors for the Contemporary A Cappella Society (CASA), as an a cappella educator and clinician at various festivals and private master classes, and as music director for a local church, so I'm also devoting time to those endeavors as appropriate and necessary.

How many people would you guess are doing this professionally?
Arranging a cappella full-time, as their day job/principal source of income (and genuinely making an "adult" living at it)? I would guess that's probably a single-digit number. The number who do it as a significant component of a broader basket of ongoing musical endeavors, though—people who are also doing, say, music production/engineering, teaching music, or performing and recording with a vocal group, but who also regularly and dependably earn a meaningful percentage of their income from arranging—is without a doubt much higher. Dozens, probably.

What percentage of your income comes from this?
It varies, but generally it's in the ballpark of 75 ± 10 percent.

What advice do you have for someone starting in this field?
Never stop creating. Never stop learning.

In what ways do you see this field growing or changing in the future?
The biggest change that I hope will come, and one that I think is necessary for what we do to thrive, is the legal landscape for arrangers. As it currently stands, while there's a cut-and-dried compulsory mechanical license for recording and releasing cover songs, there's no equivalent compulsory license regarding arrangements. The owners of publishing rights can say, "Sure, go ahead," and not charge you a nickel. Or they can charge you a million dollars. Or they can just flat out say no. It's the Wild West. There have been indications in the recent past that, with the advent of streaming services, Congress might revisit the current (antediluvian) music copyright statutes, but whether that actually occurs is anyone's guess, and whether there are revisions that work in favor of the independent arranger rather than the publishing industry . . . I wouldn't hold my breath.

COACHING—J. D. FRIZZELL

When most people think about a coach, they imagine a sports team with a gruff, former player at the helm, making decisions about who plays and barking out tough love, in hopes of bringing home a trophy. An a cappella coach is a very different breed; usually brought in for a day or so, this person needs to quickly connect with a group, understand their level and goals, and work with them on all aspects of their performance, musical, technical, physical, emotional, and so forth, all while creating a supportive environment that pushes the singers to remain focused while doing the best singing they've ever done.

J. D. Frizzell is just that sort of individual. He understands all styles of vocal harmony, from his DMA in choral conducting to his work with Briarcrest Christian School's amazing high school a cappella ensemble and Sony recording artists OneVoice. He works with singers of all ages via ACDA, the National Association of Teachers of Singing (NATS), the A Cappella Educators Association (which he founded), Camp A Cappella, and the Choir Coach.

It should be noted that no one is a full-time coach, be it in the pop a cappella, barbershop, or classical choral realms. Rather, this is the kind of opportunity that increasingly presents itself to successful directors, be they educators, conductors, or music directors of a contemporary a cappella group. Groups reach out to people they respect and trust for their insight, and in time those people's reputations become known by organizations, who invite them to teach or coach at festivals, workshops, and conferences. No one starts as a coach, and those who do it learn the craft of quickly assessing, polishing, and motivating a wide variety of groups over time.

What drew you to this field of a cappella?
I did vocal jazz in high school and college, and some light pop things like King's Singers charts, and some of your [Deke Sharon's] early songbooks, but I didn't really do what we now call contemporary a cappella until I was teaching at Briarcrest. It was my second year, and we started a vocal jazz group, which is what I knew and grew up with. The kids liked it. We did lots of very challenging charts, but the public did not connect to it in the way I had hoped. They loved the kids, and they loved the way they sang, but the music itself didn't get them very excited. My friend Matt Velker kept pushing me to do contemporary a cappella: "It's the wave of the future! It's what everybody's going to be doing; it's what you need to be doing with your vocal jazz group."

So we dipped our feet in a little bit and did a Robert Dietz arrangement of "She Will Be Loved." We sang it at a middle school gym, and the kids went insane. It was incredible. Suddenly the boys who had the two solos in that song were the most popular kids in school. That was a huge moment, so we started to do a couple more a cappella charts, and I thought, okay, we're gonna do a cappella, and by the third year we were doing about half-and-half a cappella and vocal jazz, and by the fourth year we were doing all contemporary a cappella. That was the year we did our first album, which got a lot of attention and affirmed that this was the right thing for our program to be doing.

What specifically drew me to a cappella? First of all, you have to have really strong reading ability, the ability to hold your own part. Even if you have two or three people on a part, it's more demanding than in a choir where you'll have five, ten, or fifteen people sharing a part. Second, everything is without instruments so your pitch, intonation, tone, blend, and balance all have to be impeccable or else it doesn't sound good. I love that it pushes the musicianship of my singers. Third, it's all popular music that both my singers and audiences connect with and love. That's where I think a cappella truly has the ability to be a substantial element in choral music education and in schools for quite some time, because it has this magical combination of pedagogical influence and popular appeal.

What experiences and education do you find have been most useful? What skills and knowledge do people need coming into this kind of work?
     I did a lot of training as a choral education student as an undergraduate in college, and then in my master's program I was doing a choral conducting degree, and so I was in charge of the vocal jazz group for a year. A lot of those elements and methods are similar: empowering singers to be able to sing freely and to be expressive yet doing so within the bounds of ensemble, to express, to balance with other parts, to be able to hear and interact with the solo, and to connect and feel the groove. Those are all elements that vocal jazz and contemporary a cappella have in common.
     A lot of what tends to make OneVoice successful in the eyes of the outside world are choral fundamentals. All of the members are in my honors concert choir class, which is where I work on fundamentals: tone, breath support, pitch, dynamics, articulation, phrasing, placement, and phonation. When we get into a cappella those things are just a given.
     What skills and knowledge are needed? They need a background in solid choral pedagogy. I know there are people who have been able to make a career in a cappella without that, but then you have to rely a great deal more on the instincts and training of your singers, and you have fewer tools to go in and triage when things don't sound the way they should. And then you need to understand how a cappella is different: how the rhythm section plays into the equation, what makes a good bass in a cappella singing (which is far different from operatic or choral bass), and how vocal percussion integrates (snare, kick, toms, hi-hat, etc.). You need to have a basic understanding of those sounds—what they are and the role they play in different styles—so you can clearly communicate that to your vocal percussionists. You certainly don't have to be able to

do it yourself—I'm a perfect example of someone who can't—but I know enough to be able to empower the people that I work with.

You also of course need to have leadership skills, which could be a book in itself. The ability to lead through example and empowerment is something I've tried to focus more and more on each year. With a cappella groups it's very different from a choral setting because you don't get to stand in front of them and wave your arms or will them in any way to do things differently in the middle of a song. It's wind up and go. That means the more you're able to lead through the empowerment, the better your singers are going to perform in a contemporary a cappella setting.

How has the field changed since you started?

This is my seventh year of doing contemporary a cappella of any kind. When I first started, a cappella was sort of this nerdy niche of the vocal music world. There were very few people arranging for it that we knew about, and it wasn't cool or something that was recognized at all within popular culture. Now that's different, with the advent of *The Sing-Off* and *Pitch Perfect*, and then Pentatonix and Home Free—these groups that have infiltrated popular culture, the Billboard charts, and iTunes charts—that's a game changer. When students hear a song on the radio and then you tell them this song is what we're doing . . . we've never had that before in choral music. I've never been able to point to something that we're singing that the singers have such a strong connection to in their outside lives. Plus, the audience has never had that kind of connection from their daily pop culture perspective as well.

There has also been a raising of expectations for recorded a cappella. When we did our first album with Dave Sperandio in 2012, there weren't many high school groups doing high-quality recordings. Very quickly, even in a year, that bar had been raised, and at this point, the level of a cappella production is so high that it's no longer a barrier to creating something really viable, really powerful, with your high school group, as there are so many people out there producing high-quality contemporary a cappella. It's easy to do so long as you have the resources and knowledge.

In live performance, in the past few years I've seen a trend toward lots of dancing, lots of choreography, almost like a show choir, and recently I've seen a bit of a reduction in that. I think it's like any art form: there's action and reaction. I imagine that will always ebb and flow based on what people are seeing and doing in competition and festivals.

There are also way more opportunities to get involved and connect than there used to be, with the events from CASA and the AEA (A Cappella Educators Association). There are also at least fifty a cappella festivals and workshops around the country, large and small, with a new one popping up seemingly every month in a new state. That gives us all more access to materials and information than any of us had when I started.

What are the technical aspects of your work that most people don't understand or know about?

I'm really big on process, the rehearsal process. I have a five-step method that I've outlined in various forms that I think is very important toward creating honest expression in singers. It's based on the concept of removing barriers to expression, the things that get in our way: notes, rhythms, dynamics, our own insecurities, our egos, our fear of failure, and maybe technical issues within the range of our voice. There are so many elements that get in the way that technically my job from the naissance to completion of a new song is to remove those barriers so the singers can best tell their story.

What is the scope and range of what you do?

When you're an a cappella coach, your job is to help guide the group and help them understand the musical concepts, vocal elements, and emotional elements that they need to master in order to create a final product for the audience that is powerful and that has the proper intent for the song. You're playing multiple roles as an a cappella coach. Musically you have to think about the different parts of each song and how to play to the group's strengths. Vocally you have to be a vocal technician, a voice teacher, so you can coach the soloists, the group tone, and placement and technique. You have to be a choral director in a way, making sure the parts blend, vowels align, and people are using the same phrasing. On top of all this, you're also looking at movement and choreography: Do the things they're doing highlight the music?

What does a typical day or week look like for you?

There is no typical day as a coach, as I spend most days working with my groups. Coaching is something that happens at festivals (such as the AEA), on the weekends, whenever I'm free and available to travel.

How many people would you guess are doing this professionally?

I would say there are around a hundred people doing this profession-ally to some degree. You'll see them at CASA and AEA festivals coach-ing; they're a combination of people who are directing at a high level and people who have performed at a high level (in a professional group).

What percentage of your income comes from this?

Just a cappella coaching by itself? Probably 2–3 percent of my in-come, perhaps more for others. It's not a full-time job for anyone, but it is a good way to stay engaged with the community, and it fits well around a variety of other careers, both musical and not.

What advice do you have for someone starting in this field?

I think you have to at some level be a part of a successful group before you can coach one well. I haven't specifically sung in a contemporary a cappella group, but I have been in a number of great vocal jazz and small vocal ensembles that were successful. If you haven't practiced the art and craft of a cappella, it's going to be hard for you to be an a cappella coach. Most a cappella coaches have significant performance experience, choral experience, and arranging experience.

For people who are trying to become more known for doing this, vol-unteer at a festival (CASA, AEA, etc.). They're always looking for people to help out. Or if you know any high school or middle school groups in your area that are just getting started, even college groups, offer to go in and give a critique. You'll have to do it quite a bit for free before people are willing to pay you to do it.

In what ways do you see this field growing or changing in the future?

There is going to be much more of a need for coaching as we see hundreds of new groups forming every year. I think you'll find a lot more choir directors becoming known for a cappella coaching, espe-cially those directors who sang a cappella themselves in college and high school before becoming music educators. Currently a higher percentage of coaches are people who sang in groups but don't have the pedagogical and educational experience, but I think this will change over the next five to ten years.

17

BEHIND THE SCENES

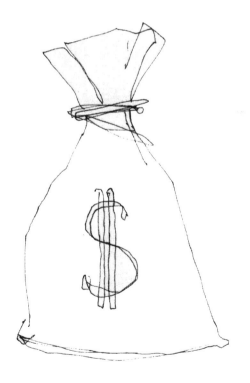

Some a cappella careers don't fit into easy categories. Others require an element of risk and entrepreneurship. Whether you'd like to start your own production company, a tournament, or a group, the first step is knowing you're not alone. Rather than reinvent the wheel, read on to learn how some of a cappella's most successful business pioneers have made their mark:

NEW GROUP PRODUCTION—BEN SPALDING

The professional a cappella field is far from glutted, with local, regional, national, and international a cappella festivals always looking for new groups and new sounds. Some groups are formed because there's a specific purpose (such as Pentatonix and others on *The Sing-Off*), and others because some college grads want to keep singing. Regardless of the reason, there is money to be made when a new group is launched, whether or not the instigator is one of the singers.

Ben Spalding is no stranger to a cappella, as he directs his own International Championship of High School A Cappella (ICHSA) champion high school group, Forte, writes (he cowrote *A Cappella* with Brody McDonald and me), and recently created a new young quintet: Vocalight.

What drew you to this field of a cappella?
My true love of a cappella started when I was in high school. I was in the top choir (called Varsity Ensemble) at my high school starting my sophomore year. One of the highlights of being in that group was that we put on a variety-type show of vocal performances at the end of the year and the students got to choose their performances. I was in high school from 1994 to 1998 when groups like Boyz II Men were in their prime. This was back when Deke Sharon had just published some of the very first doo-wop books. For the show, I put together a doo-wop group three years in a row, and we performed "In the Still of the Night" the first year, "For the Longest Time" the second year, and "A Song for Mama" my senior year. During high school the groups that I performed with arranged a few songs here and there. "A Song for Mama" was arranged by myself and the group for our performance. There was something about a cappella music that I really loved, and I loved how much

enthusiasm those performances generated. You could say that I got bit by the a cappella bug at that time.

I went to college at the University of Kentucky and studied under Dr. Jefferson Johnson and Dr. Lori Hetzel. At the start of my sophomore year, I auditioned for and made the AcoUstiKats, which would later be featured on NBC's *Sing-Off*. I remember touring around to local schools from elementary to high school, and I was always dumbfounded as to why the audience was always way more into those performances than into traditional choral music performances. When the AcoUstiKats performed, we completely grabbed the attention of the audience, no matter who it was. I will say, I absolutely love choral music, but I found it extremely fascinating how contemporary a cappella really held the attention of an audience.

From both my high school and my college experiences I knew I wanted to incorporate a cappella music into my professional career in some way.

How has your career progressed, what experiences brought you to where you are today, and what role has a cappella music played?

In my second year of teaching, I was working at Northwest High School in Cincinnati, and I started an after-school a cappella group there that was met with great enthusiasm. I went on to teach at my alma mater Winton Woods High School, which was also in Cincinnati. I was the assistant director there, and I focused on my passion for a cappella music by starting three different a cappella groups. I found out about the Kettering AcaFest (which is now the largest a cappella festival in the country), and I took my groups to that festival. I met Brody McDonald, and I was really inspired by his top group Eleventh Hour and everything he was doing related to a cappella music. Brody and I got to know each other and became friends, and a few years later he called me when the high school choral director job opened at Centerville High School, which was in the neighboring school district to his school. I interviewed and was offered the position. That was a pivotal moment in my life; I was working on a master's degree in school counseling, and I thought I would head down that educational path, but I gave that up and moved to Centerville and the rest is history! I made the decision to switch the top chamber choir at the school (Forte) to an a cappella group, and I have worked my tail off to build the entire choral program at Centerville High School to what it is today.

What skills and knowledge do people need to be successful coming into this kind of work?

For me the most important aspects of success have been hard work, passion, and an understanding of the psychology of people. To be successful in this kind of work, you have to be willing to work hard and then work even harder. The work never really stops, and you have to keep pushing and persisting. I think you also have to be willing to ask questions and reach out for help. Along the way as I have become successful, I have never been afraid to ask for help or reach out to others whom I considered the best of the best. The best way to learn is to learn from the best and find out what has made others successful. If you don't know how to do something or have a question, then ask!

I truly feel that one of the other biggest contributors to my success is the understanding of people. I'm always reading the room and pushing the envelope. Do the kids need me to be energetic today? Do the kids need me to slow things down because they're all over the place? How are the kids emotionally, physically, and so forth? I am always focused on how I can adapt on a daily basis in the classroom as well as with any group I work with. Every single group that I direct is different, and within that group are individuals that all have different buttons to push and different ways that they get motivated. There's no single method that works for everyone, and finding the method to reach every individual within a group to get to the root of them as people is more important than all of the music theory in the world. Don't get me wrong; it's all important. Every single detail of everything is important, every crescendo, pitch, and rhythm. It's all important, but how do you get people to care about that? Sometimes to teach someone how important those things are you first need to get to know the person on a human level. At the start of a student's career, he or she is not going to care as much about music as I do. In fact, some never will. But I know it's my job to get every ounce out of a kid or student that I can. It starts with caring about them and getting to know them. Kids are also a reflection of their directors. Everything we do matters, and every single person from the sound guy to the director and the kids is equally important.

It's my job to make them feel that way and understand that they all have a purpose and a role.

How has the field changed since you started?

The field has changed a lot since I first started. One of the songs I performed in college with the AcoUstiKats was "Insomniac." I also remember the recording that I got from Napster (anyone else remember Napster?) of the Brown Derbies singing "Eye of the Tiger." Those songs were groundbreaking at the time. When I was in the AcoUstiKats we were learning from Straight No Chaser (yes, I'm the same age as those guys!)—that and the very early days of m-Pact with "Higher and Higher," "Love the One You're With," and "29 Ways." My college group would learn these charts by ear. I don't remember, other than possibly Napster, how we got these recordings. Now there is an abundant library of a cappella music out there for groups to perform.

When I first started, simple mouth drumming was mind blowing, and the days of Wes Carroll and his early training videos were just starting to come out. What vocal percussionists are doing today is truly mind blowing and blows simple mouth drumming out of the water!

Also when I first started, sound and the use of microphones was very different than what it is today. I remember recording the first AcoUsti-Kats album with all of us in a circle around a microphone and Dr. Johnson keeping time visually for us. Dr. Johnson would wear headphones, and we would all sing the backing vocals together at the same time. When I first started with Forte, all of the groups competing in the ICHSA and the International Championship of Collegiate A Cappella (ICCA) would use zone microphones. Your choreography had to be strategic in order to get the best sound. Only the vocal percussionist, and sometimes the bass and the soloists, would use individual microphones.

What are the technical aspects of your work that most people don't understand or know about?

I think one of the most important things that people don't understand is that the work really doesn't ever stop. I guess I could make it stop if I wanted, but that's not how I'm hardwired as a human being. I have found that in order to have great ideas and push the envelope, you can't turn your mind off very often. Even when I leave to go home from my job, I'm constantly thinking about what's next. Should we add an extra rehearsal? What songs should we do next? What songs are working right now and which aren't and why? Do I have enough amazing kids for next year's group, or do I need to spend more time recruiting? Honestly my wheels pretty much never stop turning! In terms of Vocalight, I will get down to the nitty gritty of what I do for them a little later.

What is the scope and range of what you do?

I'm the head choral director, not to mention the only choral director currently at Centerville High School, and I direct seven groups. At the time of this interview, I'm also finishing up my master's in music at Kent State University. I also within the last year started a professional a cappella group called Vocalight, and I will focus on the scope and range of what I do with that group. But first I will first give you a brief background of the things that Vocalight has done this year and then go on to talk about all that I do with the group.

The first part of the process with Vocalight was putting the group together. I think it's very important that the group you put together is full of people with the passion and drive to want to do this for a living. Vocalight has had some trial and error with this, and some of the members have changed since its inception, but it's not often that you're going to put five people together and everything is going to click and you're not going to have any growing pains. After putting the group together, it was extremely important that we learned as much music as possible and as quickly as possible. I put the group on a weekly video release schedule right out of the gate. We knew that the music wouldn't necessarily be perfect every single week, but we knew we would learn a lot about one another over time. By doing a new song and arrangement every week, we knew we had a crazy goal. We achieved that goal for a couple months until we booked a few major gigs and had to polish a live show. Over Christmas break, we were hired to do eleven Christmas shows in a five-day span. We took that gig because it was a great opportunity to perform for a large number of people, so it was great exposure and we knew it would help our live sound develop quickly. After that we headlined a couple a cappella festivals from January to March. We were the main headliner at the annual Milwaukappella festival, and we headlined alongside the Exchange at the annual Voices in Harmony Festival in Lexington, Kentucky. Our next major gig is at Town Hall in New York City headlining the ICHSA finals. We're now working toward an album as well as continuing to arrange, write songs, headline, take gigs, and so forth. We're in talks and about to sign with an agent to plug us into the college circuit and book us gigs in the National Association of Campus Activities (NACA) and the Association for the Promotion of Campus Activities (APCA) circuits. We're looking at signing with the agent whom the Filharmonic and Dakaboom are both signed with. You have to have a booking agent to book gigs in the college circuit, and a lot of famous musicians started in these circuits.

Here are the things that I do or assist with in Vocalight:

- Help develop and keep up a website
- Assist with social media
- Make sure the group members stay in constant communication with one another in a group texting app called GroupMe
- Talk to arrangers and the group members to help figure out what songs they want to cover
- Put together a Patreon for the group
- Help put together and maintain their schedule
- Coordinate all of the videos as well as film and then send it off to someone to edit the footage
- Play "psychologist" for Vocalight as well as all groups that I direct. This is not in a bad way, but I'm always feeling out the group mentally to see where everyone's head is, whether they know I'm doing it or not.
- Network with the a cappella community, local community, and as many people as I can
- Book gigs
- Answer e-mails
- Manage a group calendar
- Run sound for the group, especially locally
- Help audition new members when or if the need arises
- Most importantly, I do everything that I can to make sure that the group can focus on learning, arranging, and writing music.

I think one of the important things about what I do is make things happen. I'm a coach, friend, mentor, investor, musician, arranger, and sound engineer. I wear whatever hat is needed on any particular day, and I make sure the group is constantly moving forward. Goals, goals, goals . . . content, content, content . . . network, network, network . . .

What does a typical day or week look like for you?
A typical day or week for me revolves mostly around my day job. I'm the head choral director at Centerville High School, and my contracted hours are from 7:40 a.m. to 3:10 p.m. daily. This job goes way beyond the contracted hours, per my choice, but that is my required schedule. I'm also currently working on finishing my master's in music education at Kent State University online. I spend around ten hours a week after school hours reading, studying, writing, and doing the required coursework to complete my master's. Vocalight is fit into all of this. The nice thing about Vocalight is that I don't have to be at every rehearsal, but I try to be there as much as I can be. If they are rehearsing the music, I don't always need to be there or want to be there until the notes and pitches are learned.

Typical Week for Vocalight

Sundays: Rehearse for two to three hours
Mondays: Rehearse for two hours

Typically we will rehearse on another day during the week, usually Wednesday or Thursday, or we will film a video or record a track. If we have neither of those to do, we will meet at a local donut shop called Bill's Donuts or the choir room at Centerville High School to talk about our upcoming goals and plans. This group spends every free second rehearsing. If we have a Saturday free we're probably filming a video, arranging, rehearsing, or tracking our upcoming releases for singles and an album. We all have a combined calendar that we keep our schedule in, and we also put conflicts on that calendar.

How many people would you guess are doing this professionally?
This is a tough question. The way that I can best answer that question is to say not enough. That's one of the reasons I started Vocalight. There are so many great a cappella people, including the members of

Vocalight, that just need help and need to be given a chance. Having more professional a cappella groups performing out there is the only way we're going to have more groups reach the level of success groups like Pentatonix have achieved. I've heard from many in the a cappella field that the market is saturated and that Pentatonix has a stronghold on it. I highly disagree with this. There aren't enough groups to make a difference. If there are only twenty or thirty highly successful a cappella groups touring and making a living doing a cappella music, then that's not enough to make a splash like Pentatonix. Think of how many rock bands there are. Think of how many musicians there are trying to make it out there. *The Sing-Off* gave Pentatonix a great jump start, but unlike some of the other groups on the show that could've made it bigger but didn't, Pentatonix kept pushing and working hard. Content, content, content! They kept releasing more and more content. They had that along with a relentless drive to succeed. Pentatonix isn't better than every group out there (although don't get me wrong they are amazing!), but they kept pushing and learning. We need more groups with a tireless passion to succeed, take risks, fail, and push the envelope! If we have that, then I know there are more groups that will reach their level of success.

What advice do you have for someone starting a pro group?
   My advice is to only get in this field or start a pro group if you love it and if you are willing to work hard. There's plenty of mediocre groups out there, and we need more groups that are incredible and amazing. I think we're starting to see this shift. This is the only way we're going to have more than just Pentatonix topping the charts.

In what ways do you see this field growing or changing in the future?
   The future is very exciting for contemporary a cappella. I think you're going to start to see the stars of high school and college a cappella really help transform this art form in the future. We need more than just the pioneers of high school a cappella such as Brody McDonald, Lisa Forkish, and J. D. Frizzell to help carry the torch as we move forward. There are a lot of amazing kids coming from those directors as well as many others that are going to have the passion to help carry this art form further and further. The A Cappella Education

Association (which I helped to create to be a resource for educators interested in a cappella) will continue to grow, and I think it will become as large as the American Choral Directors Association. There's a reason more and more directors are starting to have contemporary a cappella groups in their school programs. For one, we are finally seeing groups that are truly amazing, and they are good enough to get even the skeptics to think about starting a group. Pop music, and any kind of music for that matter, can be made very complex.

What do you see the future holding for you and Vocalight?
I think the future looks very bright for Vocalight! They are an amazingly talented group of individuals as well as being some of the nicest "kids" I have ever met. I think they have the talent, the work ethic, the drive, and the star power to make it big, and I sincerely hope they do.

For me, I know I will continue to work hard and find ways to continue to push the envelope and spread my love of a cappella music. I hope to have a long career at Centerville High School working with Forte and all of my other choirs, and I hope to see Vocalight through to success.

No matter what, I am just thankful to have all of the opportunities I have had in my life to spread my love of a cappella music to the world and meet and work with a lot of amazing people along the way.

EVENT PRODUCTION AND PROMOTION— AMANDA CORNAGLIA

Producing a concert is both one of the most exciting and one of the most dangerous careers in a cappella: exciting because you get to rub elbows with groups and bask in the roar of a happy crowd, and dangerous because the bigger the event, the greater the financial risk. A producer in general does "whatever it takes" to bring something to successful completion, and in the case of concert production that can mean everything from scrambling when a monitor stops working during a sound check to dealing with the occasional emotions that can swell backstage.

Amanda Cornaglia is a true a cappella Renaissance woman: performing and managing two a cappella groups (Snowday [scholastic educational gigs] and Euphonism [vocal band]), arranging, coaching, overseeing the Contemporary A Cappella League, and heading up a new online video initiative for vocal groups (FloVoice); and in the midst of it all she has been producing and promoting concerts and events for over a decade, starting from her days on the Contemporary A Cappella Society (CASA) board as director of programs and director of events.

What drew you to this field of a cappella?

Concert promotion and production was a natural combination of my skill set and experience. As a longtime performer with extensive event planning experience, putting together concerts and festivals allowed me to share something I was truly passionate about with a broader audience. Once I added a deeper knowledge of sound support, I realized my unique background made me a great asset to musicians, venues, and promoters because I could understand and communicate the needs of one to the others. I started with just a few a cappella–focused shows and have since moved on to work on all different styles of music and larger festivals.

What experiences and education do you find have been most useful? What skills and knowledge do people need coming into this kind of work?

The benefit of wearing many hats is that I've also walked in many shoes. Having direct experience and intimate knowledge of all angles of a production has made everything go smoother. It allows me to develop relationships that lead to better end results.

If you're a musician looking to get into production, spend some time planning events—not just concerts. Working in events, whether it is as customer service or at weddings, corporate affairs, meetings, or public festivals, will give you a much better sense of what people are looking for when they attend or plan an event. It's a shortcut to understanding the psychology and sociology of why people are drawn to some events over others, learning the benefits and consequences of setting expectations, as well as giving you a much bigger picture of what goes into planning and executing something bigger than yourself.

If you're coming from the event planning side with little or no performance experience, find a way to put yourself in a performer's shoes. Sign up for a community chorus or sing in the church choir. Sing, play, or tell jokes at an open mic. If you don't have a performance bone in your body, find a friend that does and tag along with him or her. Try out performing in a variety of environments. Just a few times through and you'll see all: how last-minute changes, less than ideal conditions, missing rider items, and other seemingly small mishaps can take its toll on a performer.

If you're starting as a venue owner or manager with no experience in events or music, get some help before you dive in. So much of what needs to happen in a concert-planning process is hard to convey without hands-on experience.

Speaking directly to skills and knowledge, it's indispensable to have the following:

- Project management: Understanding how to see something through to the end before you start the process will help you address most logistical items up front, rather than scramble to find solutions at the last minute or do without. Foreseeing risks, issues, or other problems allows you to plan ahead and move through the event proactively rather than reactively.
- Impeccable time management: Both in preparation and the day of, keeping to a schedule is important. Knowing how much time you need to get something done in ideal and less-than-ideal circumstances will help you plan a schedule that works for everyone that doesn't feel rushed or crumbles when something doesn't go as planned.
- Strong networking skills: You'll need to develop relationships with performers, venues, contractors, agents, police/security, fans, and potential fans, and that's just the beginning. Events built on trust always run smoother. If all parties trust you and your judgment, they react and follow direction better. People also give you a better version of themselves if you treat them like a friend (or at the very least, a human), rather than a product.
- Basic marketing knowledge: Don't believe the adage "if you build it they will come." Even great events can flop if no one shows up. Make sure you have people there to enjoy all your hard work. Spend some time getting to know your audience and finding your potential audiences. Figure out where they get their news, how they plan, and what entices them to come out. Put out quality materials that best represent the high quality of the event. Give

people a reason to join you. There are a lot of other things competing with you for their time and money.

- Budgeting and finance: Anyone could put on a good event if money came in endless supply. Knowing how to set a realistic budget up front and sticking to it will keep you from bankrupting yourself or your organization. Having some idea of where you can get funding legally and reliably is also important. And if you are operating on your own, understanding tax law will keep you from falling into a panic at tax time. Diversifying your support is also good practice. Not all event producers have deep pockets, and you don't want to find yourself beholden to one key sponsor.
- Hospitality: Everything comes back to customer service. People will always remember how well they were treated and if their needs were adequately met. Your reputation will precede you, for better or worse.
- Basic understanding of sound engineering: A good sound system and a competent engineer is the key to a great concert. Even the best performers can have a terrible show if the sound equipment or engineer fails them. If you take the time to understand how and why it works, it will reduce your stress level and will also give you a larger toolbox if something goes wrong.
- Patience: Your mood and reaction will reflect on the event. If you lose your cool, this will trickle down to everyone working on the event and even possibly the attendees.
- Ability to focus in stressful and loud environments: Once an event starts, you'll need to be able to operate in chaos. A quiet space to think is not always guaranteed!

How has the field changed since you started?

Over the last ten years, touring has become a much more important part of a musician's income. With declining album sales and the advent of streaming, artists rely on concert ticket sales or performance fees to make ends meet. However, with the advent of social media and the swift advances in technology, the cost of entry has also decreased, leading to a large influx of "garage bands." Promoters must have the ear to know the difference, trust their gut, and dig through deep piles of EPKs, reviews, showcase rosters, and agencies to find the best. The "best" is a moving target though and is not the same in all situations. Building personal relationships is becoming even more important as the world moves to more sterile, indirect forms of communication.

In my very niche market of a cappella, we've seen the style move mainstream. It's been far easier to convince venues to host an all-vocal show with promises of real live *Pitch Perfect*. While this has been great for booking the acts I'm most passionate about, the stakes are now also higher, as audiences are savvier and expect more from an a cappella group.

What are the technical aspects of your work that most people don't understand or know about?

A trained musical ear, while not required, certainly gives you a better perspective when making talent decisions. Those who are musicians, if booking or promoting outside of your niche, need to be willing to expand their horizons and recognize talent outside of their preferred style.

Likewise, at least a basic understanding of how the sound system works, what type of sound works best for your venue or artist, and how to speak to your sound engineer ensures that you have more control over one of the most critical pieces of the concert.

As with most any job now, a good working knowledge of computer programs and how to navigate the Internet effectively and efficiently is now a requirement. Specifically, use of project management tools (whether as simple as an Excel document or as complicated as more robust project management software) is also needed. There is a lot of data management that goes into building and producing a good event.

What is the scope and range of what you do?

I've worked on everything from one task on an event to running the entire thing alone. There are pros and cons to both. When I am assigned one small part of the event, I can really focus on the small details. I also can rely on a larger team for support and inspiration. Learning to fit in your plans with a larger picture is a great challenge and often pushes you to create something that's even bigger or better than what you would have come up with on your own. Watching all the small pieces come together on the day of the show is really something quite magical. On the other hand, having complete control over an event can also be quite empowering. I find blank slates to be exciting, and for a slightly OCD control freak, knowing that everything is in your control can actually be less stressful than delegating or chasing after teammates.

In terms of what goes into my job, here are some of the highlights:

- Envisioning and executing a new concert, series, or festival
- Improving on existing concerts, series, and festivals
- Adding a music component to an existing event
- Building and managing an event team
- Creating an event budget
- Securing funding through existing budgets, fund-raising, grants, ticket sales, and so forth
- Screening and hiring talent
- Finding and securing venues
- Recruiting and scheduling staff members and volunteers
- Liaising with the venue staff
- Providing or hiring sound engineers
- Creating and maintaining a web presence (website, social media, and online advertising)
- Graphic design
- Creating marketing materials
- Building and executing a marketing plan
- Reaching out to press contacts to promote the event
- Planning social media posts
- Evaluating concert "extras" (opening acts, food, drinks, and other special features)
- Arranging talent and staff hospitality (travel, lodging, and food)
- Networking with sponsors and fiscal supporters
- Scouting for talent and ideas at other events
- Safety and emergency training (first aid, crowd control, managing evacuations, etc.)
- Logistics (scheduling, communications, maps, etc.)
- Reviewing and fulfilling technical and hospitality riders
- Creating event schedules for the staff, the talent, and attendees
- Jumping in when needed on just about any task—food runner, chef, host, driver, emcee, stage hand, or custodian. You name it, I've done it.

What does a typical day or week look like for you?

Since production isn't my only job, I don't have a typical day or week. I typically squeeze in the work that normal people agonize over while in transit to my next concert or appointment. Each time I take on a new assignment, the first thing I'm asked, without fail, is how I manage it all. To be honest, I'm not even sure if I know the full answer. However, keeping a packed schedule doesn't give me the luxury to draw out any one task or decision. Because of this, I've learned to think on my feet, trust my gut, and follow through even in less-than-ideal circumstances. I try to keep myself to a "touch it once" philosophy where I either do the task immediately or schedule the time when I'll return to it and complete it. I've also learned to find joy in long hours of running around and the equal satisfaction of my head hitting the pillow at the end of a long day or several days.

The biggest mind-set change for your day-to-day as a producer is that you have very distinct times when you are living in the now (at the concert) and when you are living in the future (planning the concert). I spend my summers thinking about the holidays and my winter holidays thinking about the summer. Given my innate competitive side, I try to finish my programming earlier and earlier each year. The earlier I can plan the big pieces of an event, the more time I have to be creative with the smaller pieces and put more focus on the "experience."

Some clients that hire us for live sound production come to us twelve to eighteen months in advance and always seem apologetic. Don't apologize! Committing to something that early ensures that we have the time to really do it right.

How many people would you guess are doing this professionally?

Concert production and promotion is a pretty viable profession. Specifically working with a cappella, though, there are far fewer people, and most work in the field on a volunteer basis or in exchange for expenses to an event they'd really like to attend.

Volunteers are great and usually *very* enthusiastic about working on an event they really love. At least at the beginning. However, unless volunteers are responsible for just a small task, burnout is common. I see many bright-eyed volunteers push very hard for a few weeks or months and then lose interest or simply feel tired or overwhelmed. To keep something progressing in the long term, you'll find the most success with paid staff or a mix of paid staff with a very large pool of volunteers.

What percentage of your income comes from this?
Promotion and production makes up about 40 percent of my income. However, all of my other work is music and event related, through performance, education, or administrative tasks.

What advice do you have for someone starting in this field?
Start early! Even planning a small party or taking on responsibilities planning a school or community concert will give you valuable experience. Pay close attention to how you feel while doing each task during the process. If overseeing an entire event causes you insurmountable stress, this field is probably not for you, no matter how much you love it. However, in the process you may discover that you enjoy a part of the process—sound engineering, marketing, hospitality, or something else.

Be honest with yourself. Planning and promoting a concert correctly is just as much a job as are more traditional lines of work. Being heavily involved in planning concerts can also take some of the joy out of it. If attending concerts is your top source of entertainment, you may want to reconsider making it your job. Or if you do choose to make it your job, actively find another hobby to fill the void that's created.

Learn from your mistakes. Things can and will go wrong, and you'll need to engage your fight-or-flight mode appropriately. In the moment, you'll need to be quick with Band-Aids, but once everything is over, take the time to look for the cure. The postconcert debrief is an important part of the process that many amateurs often skip.

In what ways do you see this field growing or changing in the future?
Hopefully live performances will continue to stay near the top of the list for entertainment options. We are seeing a slight shift to more of a virtual audience, meaning we'll see more live streaming and online concerts. With the advent of streaming, we'll also see a new legal battle in performing and streaming cover songs, with more attention paid to lower-level shows that have traditionally operated under the radar.

VIDEO PRODUCTION—LAYNE STEIN

Video did indeed kill the radio star—or, to be more precise, forced the radio star to make videos. That was back in the 1980s, and nowadays it's even more crucial for groups—professional and amateur—to have a visual component to their music, be it a live concert video, a fully produced music video, animations, or lyrics.

Enter Layne Stein: a former Disney singer, currently performs as the vocal percussionist of VoicePlay, which was an early adopter of video, resulting in several viral videos and a fan base worldwide. His video skills have been finely honed, and coupled with his inside knowledge of a cappella, he formed a video production company that creates great videos for professional and amateur groups.

What drew you to this field of a cappella?
In high school, a cappella was introduced to me via Rockapella, the Bobs, m-pact, the House Jacks, and so on, and I have been hooked ever since! I would spend hours every week researching and learning everything I could about the music and how to write arrangements. This then led to learning how to record and mix audio, and in the more recent years has now evolved into a passion for video production of music videos.

What experiences and education do you find have been most useful? What skills and knowledge do people need coming into this kind of work?
I can pinpoint two pivotal things that have been instrumental throughout every step of my career. Both of these were things that my parents pushed me to do, and I am so appreciative to them now, although I didn't always feel that way.

The first was taking violin lessons from a very early age. This exposed me to many genres of music, the experience of playing with an orchestra, learning how to be competitive in music, and of course one of the most important things—reading music!

The second was getting my computer engineering degree from the University of Central Florida. My original post–high school desire was to attend Full Sail University's audio engineering program; however, I was "strongly encouraged" to pursue the computer engineering degree instead. Throughout my years in college I learned about audio circuits, programming, and anything else nerdy you can think of. This education has helped me on an almost daily basis troubleshoot technology issues that are a part of the audio/video production creative process.

Together, these two experiences have specifically helped my brain understand how music works, and why it affects people in the way that it does.

How has the field changed since you started?

I am so grateful for the way that a cappella has become accepted into the mainstream. When I first started, I never would have dreamed that there would be TV shows, movies, Grammy Awards and performances, sold-out arena shows, and so forth, for a cappella groups. This acceptance as a valid genre of music by the general public is the biggest change, and it has allowed so many more people to be exposed to my work.

What are the technical aspects of your work that most people don't understand or know about?

People don't see the hours that go into the details of the work (just like any other job): from the simplest writing/drawing of a concept so other people can understand your ideas, to something as specific as compression on a vocal, lighting a set "just right," finding the perfect location, or spending hours watching tutorial videos on how to make specific video edits. The beauty of the finished product is when all of these details, from the simple to the complicated, come together to create the exact feeling you imagined from the beginning of the concept formation.

What is the scope and range of what you do?

I create content from start to finish, or as I like to say, from concept to creation. This includes everything from storyboarding the idea to creating musical arrangements, composing, editing audio, mixing, mastering, location scouting, being strapped into a Steadicam setup for eight to ten hours at a time, lighting the set just right, editing video, and so forth. Here's the biggest key to success in my opinion: surround yourself with a team of people that you trust and that share your same work ethic—and bonus points if they are smarter than you!

What does a typical day or week look like for you?

There is no such thing as a "typical" week; however, every day has similarities. As a member of the a cappella group VoicePlay, I find myself in and out of airports on a regular basis. Even when I am traveling, I find time each day to work on creative projects. Although every day is different, they are also the same—I never stop creating, and my mind is always thinking about the next idea or the current labor of love I am working on. When I am home in Orlando, I spend the days in my studio working on content, arranging music, recording and mixing vocals, editing videos, researching the latest and greatest technology, and so on.

How many people would you guess are doing this professionally?

I think there are a lot of people in the video production industry, and it's for sure competitive! However, the niche of creating content and producing videos inside of the a cappella genre still feels like a small community of highly specialized individuals.

What percentage of your income comes from this?

Creating content and performing is 100 percent of my income. At one point in time it was 0 percent, and it was a journey to get to where I am today, and the story continues on every day.

What advice do you have for someone starting in this field?

Jump in and just start creating. Don't overthink it; just dive in and see where your ideas take you. Fill your brain with as much knowledge as you can along the way; utilize every resource you can get your hands on. Scour the web, learn from your peers, go to school, and get an internship—the opportunities for learning are endless. You don't need a fancy camera or expensive lights to evoke an emotion; you need a great idea and passion. The rest will fall into place as you invest your time and energy into learning about your craft.

In what ways do you see this field growing or changing in the future?

I believe we are going to see the a cappella industry's reach extend even further into live theater, film, television, and especially on social media. I see this happening in ways we haven't seen before—and I am so excited to have the opportunity to be a part of it! Many people are still being exposed to a cappella music for the first time, so using inspiration from new and different places is going to be the key to its continued growth!

WEB DESIGN—MATT ATHERTON

Every group that wants to attract fans, get paid bookings, and hang a virtual shingle for the world to see needs a website. It's a simple fact of twenty-first-century commerce that you don't just need to publicize your existence to a few locals; you want the world to know, as the people who will purchase your albums, watch your videos, and potentially invite you to perform are located everywhere and anywhere. And although you can create your own Facebook page and Twitter account, maintain your own Instagram and YouTube page, a good website that works on multiple platforms (computers as well as laptop screens) requires a professional programmer.

That's where Matt Atherton comes in. As an a cappella singer and performer for many years, he knows what a cappella groups want, and as a web designer he knows how to make it happen, so along with Ron Heaton he formed A Cappella Web Design, which now boasts a very impressive worldwide client base (including yours truly).

What drew you to this field of a cappella?
Since the age of nine I've been singing on a regular basis, from church choir to cabaret, operetta to a cappella. For the last fourteen years, I have been part of an a cappella group, which rehearses and performs locally where I live in the Odenwald region of Germany.

I started building websites in the early nineties, before the world had even heard of Flash. While working for a corporate training company, I began with the basics of HTML and CSS, and over the years have built my knowledge and understanding of a very fast-paced industry.

At the start of 2014, the time was right to combine my hobby with my profession, and A Cappella Web Design was born—the idea being to supply a cappella groups, small and large, college and professional, and producers, engineers, and all a cappella–related people with a one-stop shop for branding, design, web development, and digital marketing.

What experiences and education do you find have been most useful?

I have been fortunate enough to have had the honor of working with the most extraordinary mentors, both in my web-development career and on several occasions throughout my passion for singing harmonies. When I was nine years old, I joined the Cirencester Parish Church Choir, in the heart of the Cotswolds in the UK, under the tutelage of the late Father John Beck. The lessons learned over the following ten years have had a profound influence on my singing hobby and my professional career. Possibly the most important part of this education was that of listening, rather than just hearing. In harmony singing, this translates to finding where one's voice fits in with the whole sound—in my job, it's about listening to and understanding a client's requirements, and making sure their expectations aren't just met but also exceeded.

What skills and knowledge do people need coming into this kind of work?

I came into this career via training: learning the Microsoft Office suite to an advanced level and teaching those products to small groups over the course of several classroom sessions. My educational background, however, is one of design. Having studied maths, physics, and graphic design at college, I wanted to design cars. This was ultimately not to be the case, but the design skills I was taught stood me in good stead to move into the field of web design, with the development and code-writing coming later. Design and layout of websites is still my key role in the company today, with others in my team, more experienced in coding and development, translating my design ideas into living, breathing web systems.

How has the field changed since you started?

Best practices in web design and development are changing on an almost daily basis. Hanging on to the "cutting edge" of this industry is a full-time job in itself, and one must choose to specialize in a small selection of technologies, in order to keep up with the latest trends, techniques, rules, and coding methods. At A Cappella Web Design, we chose to specialize in WordPress, a so-called content management system (CMS) that allows us great flexibility in designing and building custom, unique web experiences for our clients, while allowing them, with the minimal amount of training, to administer their own content, images, blog posts, and slideshows. This is especially practical in the world of a cappella, specifically with college groups, where the person responsible for looking after the web content is changing on a fairly regular basis, and their successor is quickly trained in how to maintain the website.

What are the technical aspects of your work that most people don't understand or know about?
With so many "build-your-own" alternatives available for users with little or no knowledge to create their own websites, potential clients often struggle to understand why they should contract a professional web-development company, instead of simply creating their own website. The advantage of utilizing the services of purpleplanet (my primary web design company) are that we don't just build the website; we offer consultancy from the first contact with the client; we advise on best practices, current trends, and modern layouts; and we are able to customize to the finest detail, without having to remain within the limitations of a product that builds the website with no professional human interaction.

What is the scope and range of what you do?
At A Cappella Web Design, we're involved in the process from the very beginning. When a client contacts us, it's important that both parties understand what is required and what is possible. A mantra learned from my first web-development mentor, Kevin Gray, is one I still use regularly today: "The customers know what they want, but they don't know what they need." It's our job to listen to what the client wants to achieve and to use our experience and knowledge to provide a solution that goes beyond their original expectations. Once the scope of the work has been agreed upon, we design and build the website to the agreed specifications and, most importantly, offer our postlive maintenance services. Many clients don't appreciate the ongoing requirement to update and generally maintain a website. There's very often the belief that once a website is live, it will look after itself, or not require any more to be done. Core code and added plug-ins (slideshows, image optimization, social media connections, and many other added functionalities) need to be maintained to remain secure,

efficient, and optimized. Regular backups are also essential, in case of malware, direct attacks, or server failure.

What does a typical day or week look like for you?
With most of my clients several time zones away, my day begins fairly quietly. I get a chance to catch up on e-mails that have arrived overnight and to plan tasks for myself and the rest of my team. If clients have answered feedback, then that can be acted upon before they are online later in the day. Come the afternoon, clients start coming online, meetings take place, and my workday tends to continue until around 10:00 p.m.

How many people would you guess are doing this professionally?
There are thousands of web-development companies around the world, but there aren't many (if any) others who specialize in websites for a cappella groups.

What percentage of your income comes from this?
Income from a cappella websites probably accounts for about 5–10 percent of my income.

What advice do you have for someone starting in this field?
Given that so many companies offer web-development services, and there are also many online "do-it-yourself" options, my advice would be to specialize, and find a niche market. We had the advantage of understanding a cappella and the needs of those involved.

In what ways do you see this field growing or changing in the future?
There are many theories about the future of web design and development. Some say tech will get smaller; others predict that wearable gadgets will become increasingly popular. I think that websites and social media will gradually come together, to form a seamless web presence, accessible as a single source.

Personal Internet connections, whether through touch pads, voice-activated wearables, or something else will most likely become popular, particularly given the growing possibilities in the field of voice recognition and AI learning. Whatever happens, staying at the forefront of the industry is always the key to making a success of web design and development.

MULTIFACETED ADMINISTRATION—DAVID LONGO

A cappella as a field has grown beyond being a smattering of individuals working on their own as independent contractors. Corporations have arisen, such as Varsity Vocals, which has a staff of specialized workers, from local concert producers to publicists, with Amanda Newman at the helm.

David Longo is just such an impresario, at the helm of the Vocal Company, a multifaceted company that offers services in recording, live production, education, video production, arranging, songwriting, and so forth. From his home base, which includes a studio and educational space, he oversees a diverse range of employees who work together to help a cappella groups. Becoming such a jack-of-all-trades requires many things, including a wide-ranging understanding of the a cappella community, as well as skills both in the technical aspects of his company's offerings (recording and live sound) as well as overarching leadership and managerial skills.

What drew you to this field of a cappella?

I was always a music nut. I played trumpet and sang in elementary school. When I started high school, I joined every musical ensemble possible. I was in band, jazz band, and marching band, but it was a little tougher to be in the choir. See, there were forty-nine girls and . . . me. If you want to know a quick way to "get in with the ladies" as a high school nerd, join choir.

My choral director, Thomas Paster at Northern Highlands Regional High School in Allendale, New Jersey, brought in Five o'Clock Shadow, "Boston's A Cappella Rock Band," to give a performance at our school one day. I was so impressed by the Stack's percussion and the band's treatment of vocal trumpet on Cake's "Never There" that I was hooked. "Stack" is a nickname for David "Stack" Steakhouse, a Berklee grad who was the first professional vocal percussionist to sing vocal bass at the same time—a technique he named "beatbass." It was truly a unique sight: Stack was a charismatic bald man who wore a black collar microphone (Vocomotion's Thumper mic) around his throat. Somehow, with Stack onstage with nothing more than a microphone in his hands, my ears were hearing rumbling low end, as if performed live by Flea, and driving drums. The energy onstage was electric, and as a high schooler, I was enthralled. I later started researching and fell in love with Rockapella and Take 6, and oddly enough, I listened to the 4:2:Five album on repeat. (4:2:Five was made up of high schoolers at the time and later became VoicePlay, which most know from their time on NBC's *Sing-Off*.) Napster and Kazaa were coming into themselves at the time, and I downloaded anything I possibly could relating to a cappella. So, naturally, I'm sure I listened to hundreds of tracks likely having nothing to do with Rockapella, which were improperly credited to Rockapella in Napster's and Kazaa's software.

At school, Tom started a chamber choir called Highlands Voices. We performed mostly madrigals and small-format jazz pieces. It was an imperfect vessel for a love of the contemporary a cappella I was falling in love with, but it served its purpose. More importantly, Tom was fantastic at directing students' passions into his current curriculum. A few years after I left high school, a classmate of mine wrote Tom to tell him about ICCA/ICHSA: "Why haven't we done this yet? You could be really successful at this competition." Sure enough, Tom called on some House Jacks alumni, Roopak Ahuja and other friends in the field, and converted the small madrigal group into an ICHSA powerhouse, later winning ICHSA finals.

When I graduated from high school, I started college at the Rochester Institute of Technology. I started as a computer engineer in the College of Engineering and later switched to computational mathematics in the College of Science. I wanted to continue singing so I joined the only choir at RIT, the RIT Singers. At the first rehearsal, there was a showcase of all the a cappella groups going into auditions. There were four at the time: Eight Beat Measure (male), the Brick City Singers (male), Surround Sound (male), and Encore (female). They each piqued my interest, relating back to albums I had obsessed over in high school, in different ways. Eight Beat reminded me of a mix between Da Vinci's Notebook, 4:2:Five, and Boyz II Men; BCS was closer to Rockapella; and Surround Sound was a barbershop group reminding me of my days in *The Music Man*. I auditioned and had to choose which group I'd have liked to join. Eight Beat (the Da Vinci's Notebook/Boyz II Men guys) oozed confidence and cool. Their music was inviting and emotional. I was drawn to the connectivity, to the obvious fraternity in front of me. The group was made up of rowers and network security analysts, and soccer fanatics and engineers. Eight Beat gave me a place to find confidence, brotherhood, and a platform for exploration.

What experiences and education do you find have been most useful? What skills and knowledge do people need coming into this kind of work?

I have an unusual education. I have studied British debate at Cambridge, economics at Stanford, and US-UK relations at Georgetown. I led a hacking challenge lab for the National Youth Leadership Forum on Technology. I majored in computational mathematics at the Rochester Institute of Technology with minors in economics, finance, music, and music technology. My research studied social network construction and the dynamics of rumor spread. I gave a lecture to the Department of Defense on finding terrorist cells in larger networks only to realize that the field made me miserable. I registered the next day for Berklee Online.

My master certificate in music production using Pro Tools from Berklee taught me the mechanics of how to produce, how to hear, and how to use the studio as an instrument. This foundational education allowed me to walk into any studio and, at minimum, know how to use the tools. The rest was on me, and that came less from a class and more from constant collaboration with artists who were objectively better than me.

My major taught me to think and, more importantly, taught me to think logically. Mathematics allowed me to break down components of the system in front of me to question the foundation of each step. Why are we working in a Western modality? Why are we using a microphone rather than a speaker? Why are we using our mouths to sing rather than our lips to buzz? My economics and finance background taught me to price myself appropriately, searching for the number the market would bear. Finance also taught me the time value of money and how to manage debt.

People coming into this need a foundational understanding of music. Coursework in music theory and some music history is a help. Some business foundation is necessary to understand the market. A basic corporate finance class is useful.

How has the field changed since you started?

Much as the world is a wholly different place—faster, less attentive, and perhaps higher quality—the field of a cappella has come of age. The quality has increased across the board. Trends occur at a faster rate. It is easier to get involved, easier to share the art, and easier to connect with groups from across the globe. YouTube and Facebook Live are bringing groups from Taiwan into rehearsals in Kansas and vice versa. ICCA finalists are studying finals of old day in and day out to analyze dos and don'ts and apply those to their own group.

When I was coming up, arrangements were harder to find, performances were harder to share, and a cappella was the nerdy thing to do on campus. I remember buying the House Jacks' arrangements of "Sound Check" and "The Star Spangled Banner" on a-cappella.com and e-mailing Deke back in the day to get an arrangement of "Zanzibar" by Billy Joel. Deke was more or less the center of the arranging world at the time and the non-Deke arrangements were few and far between. There was no A Cappella Arranging or the Heart of Vocal Harmony. Now there are "professional" arrangers at more or less every university and city center. We didn't have the Vocal Company offering internships every semester. We didn't have the Vocal Company offering full-time, benefits-bearing salary.

What are the technical aspects of your work that most people don't understand or know about?

Most of the difficulty surrounding my role is the management of a remote workforce. We are a bunch of musicians strewn about the globe. We communicate via text constantly using Slack. We have regular meetings via GoToMeeting videoconferencing. We keep track of tasks via Asana for project management. We share files via Google Drive in the cloud. We manage quotes via Quotient and manage books via Xero, all in the cloud. It's consistently trying, and the moments we spend at events or at Sled Dog Studios are breaths of fresh air.

What is the scope and range of what you do?

My role is somewhat unique in our field, though I suspect we'll see more of it soon. I stand not only as the vehicle for the service (i.e., recording engineer, mixing engineer, etc.) but also as the central talent curator for our portfolio of offerings. I am involved in the hiring and firing, growth, and management of our entire team. I handle vision calls with bands. I teach business directors to raise funds. I send payments for paychecks. I distribute music via online services. I teach.

What does a typical day or week look like for you?
A typical day for me starts at 6:00 a.m. I start with some light meditation or reading. I triathlon train for anywhere from thirty minutes to two hours depending on the day. After a shower, I make myself a Bulletproof Coffee and prep for the day.

My workday begins with mixing as it is one of my more difficult tasks. Sessions will have been prepped for me by my assistant (my mixer in training), so I can just bounce around great tracks with ease. I will try to get through a few Pomodoro rounds (twenty-five-minute complete focus rounds, with five-minute breaks) before getting into the rest of the world. Once I've expended some creative energy, I'll check e-mails and our internal chat system, Slack. This means following up on sales e-mails, checking in with projects and groups, and managing the team. Often I'll have calls scheduled from 10:00 a.m. to 2:00 p.m. with groups from around the world. Those calls will talk about where they are looking to go this year, what is getting in their way, and best practices. A quick lunch, usually checking in with the team and any issues they might be having, precedes either more calls or more mixing. After a long day of work, my evenings are spent winding down, checking where we're at and what we might have forgotten, and planning the next day.

My weekdays are normally spent mixing and managing, and I'm usually at shows or festivals on weekends. There are periods of my life where I spend two months away from my home and periods where I don't leave the studio for a whole week.

How many people would you guess are doing this professionally?
I would say there are exactly three sets of people doing "global a cappella entity management." There are maybe five hundred doing a cappella full-time inclusive of producers, singers, arrangers, and high school directors. But, that's just a guess.

What percentage of your income comes from this?

All of my income is derived from music. My income is broken up into the following:

- Active income: My active income is my labor pay. Any time I am teaching or producing, I am paid some rate for my hourly or daily work. If I don't work, I don't get paid. I follow economics 101 here. By nature, I have a limited supply. Let's say I aim to work forty hours in a week. If I am only demanded twenty hours per week, my rates are too high. If I lower them, demand for my time might meet my supply of time and I know that I've set my price correctly. Hopefully, my demand will increase with the quality of my work. Maybe then the world will demand sixty hours of my week, but I only have forty. So, I raise my rates. Now, out of the people looking to hire me, those willing to pay more will still demand my time, and those not willing will not. My demand and supply will balance again at forty hours. I can play this game forever, ideally constantly increasing the value of my time as my quality of my work and the size of my network increases.
- Passive income: Passive income is where stability and regularity exist. Examples of my passive income include the following:

  - Royalties/release revenue: For the once free tracks I've released, for collaborative works I've done with clients, and for fun projects I've cranked out with my team, we receive regular payments from iTunes, Spotify, and the like.
  - Gear rental: In order to produce a live concert, one needs gear: wireless microphones, speakers, and a mixing console. When you're starting out, you can rent equipment from a local vendor and have your client cover that expense. Over time you can save up and purchase some of the equipment, cutting out the middleman and starting a steady stream of rental income. At first this may be as irregular as your labor hours, as you only rent equipment when you are using it. But if you smartly package and market the equipment you acquire, you may find that rental stream growing more and more regular. A simple trick: Pretend everything you own is a rental. How would you want the gear presented to you if you were a rental client? Pretending

everything you own is a rental might mean racking your fancy new outboard compressor in a portable rack rather than a studio rack, and wiring the rack with a quick disconnect or a portable power strip. Maybe you package your band's mixing console in its very own case rather than as a package with your mics and ears. By separating the components, you can now rent the mics, the ears, and the console at any given time.

○ Real estate: My home is a mixed-use home/studio. When I say home/studio I don't mean home studio but home and studio. When designing the house, we built in room for a proper studio construction in an abnormally deep basement (twelve feet rather than the usual seven or eight). We have an external door to the basement so you don't have to bother the residents in order to enter and exit the studio. The basement has two studios, one large and one small, with room for bands to crash in the lounge and shower in a private bathroom. When artists come to the house, they pay me a day rate for use of the studio, regardless of what I might be doing that day. A friend of mine takes this one step further. After he spent so much money on making his studio a beautiful space for creativity and freedom, he realized that it looked like a great place for photo shoots. He called local modeling agencies and photographers and quickly lined up a steady stream of space rentals. Now he sips his morning tea while models are photographed in his studio across the glass, before heading into the studio later that day to mix.

What advice do you have for someone starting in this field?

My advice to someone starting in this field revolves around becoming a self-starter. What gets you ahead in the field of music is only that which you yourself have created. That creation may be a melody, it may be a lens through which another act is performing, or it may be a sonic imprint. But your advancement comes only from you and your sweat equity.

Steve Pressfield wrote a fantastic book called *The War of Art* that describes the struggles of daily creation. The central exercise of the work is simply sitting at the desk (or board, piano, or practice room) each day for a set period of time and letting yourself create. The creation does not need to be "great"; it hardly needs to be "good." It simply needs to happen. Our creativity is a muscle just like our biceps or our attention span. Many before me have seen great success from regular creation. At first our work will be imperfect. But after many repetitions, patterns will emerge and we will find our groove. This repetition could be a low-stakes activity, such as singing circle songs with your roommates each day. Or, preferably in my opinion, this repetition could have some pressure attached to it.

Nick Girard started a "Free Track Tuesdays" program when he was starting Overboard. Each week, the band would arrange, record, edit, mix, master, and release a track to the world completely for free. He did this for fifty-two weeks. When I started Sled Dog, my buddies and I went through this exact process (though we took Fridays). The "free track" idea has many purposes.

1. There is an external pressure to create.
2. Each "track" you release hones your skill set a little bit more.
3. People notice, and connections build quickly.
4. A portfolio is built before you know it, and work opportunities find their way to you.

There is an external pressure to create: By committing to some regular, recurring release, you promise the world that you will release X material every Y time periods. Your commitment to your release schedule will hold you accountable for not trying or not finishing. When you don't release, the world will beckon.

You hone your craft: When we did Free Track Fridays, we actively chose a varied repertoire: Jessie J one week, Bublé the next, a Christmas tune to follow, and an AWOL Nation track after that. It becomes a genre study. Maybe one week we recorded everything individually and edited the parts in Auto-Tune the way Bill Hare used to do it. Maybe the following week we recorded parts in a group fashion and did the individual editing in Melodyne the way Dave Sperandio and Ed Boyer do it. Maybe one week we arrange the song TTBB, but the next SSAA. It becomes a technique study.

People notice, and connections build quickly: The more collaborative this effort can be, the better. Your first iteration might be just you as you find your footing. The next iteration might be you and a friend. As you find your footing, you may start including others, even those from places you would never have imagined. Only seven weeks into our Free Track Friday releases, we posted a call for collaborators on CASA's Facebook group. We were doing a Tom Anderson arrangement of Michael Bublé's "Sway." Tom gave us the vocal percussion. We had Andrew DeLong, a Hyannis Sound alumnus, commit to the lead. Within hours, the group erupted with excitement. We had commitments ranging from LA to Singapore. On a whim, we contacted Jo Eteson of the world-famous Swingle Singers. At that point, I had only met Jo after a Swingles performance in Boston. I'm not sure she would have remembered me or have had any reason to give me the time of day. Jo is known (among other talents) for her vocal violin, so we asked her to cover a beautiful line in the middle of "Sway." Mind you, we were in Rochester, New York, and Jo was in London. She excitedly replied and recorded her part that day, on the back of a train.

A portfolio is built before you know it, and work opportunities find their way to you. In music, you are only as good as your portfolio (or your audition if you make it that far without one). You may have gone to school for music or production, but if you can't perform, you are no use to the band, the artist, or the producer who is searching for you. By committing to a regular, recurring release of material, your portfolio grows with each release. The first releases will be rough, but they will be indicative of the height of your capability. As you release more, your portfolio will not only grow bigger but also grow better. You will be surprised at how quickly opportunities present themselves. Here are some examples:

- "Who arranged that track? I loved it and want to perform it with my group!"
- "Did you do the mixing on this one? I loved what you did with the wubwubs. Would you be willing to mix this track for our next album?"
- "That beatboxer is amazing! Our group is looking for a beatboxer!"

In what ways do you see this field growing or changing in the future?
I believe we will see more of the moments of change that we have seen: an expansion from the collegiate realm outward. We just saw a middle school group beat college-age contestants at a festival. A profes-

sionally led high school group won a competition across scholastic ages. There is now an all-ages competition with twenty-five thousand dollars on the line by Varsity Vocals.

In the postcollegiate realm, we are seeing more pop culture crossover: a cappella groups on TV shows, a cappella soundtracks to commercials, and a cappella–nut family members in movies. The pervasiveness of a cappella will only grow.

Video has continued to be a hotbed for innovation in the field. We see more honest musical displays of protest music, love songs, and everything in between. Groups in stairwells are getting two million views. Religious music videos are clearing three thousand views easy. I believe Facebook Live is the next spark. More live-streamed concerts, rehearsal check-ins, and tour streams will grow quickly.

Finally, I do believe the market for a cappella education is in its infancy. Camp A Cappella has become an enormous offering, bringing in hundreds of campers each year. Graduates of A Cappella Academy are taking over the a cappella world. Groups are demanding master classes and lessons more and more. Importantly, universities and high schools are beginning to see the return on investment of investing in a cappella, meaning a huge growth market is available for educators.

FINAL THOUGHT: "HOW TO BREAK INTO THE MUSIC BUSINESS"

Hopefully these various profiles give you an insight into the various options within the field of a cappella. There are a few more things to know about this industry:

- The community is a relatively small and rather tight-knit one. Most people know most other people, and with very rare exception everyone gets along well and is excited to cross paths at events, festivals, and concerts.
- People find themselves working together on various projects (I have worked with all of the people above, many more than once, and many over several years). The nature of various projects usually results in the need to work with different individuals and groups in different settings.

- To this end, reputation is paramount. You must be kind, responsible, responsive, forthright, and as they say, "play nicely with others." You will start unknown with only a couple of contacts, but before long your name and reputation will spread if you do good work and your peers had a good experience.
- Moreover, the people who will get the most requests for future work are those who work hard. Most of the people above are freelancers, self-employed, and rely on getting each job done well to attract future work. Not replying to e-mails because it's the weekend, turning off your phone for a day, and only working eight hours are not generally a good idea unless you have a personal emergency, because if there's a crisis or rush, people may be relying on you and you don't want to be the one to drop the ball.

None of this is meant to scare you away, but it's important to know the truth about working in the twenty-first century. In the end, your clients don't care how hard it was for you or what unexpected hurdles arose; they just need the product, whether it's a major movie studio or the local college group.

I wrote a blog a couple years ago that was addressed to people who ask me, not infrequently, how to get into the a cappella industry. My somewhat snarky reply was along the lines of, "If you have to ask, you'll never know." It wasn't meant to dissuade anyone but rather to make it clear that the kind of person who will thrive in this environment is someone who will just dive in and make things happen, rather than wait for the phone to ring. I'll end this chapter by including this blog post below, with the caveat that if you picked up this book and read this far you're already on the right path, so I don't intend the full weight of these words to land on your shoulders.

How to Break Into the Music Business

Posted 8/25/2014

"Dear Deke,

I would really like to break into the music business, perhaps writing music for television and film, or theater. How can I do that?"

Dear Reader,

First of all, let me make something clear: there are 1,000 eager people for every music job, especially something as exciting as writing music for film. Basically, it's never gonna happen for you. Sorry about that. Best of luck in the future.

Sincerely, Deke

. . . still reading? Well, okay, so you're not daunted by impossible odds. Good. That's an important first step: knowing you'll likely never reach your goal. Gotta weed out the weak of heart, you understand.

Great! So you're still on board. Perfecto. Here's the deal: I can guarantee if you work impossibly hard for the next decade ("10,000 hours" till you reach excellence, according to Malcolm Gladwell), you will eventually land a piece of yours in a movie. However, looking at how the business is working nowadays, I do have some bad news: you'll likely never get paid. Young filmmakers will be drawn to you and your work, which you produce for free for ten years as you gain competence and get to know the business, but alas movies will increasingly be distributed online for free (aka stolen), so the amount of money will be reduced to a trickle and you'll likely not be paid more than expenses. So very sorry, but congrats on your success nonetheless!

Sincerely, Deke

. . . still interested? Well then, you might have the stomach for the current music industry. You are willing to work tirelessly for a decade, and even once you've arrived, you'll likely not make much, if any, money. Well, then, welcome to the music industry! Pull up a chair, sit down, let's get to work.

Now, I can hear some of you grumbling, "That's unrealistic, John Williams and Randy Newman make money, bla, bla, bla . . ." Yup, they do. And they're still alive, so I think Spielberg and Pixar will be calling them before they call you. Moreover, look at the scenario above: working tirelessly for no money seems like something almost no one would do, right? But you can imagine someone that would, can't you? Someone incredibly driven, regardless of level of success. Someone who stays up all night obsessing over the ways in which the Alex North soundtrack to *2001* would have been superior, someone who turns off the sound to *Midnight Cowboy* and rewrites the score for the entire movie. Sounds crazy, right?

But someone like that does exist. And that's your competition.

My money's on them.

Here's the point I'm trying to make in this blog: making music as a career sounds wonderful, fun, better than working in a bank; you can walk around in your pajamas all day, fame, fortune, love, happiness. As a result, it's a huge magnet. Just about everyone is interested in doing it, and many people who don't really know what they want to do think it sounds much better than anything else so they study music and tell their families they want to be musicians.

That's really nice, but they're about to be crushed by the giant steam-roller of reality, because they don't really want to be musicians. They just want all of the things musicians have (see list above).

Lots of people want to be musicians, but here's the fact: you don't choose to be a musician. It chooses you.

That's right: you wake up with music in your head. You think about music all the time. You are distracted in public places by the quiet background music. You get angry when someone uses a b6 (flat 6) chord when it really should have been a iv (minor 4).

And the grim reality: you'll make music no matter what, even if you don't get paid, even if no one listens, because you have to. You've always had to.

Which is why I know when I get a note from someone "wanting to break into the music business" I know they'll fail. Because they think it's a career option.

Do you want to know what kind of letter I get from someone I know will be successful? The kind that starts with a flurry of excited statements drilling down to a focused question about how to create a variable pitch snare without using so much lip pressure, or why more people don't listen to the Todd Rundgren *A Cappella* album because it's great for the following seventeen reasons, and so on. These people aren't asking how to get started because they've already started, and they don't really care if I think they can make it in the business because they're going to do it anyway. Their excitement is palpable, which will fuel them into the future, damn the torpedoes; let's go tilt at another windmill.

My money's on them.

The best music advice I can give was offered to me, unsolicited, as a high schooler in the Tanglewood Young Artist Vocal Program: "If you can see yourself doing anything other than music as a career, do that. You can always have music in your life, and you won't have to worry about anyone telling you when or how to make music. Fact is, there will always be someone who will stay up later, get up earlier, do the job for less money than you. However, if nothing I say will dissuade you, well, then, welcome to the club."

That's basically how it works. There are flukes: the preternaturally talented, the lucky savant . . . but I'm guessing if you're writing me as a college grad, those trains have left the station. What is it they say about Berklee graduates? The successful ones are those who never graduate because they're already signed or off on tour? It's kinda like that. Or, if you do graduate, you've got a shovel in hand, already furiously digging and laying your own foundation.

So, in the future, please don't ask me how to break into the music business. I wish you the best, and hate to be the bearer of bad news. To paraphrase Louis Armstrong when asked the definition of jazz, "If you have to ask, you'll never know."

One last thought, because I don't want you to leave this section of the book discouraged: if you love a cappella, let that love motivate you. In college I would stay up late nights thinking about how to create the perfect arrangement for the Beelzebubs, and this is how successful people push themselves to the next level and discover great things, be it a football coach mapping out new football plays or a scientist searching for a new hypothesis. Greatness is not bestowed upon people; it comes as a result of lengthy, focused work, which itself is driven by passion.

If you have purchased this book, if you're reading these words right now, you must have a love of a cappella and a passion for vocal music. When you're discouraged, when you're exhausted, or when you're not sure what to do next, or how to make your career grow, return to that passion. Remember how it feels when you lock harmonies with others, how it feels when you see your name at the top of an arrangement or in a program, how it feels when you hear the cheers of the audience, or when a young audience member comes up to you after a performance and tells you she is going to join choir because you inspired her.

All of us have difficult days, dark days, times when we question ourselves. However, a cappella is as old as human culture and is deeply ingrained in who we are and how we connect with other people artistically. When you're stuck, return to this well: listen to a recording that you love, or watch a video that inspires you. Reconnect with your passion. Remember who you are and what you bring to music, how you are different, and how your unique set of experiences, taste, knowledge, and craft creates a sound and style like no one else's.

And when you think about it, the surface has only been scratched. Where's that great reggae a cappella group? Why is there no contemporary a cappella group in Hawaii? How can it be that no one has integrated a cappella into club DJing or created a dance troupe that has its own exploratory vocal ensemble providing all the music?[1] If you think it has all been done before, you're completely wrong. Almost none of it has been done. It was only a couple years ago that *The Sing-Off* launched Home Free on a career of being the first country contemporary a cappella group. Pick a style; I can almost assure you no one is doing it a cappella. Pick a region, and it's quite likely it doesn't have a professional group regularly playing the clubs and colleges.

We are right now at the very beginning of a huge Renaissance in vocal music, and you're poised to make your mark and bring something new into this world that has never existed before, with so very much to choose from. Carpe diem.

NOTE

1. The dance troupe ISO built a performance around songs by the Bobs and the two toured together, but that was fifteen years ago and it hasn't happened since.

WHY

The Reason A Cappella Matters

⓲

HARMONY THROUGH HARMONY

For all of human history, singing was a central part of every culture around the globe. People sang during the holidays, at parties, at sporting events, at state fairs, after a meal when friends came to visit, at work (singing while working extended through the Industrial Revolution when many companies had company songs), in the local pub, and so on. From kindergarten through college everyone sang. Everyone knew several songs from their alma mater, including their school song, fight songs, and the like.

And then everything changed.

The first step was the invention of recorded music. It used to be if you wanted music, you made music. Christmas carols? Start singing. Music after dinner? Gather around the living room and make it yourself. Concerts still happened, of course, but almost all of every day was without music. Recorded music would seem to be a good thing, as it brought music to us everywhere. However, the ubiquity of music meant music was no longer something in which we as a people needed to actively participate. John Philip Sousa, the famous American composer, stated, "I foresee a marked deterioration in American music and a host of other injuries to music in its artistic manifestations, by virtue—or rather by vice—of the multiplication of the various music-reproducing machines." He was correct.

The promulgation of recorded music made each day more melodious, filling our stores, commutes, and elevators with sound that soothed us and lifted our moods, but there was a terrible side effect: music making was no longer seen as something that everyone needed to do. The specialization and focus of skills and labor that came from the Industrial Revolution and modern economy has led to a great increase in output, but the act of music making was not a product to be maximized in quantity and quality; it is an essential part of our biological being. Like birds, crickets, and whales, music is a part of us—not only experiencing music but also making music. Tens of thousands of years of human evolution included singing, and then over the last century the experience disappears for most people after a couple of years of grade school, with only the most driven and talented pursuing it; everyone else stops singing.

The result of this is devastating, as the combination of lack of experience and a culture that expects perfection from music is that a significant percentage of Americans believe they "can't sing" or are "tone deaf," a physiological condition that indicates the inability to differentiate different pitches. People can most certainly differentiate pitches and in fact are quick to judge the imperfections in themselves and others when singing, a situation made worse by shows like *American Idol* that relish mocking inexperienced singers (after spending all day building them up behind the scenes so they believe they're great, only to roll the cameras when they have their egos punctured by celebrity judges).

The fact is that most people would be very happy with their singing level if they only did it more often. The analogy I use when explaining this to self-assessed tone-deaf individuals is that of basketball: "If you had never or rarely picked up a basketball, how good do you think you'd be at shooting free throws? The human voice is a muscle, and matching pitch is something almost every person on this planet can do well; it just takes practice. You may not be Michael Jordan or Steph Curry, but that doesn't mean you can't have fun shooting hoops with friends." Sadly, whereas most people can pass by a schoolyard on a weekend and see some forty-year-olds playing two-on-two and think nothing of it, if they saw the same people at the local farmers' market singing as a quartet, they'd be quick to judge them. We don't expect perfection from amateur chefs, but for some reason when it comes to music everyone's an expert and quick to point out the slightest flaws.

And what of the flaws? A generation ago imperfection was baked into music. The best-selling jazz album of all time, Miles Davis's *Kind of Blue*, has mistakes in it: sloppy notes that add to the character of the recording because you can hear the humanity in it, and more importantly appreciate his understanding that there are things more important than polish in music. Moreover, some of the greatest music ever recorded is out of tune, by today's exacting standards. Motown, for instance, is full of passion, energy, personality, and soul, but if those songs were being recorded in a studio today, they would almost certainly be corrected and tuned, buffed to a high sheen. Live Auto-Tune is even used onstage to correct pitches as celebrities sing; or even more often, when you see a lot of dancing onstage, you're actually hearing a studio recording as the star gamely lip-syncs to her own voice. The result of all of this careful manipulation is that our standards have become so exacting that even the brightest stars are incapable of achieving them without digital manipulation and recorded playback. That's right: even live music often isn't live. Sousa was right: the greatest injury to music by the introduction of recordings is that now artistic manifestation often cannot occur without it.

Okay, so music is more polished now; how exactly is that a problem? The greatest loss to our society is the fact that the act of making music is something we long to do. It is a part of our biology to the extent that even the incorrectly self-professed tone-deaf members of our society sing in the shower, sing along with the radio in the car when no one is listening, and occasionally get drunk and sing karaoke. Their desire remains, a biological instinct that can't be dampened; it can only be hidden, revealed primarily when they are alone. People dream of being singers, of being rock stars—it is one of the most popular fantasy careers in the world. If only they realized they are singers already; they just need a little more experience.

Beyond the loss to the individual, a lack of communal music making has been a loss to society. People go home at the end of a long day of work and collapse in front of a screen—television or computer—and wonder why they feel so disconnected. The incredible experience of singing together is the antidote to loneliness, to disaffection, and to not knowing your neighbors. Politically we live in a time of great divide, and yet if people sang together they not only would experience the joy of creating something great communally but also would come to learn the true value of diversity.

When I joined the Tufts Beelzebubs, I was convinced every member was a musical genius and was shocked when I learned most couldn't read music. My reaction was great frustration when I started music directing: Why couldn't we only take musicians and make the group musically great? It took time for me to realize that the very diverse group of people—different backgrounds, races, experiences, and perspectives—was what made the group compelling. Just as you need high voices and low voices, you also need powerful voices and soft voices. The coming together of all of us—frat boys, computer programmers, future lawyers, jocks, theater nerds, and the like—made for a better group. No one learned and grew more than I did during those years. I learned how to understand and respect their differences, how to discuss, how to listen, and how to compromise. We needed each other, as we brought different skills to the group, and learning how to maximize our potential prepared me for the life I have today.

If only everyone had the same experience! To sing in a group with people of different religions, races, and backgrounds is to realize their value and to see them as human, just like you. This doesn't mean there won't be differences, but the vilification of others from behind a screen is rapidly eroded when you're met instead with a smiling face. Perhaps the greatest skill that is learned when singing harmony isn't the singing itself but the act of listening, to others and to the combined sound. Through listening we learn how to modify our own voices to meld with others and learn to appreciate the immense beauty that is within those different from us.

There were conflicts a hundred years ago and before, most certainly, but what existed was greater local cohesion and sense of community. As communities become more diverse there is a greater need for integration and connection, and yet people increasingly don't know their neighbors as so much of our lives can be lived impersonally, from shopping to telecommuting. Soon we'll have driverless cars and stores in which there's no need to check out as everything in your cart will be scanned automatically as you exit the door, and we'll see even fewer people during our day. We will increasingly need experiences and opportunities to connect with others, to express ourselves, and to be heard. Vocal harmony is the most powerful way in which this can be achieved, and unlike team sports, if you do it right, you win every single time.

"Harmony through harmony" is my life's work for a very specific reason: it changes lives. It has been shown that students who sing and participate in music during school have higher grades, stay in school longer, are less depressed, are more productive, and so on. Music has also been linked to higher test scores, increased linguistic and special skills, and higher IQ. I'm the first to be skeptical of studies, of which there are many and almost anything seemingly can be proven, but I do know that for myself, and so many others I have met, music making has in many different ways saved their lives and made it far richer.

What we are seeing in our culture right now is a course correction, a return to a greater level of interest in a cappella and vocal harmony after so many decades in which singing has diminished. Perhaps people are yearning for the sense of humanity that comes from the sound of voices singing together after so much mechanization and programming in music, as live instruments have given way to synthesizers and drum loops, and vocals have been tuned to the point of sounding robotic. Perhaps vocal harmony fundamentally taps into something deep inside our brains, our biology, that reminds us what it is to be human and what it means to be a part of a community, a society, in which we are all important, necessary, and valued, and in which together we are able to create something more beautiful than we ever could alone; and as such we reaffirm the importance of community and harmony.

I know it does in me.

⑲

CONCLUSION

This book should be only the very beginning of your journey as an a cappella musician, whether casual or professional. As the days turn to months and months turn to years, the words in this book should be augmented by, and in some cases supplanted by, additional information found outside these pages. The groups mentioned within will release new albums; the various careers within will morph as society and technology grow and change. The human voice is eternal, but how it is used will change, be it a result of new styles of music on the radio that inspire new vocal techniques or the result of new technologies that further push the boundaries of recording, live looping, and the like.

I hope you take these words and concepts as a first step and use them to help you find your own path. Perhaps you're a student in school and looking to join and eventually direct a group. Perhaps you're a recent grad who is moving to a region without a group and you'd like to start one. Perhaps your children all just left the house and you're looking for a new activity, hoping to start singing again after a long break. Whoever you are and whatever you'd like to do, I hope this book inspires you not only to follow in the footsteps of the many mentioned within but also, when appropriate, to forge your own paths. Most of the careers in these pages didn't exist a couple of dozen years ago, nor did most of the groups. A cappella is the oldest music, but the current sound and direction are new, and the way we keep it relevant is by continuing to grow, change, and adapt to new styles, new structures, new formations, and new partnerships with other arts such as dance, body percussion, theater, and so on.

Learn, listen, explore, and create. That's exactly what everyone else has done. There are no rules, and the potential for new sounds is immense; the potential for this community to grow is enormous. We're just getting started. Then, when I update this book in a few years, you may find yourself listed in these pages, an inspiration to the next generation of singers. If that seems far fetched, let me assure you that the people you've read about are just like you: singers who love harmony and want to create music with others and make the world a better, more harmonious place. Most everyone else on the planet wants to sing, wants to feel connected to others, and wants the immense joy that comes from vocal harmony; they just don't realize it yet. For each person you wake up, each person you convince to sing, you'll have changed a life in a profound, immeasurable way.

Theirs, and yours.

APPENDIX

A Cappella Festivals around the World

Courtesy of the Vocal Blog (Germany)

AFRICA

August

Namibia International Vocal Festival, Windhoek (Namibia)
http://www.facebook.com

ASIA

March

Hong Kong International A Cappella Festival, Hong Kong
http://acappella.hkfyg.org.hk
Youth Vocal Music Fest, Singapore
http://www.a-cappella.org.sg

April

FAN—Festival of A Cappella Nagoya (Japan)
http://fan.go2.jp
Spring Vocal Festival, Taibei (Taiwan)
http://www.tcmc.org.tw

June

Yamanashi A Cappella Summit, Yamanashi (Japan)
https://www.facebook.com/events

July

National A Cappella Championships, Singapore
http://www.a-cappella.org.sg
Shanghai A Cappella Festival (China)
http://www.vocalasia.com

August

Kanazawa A Cappella Town, Kanazawa (Japan)
http://www.nihon-kankou.or.jp.e.wp.hp.transer.com
Vocal Asia Festival (location moves each year)
http://www.vocalasia.com

October

A Cappella Society's International A Cappella Festival, Singapore
http://www.a-cappella.org.sg
Taiwan International Contemporary A Cappella Festival, Taibei
(Taiwan)
festival.tcmc.org.tw

November

Asia A Cappella Festival, Hong Kong
http://www.cashk.org

AUSTRALIA

May

Get Vocal—Melbourne Vocal Music Festival
http://www.vocalaustralia.com

July

Festival of Voices in Tasmania
https://festivalofvoices.com

EUROPE

January

Lievekamp A Cappella Evening, Oss (the Netherlands)
http://www.lievekamp.nl
London A Cappella Festival (UK)
http://www.londonacappellafestival.co.uk
VocCologne, Köln (Germany)
http://voccologne.hfmt-koeln.de

February

BALK Festival Oost, Ulft (the Netherlands)
https://balkfestivaloost.wordpress.com
International Gdansk Choral Festival (Poland)
http://www.gdanskfestival.pl

March

A Cappella Rorschach (Switzerland)
http://www.acappella-rorschach.ch
EverySing! Festival, Ville de Montlouis-sur-Loire (France)
http://www.festival-everysing.fr

Total Choral—Pop/Jazz Choir Festival, Berlin (Germany)
http://www.totalchoral.de
The Voice Festival (UK)
http://www.thevoicefestival.co.uk

April

A Cappella Woche Hannover (Germany)
http://www.acappellawoche.com
Internationaler Chorwettbewerb and Festival, Bad Ischl (Austria)
http://www.chorwettbewerb.at
Prague Aca Fest 2013 (Czechoslovakia)
http://www.pragueacappellafestival.cz

May

Aarhus Vocal Festival 2013 (Denmark)
http://www.aavf.dk
A Cappella Festival Appenzell (Switzerland)
http://www.acappella-appenzell.ch
Festival für Vokalmusik Leipzig (Germany)
http://www.a-cappella-festival.de
Stimmakrobaten Festival (Germany)
http://www.stimmakrobaten.de
Voxon A Cappella Festival, Bleiburg (Austria)
http://www.voxon-festival.com
Wetterauer Musik Sommer Akademie—Festivokal (Germany)
http://www.festivokal.de

June

Chortreffen Ibbenbüren (Germany)
http://www.chortreffen.com
Hofkonzerte—A Cappella, Winterthur (Switzerland)
http://www.obertor.ch
Odense Vokal Festival, Odense (Denmark)
http://www.odensevokalfestival.dk

Sing A Cappella Festival and Workshop Day (UK)
  http://www.singacappella.org
Solevoci A-Cappella International Contest and Festival,
  Varese (Italy)
  http://www.solevocifestival.it
Tampere Vocal Music Festival and Competition (Finland)
  http://tamperemusicfestivals.fi/vocal/en
Vocaal Festival Amusing Hengelo (the Netherlands)
  http://www.amusing-hengelo.nl

July

Crest Jazz Vocal Festival, Crest (France)
  http://www.crestjazzvocal.com
vokal total, 14th International A Cappella Competition, Graz (Austria)
  http://www.vokal.at

August

Nuits des choeurs/Stemmen onder de Sterren, Braine-l'Alleud
  (Belgium)
  http://www.nuitdeschoeurs.be
Ohrid Choir Festival (Macedonia)
  http://www.ohridchoirfestival.com
Vocal Pop and Jazz Days, Oberhausen (Germany)
  http://www.vpjd.nl
XXI Choralies, Vaison-la-Romaine (France)
  http://www.choralies.fr

September

Acappellica, Hamburg (Germany)
  http://www.acappellica.de
BerVokal—A Cappella Pop Festival, Berlin (Germany)
  http://www.bervokal.de
chor.com, Dortmund (Germany)
  http://www.chor.com

sangeslust, Bayreuth (Germany)
   http://www.sangeslust.com
Zoom+ Festival, Trnava (Slovakia)
   http://www.zoomplus.sk

October

Festival Espoochor, Espoo (Finland)
   http://www.festivals.fi
Fool Moon International A Cappella Festival (Hungary)
   http://acappella.hu
Voice Mania, Vienna (Austria)
   http://www.voicemania.at

November

BALK Top Festival, Rotterdam (the Netherlands)
   http://www.balknet.nl
Polyfollia International Summer Festival, Saint-Lo (France)
   http://www.polyfollia.org
Tonart-Festival Ilmenau (Germany)
   http://www.tonart-festival.de
Vokal Total, Munich (Germany)
   http://www.spectaculum-mundi.de

December

Stemvork Festival, Torhout (Belgium)
   http://www.stemvork.eu

NORTH AMERICA

Intensive Professional Development Opportunities

The National A Cappella Convention, late April
http://acappellaconvention.com

Over the course of two days, the A Cappella Educators Association (AEA) offers this event that features over forty different interest sessions as well as the National High School Championship, and showcases for middle school, high school, and collegiate groups. This official AEA event is the fastest-growing professional development and networking opportunity.

Camp A Cappella, late June
http://campacappella.com
This fully immersive, weeklong summer camp allows educators to be participants in an a cappella group and learn techniques from Deke Sharon and other innovative a cappella educators, professional performers, and audio specialists.

Next Level Workshops by the Vocal Company, June/July
http://thevocalcompany.com/next-level
Four different sessions are offered on topics such as arranging, directing, production, and mixing. Each session lasts one week and serves as a wonderful hands-on learning opportunity for any level of experience.

Kettering National High School A Cappella Festival, mid-November
http://ketteringacafest.com
Currently the nation's largest a cappella festival, with sixty-five to seventy-five attending groups, this event features headliners from across the country, along with performance opportunities and several interest sessions.

Major Festivals and Other Events

January

International Championship of Collegiate A Cappella and International Championship of High School A Cappella (various locations; January–April)
http://varsityvocals.com
N.E. Voices, Wilmington, Massachusetts
http://ne-voices.com

February

Bend A Cappella Festival, Bend, Oregon
http://bendacappellafestival.com
Los Angeles A Cappella Festival, Los Angeles
http://www.la-af.com
Mile High Vocal Jam, Denver
http://mhvj.org
Voices in Harmony, Lexington, Kentucky
http://voicesinharmony.net

March

Nordonia A Cappella Festival, Nordonia, Ohio
http://www.nordoniachoirs.com/acappella-festival.html
SheSings, Berkeley, California
http://www.womensacappella.org/shesings
Texas A Cappella Celebration, San Antonio
http://acappellacelebration.com

April

Boston Sings (BOSS), Boston
http://bostonsings.com
Montreacappella, Montreal, Quebec, Canada
http://www.mtlacappella.com
Total Vocal, New York City
http://www.dciny.org
VoiceJam, Fayetteville, Arkansas
http://waltonartscenter.org/voicejam

May

Harmony Sweepstakes Finals, San Rafael, California
http://www.harmony-sweepstakes.com
Highlands A Cappella Festival, Northern Highlands, New Jersey
http://www.northernhighlands.org

International Championship of Collegiate A Cappella and International Championship of High School A Cappella, finals, New York City
http://varsityvocals.com
Sing! Toronto, Toronto
http://torontovocalartsfestival.com

June

Camp Acappella, Wright State University, Dayton, Ohio
http://www.campacappella.com

July

A Cappella University, Kenosha, Wisconsin
http://www.acappellauni.com
Re-Mix Vocal Academy, Brigham Young University, Provo, Utah

August

AcappellaFest, Chicago
http://acappellafest.com
ReCALibrate, Philadelphia
http://acappellaleague.org

October

Haunted Harmonies, Salem, Massachusetts
http://www.hauntedharmonies.com

November

The Betsy A Cappella Festival, Miami
http://www.thebetsyacappella.com
SoJam, Raleigh, North Carolina
http://sojam.net

BARBERSHOP EVENTS THROUGHOUT
THE YEAR WORLDWIDE

BABS (British Association of Barbershop Singers)
http://sing2017.com
Barbershop Harmony Society Prelims and Internationals, March–
July (US)
http://www.barbershop.org/all-conventions
BinG (Barbershop in Germany) world mixed A Cappella contest
http://www.barbershop-in-germany.de
Harmony Incorporated, May–September (Canada, US)
http://www.harmonyinc.org/area-contests.html
Holland Harmony
https://hollandharmony.dse.nl
LABBS (Ladies Association of British Barbershop Singers)
https://www.labbs.org.uk/convention
Pan Pacific Convention (Australia)
https://www.barbershopconvention.com.au
SABS (Spanish Association of Barbershop Singers; Spain)
http://www.sabs.es/cm2
SNOBS (Society of Nordic Barbershop Singers)
https://www.facebook.com/snobs.bbs
Sweet Adelines International, March–October
https://sweetadelines.com/competitionconvention
World European Convention
http://ebc.labbs.org.uk

FURTHER READING

A Cappella Books and Resources

McDonald, Brody, and Deke Sharon. *A Cappella Pop: A Complete Guide to Contemporary A Cappella Singing*. Van Nuys, CA: Alfred Music, 2012.

Sharon, Deke. *The Heart of Vocal Harmony: Emotional Expression in Group Singing*. Milwaukee, WI: Hal Leonard, 2016.

Sharon, Deke, and Dylan Bell. *A Cappella Arranging*. Milwaukee, WI: Hal Leonard, 2012.

Sharon, Deke, Ben Spalding, and Brody McDonald. *A Cappella*. Van Nuys, CA: Alfred Music, 2015.

INDEX

abdominal muscles, 40–41, *41–42*

abduction, 44

aboriginal tribes, xvii

Acappella, 14, 319

A Cappella, 274

A Cappella Academy, 316

A Cappella Educators Association. *See* AEA

a cappella groups: anatomy of, 55–60; business manager of, 58, 216; health of, 81–83; logistics of, 57–59; members of, 59–60; musical components of, 55–57; music director/conductor of, 58; new group production, 284–92; placing singers in, 90; president of, 58–59; scholastic group directing, 266–70; songs known well in rehearsals, 136; stage configurations, 59–60

A Cappella Radio International, 29

A Cappella Summit, 27–28

A Cappella Video Awards. *See* AVAs

A Cappella Vocal Band (AVB), 8

A Cappella Warmups for Pop and Jazz Choirs, 134

A Cappella Web Design, 303–6

AcaWest, 31

accountant, 59

ACDA. *See* American Choral Directors' Association

acid reflux, 66

acne, 67

acoustic measurement software, 256

AcoUstiKats, 285, 287

active income, 312

adaptability, 225

ADD/ADHD medication, 67

administration, 307–16

adrenaline, 71, 218

advertising, 205, 214

advice, career: for administration, 313–14; for arranging, 277; for coaching, 282; for editing, 247–48; for event production and promotion, 299; for live sound engineering, 230; for local and regional performing, 210; for mastering, 259–60; for mixing, 251; for national and international touring, 219; for new group production, 291–92; for producing recordings, 263; for professional holiday caroling, 226; for scholastic group directing, 269–70; for session singing, 237; for singing and producing parts recordings, 242; for theme park performing, 223; for video production, 302; for web design, 306

AEA (A Cappella Educators Association), 31, 281, 291–92, 339

Africa, xvii, 19

agents, 191

Ahuja, Roopak, 308

airflow, 42, 47

air pressure, 42

albums, 218, 261, 295

alcohol, 76

alignment, 62, 73, 74

All 4 One, 15

Allegiance, 13

Allen, Debbie, 21

allergies, 66, 72

alumni, collegiate a cappella, 185–86

alveoli, 38

Amazon, 219

American Choral Directors' Association (ACDA), 33, 267, 292

American Idol, 326

American Sound Machine, 220

amplification, 49–51, 56, 79, 89, 141, 161

amplitude, 127, 142, *142*

amplitude response, in microphones, 148–52, *150*, 152

analog hardware, 255

Anderson, Tom, 270–77, 315

animal sounds, 18

animation, 300

ANS. *See* autonomic nervous system

Antares, 159

anxiety, 70–71

APCA. *See* Association for the Promotion of Campus Activities

apple cider vinegar, 66–67

Apple Music, 261

archiving, in mastering, 258

"Are You Gonna Be My Girl," 116

Armstrong, Louis, 92, 320

ARORA, 172, 274

arranging, xiii, 13, 23–24, 262; career, 270–77; complexity of, 225; horn section, 95; of the House Jacks, 310; income, 276; legal aspect of, 276; process of, 216; publishing of, 270; rehearsals and, 139–40; techniques, 55; transcription and, 273; unique, 90; violins, 97; vocal percussion, 117

articulation, 134, 279

articulation system, 37, 52–54

Arts House, 17

arytenoid cartilage, 45, *46*

assessment, of rehearsals, 136

Association for the Promotion of Campus Activities (APCA), 289

Atherton, Matt, 303–6

Atlantic Records, xii, 29–30, 212, 214, 219

attention spans, in rehearsals, 135

audience, 21, 224; appreciation from, 222; assessment of, 225; cheers of, 321; engineers and, 174, 176;

feedback from, 83; identity and, 210; virtual, 299; women in, 19
audio engineering. *See* engineering
auditions, 197, 257, 308
auditory illusion, vocal percussion and, 109
autonomic nervous system (ANS), 71
Auto-Tune, 159, 160, 220, 242–43, 327
AVAs (A Cappella Video Awards), 33
AVB. *See* A Cappella Vocal Band
Az Yet, 15

Bach, Johann Sebastian, 128
the Backbeats, 120
bagpipes, 99
Ball in the House, 26, 205
Bandersnatchers, 204
Barberpole Cat, 12
barbershop events worldwide, 342
Barbershop Harmony Foundation, 29
Barbershop Harmony Society, 6, 241
Barbershop Polecat, 27
barbershop quartet, 6, 12, 234
Barbershop Quartet, 12
Barden Bellas, 239
Basix, 251
bass, 55–56, 96, *108*, 128, 166
BBC, 32
Beach Boys, 271
beatboxing. *See* vocal percussion
the Beatles, 12, 90, 262
beats per minutes (bpm), 123
beauty, 328
Beck, John, 304
"Bed of Nails," 266
Bee Gees, 112
Beelzebub University, 18
Bennett, Tony, 12

Berklee Online, 309
Best of College A Cappella (BOCA), 25, 28
beta-blockers, 235
bias, in history, 10
bidirectional pattern, 150
big picture thinking, in rehearsals, 140
Biz Markie, 103
Björk, 103
"Blackbird," 14
"Black Horse and a Cherry Tree," 114
Blake, Gene, 13
the Blenders, 26
blogs, 260, 305
blues, 5, 48
bluetooth devices, 75
the Bobs, 11, 12, 218, 274, 300, 321*n*1
BOCA. *See Best of College A Cappella*
body percussion, 332. *See also* vocal percussion
"Bohemian Rhapsody," 13
bongos, in vocal percussion, *108*
Borge, Victor, 95
Bossa nova, 115, *115*
Boyer, Ed, 261–64
Boyle's law, 38
Boyz II Men, 15, 271, 274, 284, 308
bpm. *See* beats per minutes
brain, 70, 91
Bram, Ben, 120
branding, 303
"Breakeven," 120
breakups, 206
breathing, 56; control of, 43, 108, *107–8*; exercises, 74; management, 43, 73; posture and, 43; singing

and, 38–43; staggered, 221;
support, 279; techniques, 72
Briarcrest, 278
Brick City Singers, 308
Broadway, 32, 203, 219, 220
Brown, James, 112, *112*, 122
Brown Derbies, 25, 287
Browne, Jackson, 93
Bublé, Michael, 315
budgeting, 205, 260, 295
build-your-own websites, 305
Bulgarian women's choir, 7, 11
burnout, 298
"Bushes and Briars," 17
business, 206; collegiate a cappella
and, 181; manager, 58, 216; music,
317–21; professional a cappella,
190–93; rehearsals and, 136–37;
skills of engineer, 172–74
Buzzfeed, 255

CAL. *See* Contemporary A Cappella
League
call and response, 6
Callen, Michael, 26
"Call Me Maybe," 114
Camp A Cappella, 31, 32–33, 266,
269, 316, 339
camps, 31
*CAN. See Collegiate A Cappella
News*
CARAs. *See* Contemporary A
Cappella Recording Awards
carcinogenic substances, 76
cardioid microphones, 149, *150–51*
cardiovascular training, 70
careers, xii, 33, 190–93, 202, 203–4;
administration, 307–16; advice
for, 210, 223, 226, 230, 237, 242,
247–48, 251, 259–60, 269–70, 282,

291–92, 299, 302, 306, 313–14;
arranging, 270–77; coaching,
277–82; editing, 242–48; event
production and promotion, 292–
99; holiday caroling, 223–26; live
sound engineering, 226–31; local
and regional performances, 204–
11; mastering, 251–61; mixing,
248–51; as musician, 317–21;
national and international touring,
211–20; new group production,
284–92; part-recording, 239–42;
producing parts for recordings,
239–42; producing recordings,
261–64; recording session singing,
234–39; scholastic group directing,
266–70; student, 286; theme park
performances, 220–23; video
production, 300–303; web design,
303–6. *See also* professional a
cappella
Carnegie Hall, 28
Carroll, Wes, 287
CASA. *See* Contemporary A Cappella
Society
A CASA Christmas, 27
Cash, O. C., 6
"Castle on the Hill," 114
CDs, 260–61
cell phones, 75
Centerville High School, 285, 288,
290, 292
Cetera, Peter, 15
Chaikin, Andrew, 24
chain gangs, 5, 88
Chamberlin Rhythmate, 103
Chanticleer, 218
Charles, Ray, 12
charts, 213, 223
Chase, Chevy, 95

Chase, Walter, 211–20
"Cheap Thrills," 115
chest voice, 47, 157
Chicago (band), 95
children's choirs, 187–88
choirs, 10, 187–88, 202
choral music, 5, 285
chords, 128, 227
choreography, 59, 105, 280, 281
Christian music, 7–8
cigarettes, 76
Cirencester Parish Church Choir, 304
Clark, Jon, 252
classical music, 4–5, 10
CMS. *See* content management system
coaching, 277–82
the Coats, 25–26
cognition, 71
collaboration, 211, 316
college radio, 19, 28–29
collegiate a cappella, 7, 16, 179; administration and leadership of, 181; albums and recordings of, 185; alumni, 185–86; auditions for, 182–83; business and, 181; community of, 180; competitions, 185; concerts, 183–84; directors of, 181; ensembles, 184–85; festivals, 185; group size for, 180, 195; music videos of, 185; performances for high schools, 184; rehearsals of, 181, 183; road trips, 184; scholastic group directing, 266–70; social media and, 185; solos in, 183; vocal percussion in, 180
Collegiate A Cappella News (CAN), 23, 29

color, 96, 108
Colorado All-State Jazz Choir, 227
Comedian Harmonists, 7
commercial work, 208
Committed, 30
communication, xviii, 82, 310
community, 10, 23, 191–93, 240, 267, 316, 328; of collegiate a cappella, 180; growth potential of, 332; recreational a cappella and, 197
competitions, 30, 270, 280, 316; collegiate a cappella, 185; high school a cappella, 187; professional a cappella, 192; vocal percussion, 101
compression, *142*, 155–57, *156*, 259
computer engineering, 300–301
concerts, 83; collegiate a cappella, 183–84; production and promotion, 292–99; vocal percussion in, 122
condenser microphones, *146*, 146–47
conductor, 58
consonants, microphones and, 162
Contemporary A Cappella League (CAL), 32, 197, 293
Contemporary A Cappella Publishing, 27
Contemporary A Cappella Recording Awards (CARAs), 24, 33
Contemporary A Cappella Society (CASA), 27, 33, 196, 202–3, 250, 275, 281, 293
Contemporary A Cappella Society of America, 24
Contemporary A Cappella Songbooks, 27
contemporary Christian music, 7–8
content, 219, 291, 302

content management system (CMS), 304
cool-downs, 74
Cooleyhighharmony, 271
Copeland, Stewart, 113
Cornaglia, Amanda, 292–99
counseling, 76, 82
cover songs, 216, 219
CR-7030 "Beat Box," 103
Cranin, Andy, 13, 20
creative process, 313–14
creative skills, of engineers, 171–72
creativity, 313–14
cricoid cartilage, 45, 46
cricothyroid (CT) dominant voice, 47
cricothyroid muscles, 46
Croatia, 7
Crosby, Stills & Nash, 20
crossover, 161
CSS, 303
CT. See cricothyroid dominant voice
Cuba, 28
culture, singing and, 325–26
"The Cup Song," 31
Cusack, John, 19
customer service, 173, 174–75, 295, 305
cymbals, in vocal percussion, 108

Dakaboom, 289
dance, 280
Dancing with the Stars, 32
Dapper Dans, 220
D'Arrezzo, Guido, 4
Da Vinci's Notebook, 308
Davis, Miles, 93, 327
dB. See decibels
DeBar, Phil, 29
debt, 309
decibels (dB), 142

deep lamina propria, 45
delay, 158, 159, 170
delegation, 136, 216
DeLong, Andrew, 315
Delusions of Grandeur, 212
demand, xii
diaphragm, 39, 39, 40
diaphragm microphones, 145
diction, microphones and, 162
Diddley, Bo, 114, 114
didgeridoo, as vocal instrument, 99
diet, 68–69. See also nutrition
Dietz, Robert, 278
digestive system, 42, 68
digital processing, 228
digital reverb units, 158
digital voice processors, 160, 161
Digitech, 161
the Diners, 25
diphthongs, 52, 129
directors, xiii, 13, 270–71, 285; of a cappella groups, 58; of collegiate a cappella, 181; of recreational a cappella, 196; rehearsals and, 140; scholastic group, 266–70
Disney, 29, 203, 220, 222, 223
distortion/noise, 255
distribution, 257, 311
diversification, of skills, 237
Divisi, 272
DJs, 28–29
DJ Snake, 115
Do It A Cappella, 271
"Don't Worry, Be Happy," 15
"Don't You Worry Child," 121
doo-wop, 7, 12, 15, 226
downloads, 204
dreams, 239
driverless cars, 328
Dropbox, 275

drugs, 67–68, 76
drum machines, 14, 103
drums/drumming, 4; of Ghana,
    102; Latin American, 114; styles,
    111; tone of, 164, *165*, 166;
    West African, 19. *See also* vocal
    percussion
drum set, *106*, *109*, *123*
Dunlop, Ewart, 12
Duran Duran, 20
duration, 127, 130
dynamic microphones, *145*, 145–46,
    162
dynamics, 52, 79, 89, 157, 259,
    279; balance, 131; in new music,
    134; vocal blend, 131; of vocal
    percussion, 116

ear, 56
Earth, Wind and Fire, 111, *111*
ear training, 213, 214, 296
East Coast A Cappella Summit,
    27–28
eating disorders, 62
economy, 208, 326
editing, 242–48
the Edlos, 13
education, 309; for administration,
    309; for arranging, 272–73; for
    coaching, 279–80; for editing,
    244–45; for event production
    and promotion, 293–95; for live
    sound engineering, 227–28; for
    local and regional performance,
    205–6; for mastering, 253–54; for
    national and international touring,
    212–14; for producing recordings,
    261–62; for professional holiday
    caroling, 224; for scholastic group
    directing, 267; for session singing,

235; for singing and producing
    parts recordings, 240; for theme
    park performance, 221; for video
    production, 300–301; for web
    design, 304
educational shows, 26
ego, 213
Eight Beat Measure, 308–9
Einstein, Albert, 96
electric guitar, 97–98
Eleventh Hour at Kettering
    Fairmont High School, 268, 269,
    285
ELI CompuRhythm, 103
e-mail, 136–37, 229, 317
emotional demands, 62
emotional focus, 56
emotions, 79–80, 134–35, 238, 244
empowerment, 280
Encore, 308
engineering, 206, 295, 299; goal of,
    228; live, 226–31; sonic elements
    of, 163–67, *165*, *167*; style and,
    229; success in, 231. *See also*
    mixing
engineers, 207; audience and,
    174, 176; business skills of,
    172–74; creative skills of, 171–72;
    customer service of, 174–75;
    definition of great, 176; income
    of, 230; invisibility of, 174; job of,
    167–68; keys to success for, 174–
    76; learning of, 227–28; people
    skills of, 172–74; personal hygiene
    of, 172, 175; schedule of, 229–30;
    shortage of, 231; technical skills
    of, 170–71; trust and listening of,
    175–76
Entertainer's Secret, 64
entrepreneurship, 273

enunciation, 245
environmental irritants, 76
Epcot, 220
epiglottis, 45, *46*
epithelial layer, 44, *45*
EPKs, 295
equalization (EQ), 163; graphic, 155, *155*, 171; from ground up, 169; mastering and, 252; mixing, 164; parametric, 153–55, *154*, 168, 171; room, 167–69; shelf, 152–53, *153*; utilizing, 155; of vocal percussion, 169, 227, 228
equipment, knowledge of, 227–28
esophagus, 68
Eteson, Jo, 315
ETHOS, 268, 269
etymology and definition, 4, 10, 33n2, 88
Euphonism, 292
event production and promotion, 292–99
events, 340–42. *See also* festivals
evolution, singing and, 326
Exact Change, 226
Excel, 296
exercise, 69–70, 80
experimentation, 92, 274
exposure, 210
extended techniques, 90, 163
external factors, 208
external hard drives, 275
external intercostal muscles, 40, *41*
external obliques, 41, *42*
extroverts, 82
"Eye of the Tiger," 287

Facebook, 303, 310, 315, 316
FaceTime, 52
facial expressions, 71

failure, 273
Fairfield Four, 6
falsetto voice, 47, 92, 97, 157
family, 211
Farb, Adam, 25, 28
the Fat Boys, 21
fear, 70–71
feedback, microphones, 146
feel, 221
Fernandi, Marty, 13
festivals, 128, 203, 210, 253, 275, 280, 281–82, 293, 311; collegiate a cappella, 185; high school a cappella, 187; major, 340–42; by region, 332–38
field hollers, 5, 6, 88, 202
fight or flight response, 71
Filharmonic, 289
fills, 116, *116*
film, 223, 234, 235, 237, 253, 303, 318–19
Finale, 275
finances, 58, 208, 212, 229, 295, 309
first formants, *50*
Fisk Jubilee Singers, 6
Fitzgerald, Ella, 95
Five o'Clock Shadow, 307
Flash, 303
FloVoice, 293
flu season, 215
flute, 95
the Flying Pickets, 14, 16
focus, 295
folk music, 5
food, 62–63
forced resonance, 49
Forkish, Lisa, 119, 291
formants, 49–52, *50*
Forte, 292
"For the Longest Time," 284

Foster Street, 20
4:2:Five, 308
four on the floor groove, *114*, 115, *119*, 120
four-part harmony, 20
four-part hymns, 5
freelance work, 226
free resonance, 49
free tracks, 314–15
frequency, 47, 127; cheat sheet, 164, *165*, 166; correlations with artist's language, 164, *165*, 166; fundamental, 143, *144*; grooves and, *107*; response in microphones, 147, *148*, 149; in room EQ, 168; sound and, 142; of voice, 166–67
Fresh, Doug E., 103
friends, 211
Frizzell, J. D., 277–82, 291
fundamental tone, 47, 56

Gabriel, Peter, 19–20
garage bands, 295
gargling, 66–67
gastroesophageal reflux (GERD), 68
Gayaud, Mael, 123
gear, 58
gear rental, 312
GERD. *See* gastroesophageal reflux
Ghana, 102
Girard, Nick, 314
Gladwell, Malcolm, 318
Glee, 222, 261
glottis, 44, *47*, 49
goals, 139, 210
Gobsmacked, 32
Gold Circle, 30
Gooding, Don, 26, 28
"Good Time," 118

Google Drive, 310
Gordon, Dexter, 94
Gordy, Berry, 262
gospel choirs, 202
gospel music, 6
Graceland, 14
Grammy Awards, xi, 16, 24, 223, 301
graphic equalization, 155, *155*, 171
Gray, Kevin, 305
Green, Alex, 242–48
Greene, Richard, 33n1
Gregorian chant, 4, 55
Gregory (Pope), 4
Groove 66, 29
grooves: Bo Diddley beat, *114*; Bossa nova, 114–15, *114–15*; definition of, 111; fills, 116, *116*; four on the floor, 113, *113*, *118*, 120; frequency and, *106*; Reggaeton, 114, *114*; sound production techniques for, *107*; subdivisions of, 113, *113*, 122; swing, 115, *115*; 3:2 son clave rhythm, 114; 3+3+2, 114; vocal percussions, *106*, 111–15, *111–15*
GroupMe, 289
group melodies, 89
group tone, 281
growth, 235
guitars, 14, 49, 56

habits, 53, 63
hand movements, 91
Hanks, Tom, 26
"Hard to Say I'm Sorry," 15
Hare, Bill, 248–51, 252
harmonica, 98–99
harmonic progressions, 55
harmonics, 47–48; formants and, 52; pitch and, *144*; sound and, 143,

144; sub, 169; subharmonics, 169; vowels and, 129
harmonic series, 47, *48*, 56
harmony, 4, 7, 12, 20, 56, 214, 328–29
Harmony Festival, 288
Harmony Incorporated, 6
Harmony Sweepstakes, 13, 25–26, 27, 192, 196
Harvard, 181, 183
head-mounted microphones, 157
headphones, 259
health, of a cappella group, 81–83
Heap, Imogen, 262
heartburn, 68
The Heart of Vocal Harmony, 81, 135
Heaton, Ron, 303
Heimbigner, Adam, 117
Hendrix, Jimi, 97
Hetzel, Lori, 285
"Higher and Higher," 287
Highlands Voices, 308
high school a cappella, 186–87, 265, 285, 288–89, 308
high schools, collegiate a cappella performances for, 184
Hi-Lo's, 11
hip-hop, 102–3
historian, 59
history, 88, 202; bias in, 10; early 90s, 21–29; early and mid 80s, 10–15; late 80s, 15–21; music, 273, 309; today, early 2017, 32–33; tradition and history of singing, xvii–xviii; 2000s and 2010s, 29–32; of vocal percussion, 102–4
hoarseness, 76
Hogwarts Frog Choir, 220
holiday caroling, 223–26, 236
holidays, 215, 223

Holiday Spirits, xii
Hollens, Peter, 271, 272
Home Free, 32, 280, 321
honesty, 299
honey, 66–67
hormonal imbalance, 72
horn section, 95
hospitality, 295, 299
the House Jacks, 102, 203, 218, 226, 250, 274, 300; alumni, 308; arranging of, 310; beginning of, 24; debut album, 29; following of, 26
HTML, 303
Huerta, Tony, 226–31
Huey Lewis and the News, 15
Hulu, 219
humanity, 329
Humidflyer, 65
humidification, 64–65
Hyannis Sound, 315
hydration, 63–66, 74, 80
hygiene, 172, 175
hyoid bone, *46*, 53
hyper-cardioid pattern, *151*

ICCA. *See* International Championship of Collegiate A Cappella
ICHSA. *See* International Championship of High School A Cappella
identity, audience and, 210
"If I Ever Fall in Love," 15
"I Got You (I Feel Good)," 112, *112*
imperfection, 140, 326–28
income, 318; from administration, 312–13; from arranging, 276; from coaching, 282; from editing, 247; from event production and

promotion, 299; from live sound engineering, 230; from local and regional performance, 207, 208–9; from mastering, 259; from national and international touring, 218–19; online ad, 211; from producing recordings, 263; from professional holiday caroling, 226; from scholastic group directing, 269; from session singing, 236; from singing and producing parts recordings, 242; from theme park performance, 22–224; from video production, 302; from web design, 306
Indiana University (IU), xi, 29
industrial revolution, 326
in-ear monitors, 161, 218
inflammation, 66–67
inhalers, 64–65
inharmonic overtones, 48
"Insomniac," 287
instant gratification, 73
instructional DVDs, 270
instruments, 4, 37, 88–89, 90–100, 143. *See also* voice
intensive professional development opportunities, 339
intermediate lamina propria, *45*
internal intercostal muscles, 40, *41*
International Barbershop Quartet champions, 241
International Championship of Collegiate A Cappella (ICCA), 30–31, 185, 241, 287, 310
International Championship of High School A Cappella (ICHSA), 28, 187, 284, 289, 308
international touring, 211–20
Internet, 211, 222, 223, 251, 296, 306

interpersonal skills, 205
"In the Still of the Night," 284
In Transit, 32, 203
introverts, 82
investors, 192
"In Your Eyes," 19–20
IQ, music and, 329
Irish/Scottish/Gaelic mouth music, 5
Isicathamiya, 6
ISO, 321*n*1
Italiano, Ronnie, 15
iteration, 254
"It's Alright," 15
IU. *See* Indiana University
Ivy League schools, 180
"I Want Candy," 114

Jalkeus, Anders, 27
jaw, 49, 52
jazz, 7, 271
Jensen, Courtney, 120
Jepson, Carly Rae, 113, 118
JET, 116
Joel, Billy, 14–15, 310
Johnson, Jefferson, 285
Jones, Quincy, 93
joy, 332

Kallman, Craig, xii, 212
Katz, Bob, 259
Kazaa, 308
kazoo, as vocal instrument, 96
Kendrick, Anna, 31
Kent State University, 288, 290
Kettering AcaFest, 285
Kettering City Schools, 269
Kettering National High School A Cappella Festival, 339
keyboards, 216
Khatri, Beejul, 120

Kibble, Mark, 176, 227, 230
kick drum, *107*, 166
kids, 286–87
Kind of Blue, 327
King's Singers, 11, 218, 278
Kirk, Denise, 28
"(Na Na Hey Hey) Kiss Him Goodbye," 15
Klapa, 6–7
Klapa S Mora, 7
the Knudsen Brothers, 13–14
Koutzoukis, Alexander, 244
Kravitz, Lenny, 99
Krokodiloes, 181

Ladysmith Black Mambazo, 6, 14, 21, 271
lamina propria, 44
Lamott, Bruce, 11
language, 91, 164, *165*, 166, 236
laryngeal pathology, 72, 76
laryngitis, 45
laryngopharyngeal reflux (LPR), 68
larynx, 42, 43–49, *46*, 52–53, 62–65, 74–75
Latin American music, 114
latissimi dorsi muscles, 43
laughing, 75
laundry, 217
Lawrence, Van, 63
leadership, 57–59, 280
lead vocals, 55
learning: of engineers, 227–28; in rehearsals, 137; styles, 245; tracks, 138, 242
LED screens, 220
Lee, Spike, 21, 271
Lennon, John, 98
"Let Me Love You (feat. Justin Bieber)," 115

licensing, 208
lifestyle, 69, 214–15
light, music and, 96
Lincoln Center, 28
Linda, Solomon, 6
The Lion King, 6
"The Lion Sleeps Tonight," 6, 27
lip buzz, in vocal percussion, *108*
lips, 49, 52–54
lip syncing, 327
listening, 223, 245, 254, 255–56
live looping, 331
live performance, tuning and, 128
live sound systems, 160–61
local performances, 204–11
loft voice, 47
"Longest Time," 14–15
Longo, David, 307–16
Los Angeles A Cappella Festival, 33
loudness, 127, 130–31, 141, 254, 256, 259, 261
loud talking, 75
"Love Me Do," 98
"Love the One You're With," 287
LPR. *See* laryngopharyngeal reflux
lungs, 38–43
Lutte, Carol, 213
lyrics, 243, 300

Ma, Yo-Yo, xvii
Mach 5, 24
Made in U.S.A., 271
Madrigals, 4
Magic Kingdom, 220
magnetic tape, 254–55
Mainely A Cappella, 26
Make the Music 2000, 103
malware, 306
"Mama's Black Baby Boy," 6
mandolin, as vocal instrument, 99

Manhattan Transfer, 11
manners, 173, 223, 274, 317
"March Madness," 28
marijuana, 76
marketing, 229, 294–95, 299, 303
markets, 251
Maroon 5, 115
marriage counseling, 82
Marshall, Kathleen, 32
Martin, George, 262
Martin, John, 121
mastering, 251–61
Mastering Audio: The Art and the Science (Katz), 259
mathematics, 309
Mayflower Chorus, 13
MBTI. *See* Myers-Briggs Type Indicator
Mbube, 6
McCartney, Paul, 98, 273
McDonald, Brody, 266–70, 285, 291
McFerrin, Bobby, xvii, 14, 15, 103, 109, 218
media creation, 257
medication, 63, 67–70
Medulla, 103
melody, 55, 89
Melodyne, 159, 240, 242, 252
memorization, 135–36, 137, 224
Mendicants, 250, 251
mental health, 70–72, 77–78
merchandise, 208, 212
metronome, 123
"Mickey's Monkey," 114
microphones, 79, 275, 287;
    amplitude response in, 148–52,
    150, 152; bidirectional pattern,
    150; cardioid, 149, *150–51*;
    cardioid pattern, *150*; condenser,
    146, 146–47; consonants and,
162; diaphragm, 145; diction
    and, 162; dynamic, *145*, 145–46,
    162; experimentation with, 162;
    feedback, 146; frequency response
    in, 147, *148*, 149; function of,
    145; head-mounted, 157; hyper-
    cardioid pattern, *151*; loudness
    and, 141; omnidirectional pattern,
    151; phantom power and, 146;
    polar pattern diagrams of, 148–49,
    149–51, 152; projection and, 141;
    proximity effect, 152; reactions of,
    248; sensitivity of, 152; shotgun
    pattern, *151*; SPL, 149; super-
    cardioid pattern, *151*; technique,
    141, 156, 161–62, 268; for vocal
    percussion, 169; vowels and, 162
Microsoft Office suite, 304
middle school a cappella, 187–88
Milists, Ed, 213
Mills Brothers, 7, 91
Milwaukappella festival, 288
the Mint Juleps, 21
the Miracles, 114
mistakes, 140, 238, 260, 299, 327
mixers, 160–61
mixing, 89, 164, 166–72, 248–51. *See also* editing
mixing consoles, 228
modal voice, 47
Modern A Cappella, 22
monitors, 161, 259
Monteith, Cory, 76
Montezuma's Revenge, 16
Moog, Robert, 98
motivation, 320
Motown, 327
mouth, 49, 52–54
mouth music, 5
Mouth Sounds (Newman, F.), 100

movies, 28
MPA. *See* musical performance anxiety
mucus production, 64, 65
multitracking, 239–42
Murphy, Lisa, 13
muscles: abdominal, 40–41, *41–42*; control of, 53–54; cricothyroid, 46; diaphragm, *39*, 39–40; external intercostal, 40, *41*; external obliques, 41, *42*; internal intercostal, 40, *41*; jaw, 53; larynx, 53; latissimi dorsi, 43; memory, 73; muscular antagonism, 43; neurology and, 53–54; palate, 53; portions or bellies of, 40; rectus abdominis, 40, *41*, *42*; secondary respiratory functions of, 43; throat, 53; thyroarytenoid, 45–46; tongue, 53; transverse abdominis, 41, *41*; vocal folds and, *45*
muscular antagonism, 43
music: in Africa, xvii–xviii; business, 317–21; color and, 96; communication and, xvii–xviii; industry, 192; IQ and, 329; librarian, 59; light and, 96; theory, 213, 235, 267, 309
musical performance anxiety (MPA), 70–71
musical theater, 63
musical traditions, 100
musical vibrators, 37, 42–49, *46*
music history, 273, 309
MusiciansFriend, 161
musicianship, x, 279
The Music Man, 12
music videos, 185, 211, 261
muted trumpet, as vocal instrument, 93–94

muzak, 249
Myers-Briggs Type Indicator (MBTI), 82
Le Mystere Des Voix Bulgares, 7

NACA (National Association of Campus Activities), 26, 289
NAfME (National Association for Music Education), 267
Naked Noise, 28
Napster, 287, 308
nasal cavity, 49, 65–66
National A Cappella Convention, 339
National Association for Music Education. *See* NAfME
National Association of Campus Activities. *See* NACA
National Association of Teachers of Singing (NATS), 54
National Center for Voice and Speech (NCVS), 54
National Championship of Collegiate A Cappella (NCCA), 28
National High School Championship, 339
national touring, 211–20
National Youth Leadership Forum on Technology, 309
Native American music, 4
NATS. *See* National Association of Teachers of Singing
natural harmonic series, *48*
Naturally 7, 14
NBC, x, 30, 285
NCCA. *See* National Championship of Collegiate A Cappella
NCVS. *See* National Center for Voice and Speech
Neal, John, 26, 27
Negro spirituals. *See* spirituals

Netflix, 219
Neti pot, 66
networking, 236–37, 273, 294
neurology: MPA and, 71; muscles and, 53–54
new group production, 284–92
Newman, Amanda, 28
Newman, Fred, 100
new music, 134–35
Newmyer, Bobby, 30
Next Level Workshops, 339
nicotine, 76
"Nightingale Sang in Berkeley Square," 11
Nomura, Christòpheren, 13
the Nor'easters, 121
North, Alex, 319
North Shore A Cappella, 13–14, 26
Northwest High School, 285
nosebleeds, 67
Nota, 30
notation, 4, 89, *110–11*, 109–12
notes, for rehearsals, 139–40
Noteworthy, 120
nutrition, 62–63, 80
the Nylons, 12, 15

octavizer, 170
off-book performance, 224
Ohio State University, 31
O-Kai Singers, 6
O'Keeffe, Georgia, 97
omnidirectional pattern, *151*
OneRepublic, 114
One Size Fits All, 12
OneVoice, 279
online mastering, 261
online resources, 196
"Only You," 14
On the Rocks, 272

open mics, 210
oral cavity, 49
oral hydration, 64–65
oral hygiene, 66, 72
orchestration, 273
organizations, 196
Overboard, 244, 314
overhydration, 64
oversaturation, 248
oversinging, 225
overtones, 47, 48, 127, 128, 129, 143, 167
overuse, 61
Owl City, 118

palate, 49, 52–53
Pandora, 219
parametric equalization, 153–55, *154*, 168, 171
Parker, Charlie, 94
parts-recording, 239–42
passion, 221, 321
passive income, 312–13
Paster, Thomas, 307
patience, 295
Patreon, 191, 289
PBS, 21, 22
peers, social media and, 238–39
Pentatonix, 214, 226, 253, 261, 280; awards of, 30, 184, 187; holiday music of, 223; popularity and success of, ix, 32, 291; *Sing-Off* and, 291; videos of, 191
people skills, 172–74, 236
percussion, 19, 20, 57, *110*
perfectionism, rehearsal and, 210
performance, 13, 71; emotions and, 244; inviting friends and family to, 211; local and regional, 204–11; mistakes, 238; off-book, 224;

planning of, 210; rehearsals and, 137; selecting, 210; social media and, 211; theme parks, 220–23
personal hygiene, 172, 175, 227
the Persuasions, 21
phantom power, microphones and, 146
pharynx, 49, 64, 66–67
Philadelphia, 26
phonation, 40, 44, 62, 279
phonation threshold pressure (PTP), 64
phonotrauma, 61, 72, 75, 78–79
photo shoots, 313
phrasing, 279
physical exercise, 69–70
piano, 49
Pink Floyd, 20
pitch, 279; correction, 240, 246; formants and, *50*, 50–51; harmonics and, *144*; of vocal blend, 127–29
Pitch Battles, 32
Pitch Perfect (film), 31, 253, 261, 280, 296
Pitch Perfect (Rapkin), 18, 30–31
Pitch Perfect 2 (film), 31
Pitch Perfect 3 (film), 32
pitch pipe, 218
Pitch Slapped, 31
pitch sliding, 89
placement, 279, 281
Plaid Productions, 244
plantations, 5
plug-ins, 255, 305
polar pattern diagrams, 148–49, *149–51*, 152
the Police, 113, *113*
polishing, in rehearsals, 137
Pollstar Magazine, 218

polypoid degeneration, 76
Ponce, Dan, xiii
pop culture, 280
popular music, 57
portfolio, 314–15
posture, 43, 74
potential, 328
Powell, John, 235
power, 79
powered monitors, 161
power source, 37–43
practice, 77–78, 121–23
preparation, 71–72
president, 58–59
Pressfield, Steve, 313
Primarily A Cappella, 26
processing, mastering, 257
producing parts, for recording, 239–42
producing recordings, 261–64
production, 248, 253, 284–92
productivity, in rehearsals, 139
professional a cappella, 190–93. *See also* careers
professional development, 339
professionalism, 223, 227
projection, microphones and, 141
project management, 294, 296
promoters, 170
promotion, 205, 292–99
Pro Tools, 229, 252, 309
proximity effect, 152
psychology, 70, 286, 293
PTP. *See* phonation threshold pressure
publicity, 206
Puerling, Gene, 11
pulmonary system, 38–43, *39*, *41–42*
punctuality, in rehearsals, 134
purpleplanet, 305

quality control, 257

radiation, 68
radio, 19, 28–29, 191, 252, 300
Rahzel, 103
Rapkin, Mickey, 30–31
rarefaction, *142*
Raugh, Anne, 27
R&B. *See* rhythm and blues
real estate, 313
The Real Group, 27, 226
real-time analyzer (RTA) app, 164, 166
recorded music, 326, 327
recording, 191, 205; of collegiate a cappella, 185; editing, 242–48; emotions and, 238; equipment, 216; isolated tracks in, 237, 239–42; magnetic tape, 254–55; mastering, 251–61; mistakes in, 238; multitracking, 239–42; portable, 234; practice, 122; process, 237, 262; producing, 261–64; producing parts for, 239–42; rehearsals, 135, 138, 140; session singing, 234–39; studio, cost of, 235–36; technology, 234, 237, 242, 325; vowels and, 238. *See also* engineering
recreational a cappella, 195–97, 197n1
rectus abdominis muscles, 40, *41*, *42*
reflex reaction, 53
reflux, 68–69, 76
Regency, 26
Reggaeton groove, 115, *115*
regional performances, 204–11
rehearsals: arranging and, 139–40; assessment of, 136, 140; attention spans in, 135; big picture thinking in, 140; business and, 136–37; of collegiate a cappella, 181, 183; directing and, 140; goals of, 139; learning in, 137; learning tracks in, 138; memorization in, 135–36, 137; mistakes in, 140; new music in, 134–35; notes for, 139–40; order of, 133–40; perfectionism and, 210; performance and, 137; polishing in, 137; prioritization in, 136; process of, 133, 137, 281; productivity in, 139; punctuality in, 134; recording, 135, 138, 140; of recreational a cappella, 197; repertoire and, 140; sectional, 135, 138; of songs in progress, 135–36; songs well known in, 136; task delegation in, 136; time, 134; time management in, 137–38; warm-ups, 133–34
relationships, 294, 296
Renaissance polyphony, 4–5
repertoire, 140, 196, 216, 225
reputation, 295, 317
resonance, 46, 48–52, 62, 73, 143
resonator, 37, *144*
respiration, 62
respiratory system. *See* pulmonary system
rest, 80
reverb, 157–58, *158*, 170, 248
Rhino Records, 22
rhinosinusitis, 66
rhythm, 57, 104, 246
rhythm and blues (R&B), 5
the Riveters, 120
Robinson, Buffy, 103
Robinson, Smokey, 114
Rochester Institute of Technology, 309

Rockapella, 21–22, 103, 104, 123, 218, 252, 266, 300, 308
rock music, 48
Roland VS-880, 252
room: acoustics, 167–70, 256; correction software, 259; modification/treatment, 256
rough sounds, 48
"Roxanne," 113, *113*
royalties, 312
RTA. *See* real-time analyzer app
Ruiz, Rene, 220–26
Rundgren, Todd, 14, 319–20
Rust, Darren, 252
Ryan, Jon, 204–11

sacred harp music, 5
safety, 81
Saleman, Buddy, 29
saliva production, 68
saltwater gargle, 66
sampling, 14, 102
San Francisco University High School (SFUHS), 13
Sängerfest/Liederfest/Liederkranz, 5
Saturday Night Extravaganza, 27
saxophone, as vocal instrument, 94–95
Say Anything, 19
SBN. *See* Standard Beatbox Notation
scales, 47, 50
schedules, typical, 83; for administration, 311; for arranging, 276; for coaching, 281–82; for editing, 247; for event production and promotion, 298; for live sound engineering, 229–30; for local and regional performance, 208–9; for mastering, 258; for national and international touring, 215, 217–18;

for new group production, 290; for professional holiday caroling, 224, 225; for scholastic group directing, 268; for singing and producing parts recordings, 241; for theme park performance, 222; for video production, 302; for web design, 306
scholastic a cappella. *See* collegiate a cappella
scholastic group directing, 266–70
schools, 179–80
science, 54
Score, 17
scores, 275, 319
screaming, 75
the Script, 120
sea shanties, 5, 88
second formants, 50, 51
second tenor, 55
sectional rehearsal, 135, 138
self-employment, 202, 317
senses, 238
sensitivity, of microphones, 152
"September," 112, *112*
sequencing, in mastering, 257
set lists, 216
setup, mastering, 257
17th Avenue Allstars, 25, 227
SFUHS. *See* San Francisco University High School
Shai, 15, 274
Shanté, Roxanne, 103
shape note singing, 5
"Shape of You," 115
sharecroppers, 5
Sharon, Deke, 250, 269, 310
Sheeran, Ed, 114, 115
sheet music, 216, 220, 237
SheetMusicPlus, 26, 196

shelf equalization, 152–53, *153*

Sheridan, Fletcher, 234–39

"She Will Be Loved," 278

shotgun pattern, *151*

Sia, 115

sight reading, 214, 224, 328

signal chain, 144–60. *See also* microphones

signal flow, 171

Simon, Paul, 14

Sing, 253

singers, wellness tips from, 78–80

Singers Unlimited, 11

singing: breathing and, 38–43; culture and, 325–26; evolution and, 326; in other languages, 236; recording session, 234–39; speech and, 75–76; style, 53, 78, 88, 248; throat, 48; tradition and history of, xvii–xviii

Sing It On, 31

single line notation, *111*

singles, 261

Sing-Off, x, 202, 222, 226, 253, 272, 280; high school teams in, 187; Home Free and, 321; origin of, 30; Pentatonix and, 291; products of, 219; vocal percussion on, 103

Sing That Thing, 31

sinuses, 65–66, 72

slides, 89, 93, 128

smoking, 76

snacks, 196

snare drum, *107, 108, 166*

SNC. *See* Straight No Chaser

sneezing, 75

social media, 57, 59, 185, 187, 193, 211, 214, 229–30, 238–39, 289, 295, 303, 306

social networking, 214

society, 331

Society for the Preservation and Encouragement of Barber Shop Quartet Singing in America. *See* Barbershop Harmony Society

sociology, 293

software, 213, 216, 255, 256, 296

"So in Love," 15

SoJam Festival, 172, 253

Solomon, Rex, 23

solos, 92, 183

song breakdowns, 117–20, *119*

"A Song for Mama," 284

songs, 4, 135–36

songwriting, 243

Sonos, 172

sopranos, 65

sore throats, 66–67

sound: amplitude and, 142, *142*; Auto-Tune, 159, 160; building blocks of, 163–67; compression, *142*; definition of, 163–64; delay, 158, *159*; frequency and, 142; fundamentals of, 142–44; harmonics and, 143, *144*; perception of, 49; physics of, 127; rarefaction, *142*; resonance and, 143; reverb, 157–58, *158*; traveling of, 49, 142. *See also* compression; equalization

soundboard, 146, 268

"Sound Check," 310

sound checks, 167–70, 173, 217, 231

sound engineers. *See* engineers

sound pressure level (SPL), 149

sound source, 37, 49

sound systems, 128, 160–61, 295, 296

Sousa, John Philip, 325, 327

South Africa, 6, 14

"Southern Cross," 20

South Pacific, 12
SoVoSo, 14
Spalding, Ben, 284–92
speakers, 160–61
spectrum analysis, 51–52, 143
speech, 49, 72, 75–76
Sperandio, Dave, 251–61, 280
Spike and Co.: Do It A Cappella, 21, 103
spine, 41
Spiralmouth, 274
spirituals, 5, 6
SPL. *See* sound pressure level
Splinter, Mark, 110
sponsorship, 295
sports medicine, 62
Spotify, 121, 261
staff notation, 4
stage configurations, 59–60
stage fright. *See* musical performance anxiety
staggered breathing, 221
Standard Beatbox Notation (SBN), 110–11, *111*
Stanford, 249, 250–51
"Star Spangled Banner," 22, 55, 310
"Stayin' Alive," 112
Steakhouse, David ("Stack"), 307–8
Steam, 15
steam inhalers, 64–65
steel drums, as vocal instrument, 99
Stein, Layne, 300–303
Stein, Randy, 29
stomach, 68
Straight No Chaser (SNC), xi–xiii, 29, 32, 212, 214, 216–17, 218–19, 287
the Strangeloves, 114
streaming concerts, 316
streaming services, 261, 299
street performance, 210

strength training, 70
stretching, 74
student careers, 286
studio construction, 313
style, 293, 296, 321; engineering and, 229; singing, 53, 78, 88; vocal technique and, 88; vowels and, 129
subdivisions, 114, *114*, 123
subharmonics, 169
subwoofers, 168, 169
success, 238–39
"Summertime," 18
"Sunday Morning," 116
super-cardioid pattern, *151*
superficial lamina propria, *45*
super formants, 50
"Superstition," 112
surgery, 68
Surround Sound, 308
Swedish House Mafia, 121
Sweet Adelines International, 6
Sweet Honey in the Rock, 11
Sweetwater, 161
swing groove, 116, *116*
Swingle Singers, 11, 218, 315
syllables, harmony and, 214
synthesizers, 14, 102; as vocal instrument, 98

TA. *See* thyroarytenoid dominant voice
Taiwan, 6
Take 6, 16, 21, 55, 176, 218, 226, 227, 228, 230, 271, 308
Takei, George, 13
talent, 202, 296, 326
the Talking Heads, 11
tax law, 295
TC-Helicon, 160, 161

tea, 66–67
teachers, 273
technical aspects: of administration, 310; of arranging, 275; of coaching, 281; of editing, 245–46; of event production and promotion, 296; of live sound engineering, 228; of local and regional performance, 206–7; of mastering, 255–56; of national and international touring, 214–15; of new group production, 287–88; of producing recordings, 262–63; of professional holiday caroling, 225; of scholastic group directing, 267–68; of singing and producing parts recordings, 240–41; of theme park performance, 221–22; of video production, 301; of web design, 305
technical skills, of engineers, 170–71
technology, 52, 295, 300–301, 331
teeth, 52
telecommuting, 328
television, 28, 30, 104, 191, 219, 223, 234, 237, 253, 301, 303, 316, 318
tempo, 104, 245
tessitura, 96
Thacher, Jeff, 122, 252
theater, 202, 303, 318, 332
theme park performances, 220–23
Theremin, 96, 97
Theremin, Leon, 96
thorax, 39, 40, 41
3:2 son clave rhythm, 114
throat, 44, 48, 49, 52, 64, 66–67
throat singing, 48
thyroarytenoid (TA) dominant voice, 47
thyroarytenoid muscle, 45–46

thyroid cartilage, 45, *46*
timbre (vocal color), 46, 50, 100, 129–30, *144*
time correction, 246
time management, 137–38, 273, 294
TimTracks, 240
tobacco, 76
The Today Show, xii
the Tokens, 6
Tommy Boy, 28
tom-toms, in vocal percussions, *108*
tones, 47, 56, 279, 281
tongue, 49, 52–54
The Tonight Show, 11
tools, 4
touring, 295–96; buses, 216–17; effect on voice, 215; lifestyle, 214–15; local and regional, 204–11; manager, 59; national and international, 211–20; schedule, 208–9, 214–15, 217
Tower of Power, 95
Toxic Audio, 14, 223
toxins, 76
T-Pain, 159
trachea, *46*
traditional forms, 10
Traditional Jewish music, 4
training, 73, 77–78, 213, 221
transcription, 213, 235, 273
transportation, 58
transverse abdominis muscles, 41, *41*
trauma, 72
travel, 58
the Trenchcoats. *See* the Coats
tresillo rhythm, 114
trombone, 93
True Image, 103
trumpet, 93–94
Tufts Amalgamates, 243–44

Tufts Beelzebubs, 13, 16–17, 20, 23, 24, 26, 31, 33n3, 251, 328
tuning, 47, 55, 56, 57, 128, 131, 224
Tunstall, KT, 114
tutorial videos, 91
TVF. *See* Voice Foundation
tweeters, 161
"12 Days of Christmas," xi–xiii, 29, 212
twelve-part harmony, 20
"29 Ways," 287
Twitter, 303
Tyte, Gavin, 110

U2, 20
Unbroken, 251
undertones, 128
Unique Quartet, 6
United Group Harmony Association, 15
Universal, 220
University of North Colorado, 227
upper harmony, 56
upper-respiratory infections, 66
upright bass, 96
urine, 63

Valliere, Eric, 17–18
varicose veins, 67
Varsity Vocals, 307, 316
Velker, Matt, 278
verification, in mastering, 257
vibrato, 52, 89, 93, 95, 97–99, 221, 238
videographer, 59
video production, 300–303
videos, 185, 191, 261, 316
video technology, 204
video wall, 220
Vineyard Sound, 205

violins, 49, 95–97
virtual audience, 299
visualization techniques, 71
vitamins, 63, 67
vocal accidents, 79
vocal blend, 127–31, 221, 224, 236, 281
vocal coaching, xiii
vocal color. *See* timbre
Vocal Company, 307, 310, 339
vocal conservation, 77–78
vocal cords. *See* vocal folds
vocal damage, 48, 92, 94
vocal extremes, 155, 157
vocal fatigue, 78
vocal fitness program, 74
vocal flange, 98
vocal flexibility, 78
vocal folds, 44–47, *45, 47*, 62, 64, 80, 143
vocal health, 74
vocal hygiene, 72
Vocalight, 284, 288, 289, 290–91, 292
vocal injury, 61–62, 72–76, 78–79
vocal instruments, 90–99. *See also* vocal percussion
vocalization, in vocal percussion, 108–9
vocal jazz, 7, 227, 278
vocal longevity, 73
vocal naps, 76
Vocalosity, 32, 226
vocal percussion, 19, 20–21, 57, 91, 225, 268; advanced techniques of, 105; arranging, 117; artists, 102–4; auditory illusion and, 109; bass in, *110*; best practices for, *117*; bongo sound in, *108*; breath control in, 107, *108*; in collegiate a cappella, 180; color in, 108–9; competitions,

101; in concert, 122; cymbals in, *108*; defining, 102–3; drum set components for, *106*; drum set sounds of, *123*; dynamics of, 106; EQ of, 227; equalization of, 169; grooves, *106*, 110–15, *110–15*; hierarchy of priorities for, *105*; hi-hat sound, *107*, *108*; history of, 102–4; judging and standards of, 106; kick drum sound, *107*; lip buzz in, *108*; microphones for, 169; notation of, *109–11*, 109–11; placement in, 108; practice of, 121–23; rhythm of, 104–6; rim shot sound in, *108*; role of, 104–6, *105*; SBN, 110–11, *111*, 112; sight reading and, 214; on *Sing-Off*, 104; snare drum sound, *107*, *108*; song breakdowns, 117–21, *118*; techniques, *107–8*; in television, 104; tempo of, 104–5; tom-toms in, *108*; urban origin of, 102–3; vocalization in, 108–9; vocal scratch in, *108*; water breaks, 122. *See also* groove

Vocal Point, 118

vocal problems, 78

vocal range, 92, 100

Vocal Sampling, 28

vocal scratch, in vocal percussion, *108*

vocal strain, 215

vocal style, 48

vocal technique, xii, 14, 26, 59, 267, 331; correct, 87; extended, 90; mimicry of instruments, 90–99; style and, 88; universal, 89–90; unusual, 91

vocal tract, 46, 48–52, 143

vocal training, 221

vocal wellness, 72–76

vocal workouts, 77–78

Voctave, 222

voice, 4, 37, 331; air pressure, 42; disorders, 72; frequency of, 166–67; larynx, 42, 43–48, *46*; limits of, 14; medication and, 67–68; power source of, 38–43; pulmonary system, 38–43, *39*, *41–42*; reflux and, 68–69; touring effect on, 215; versatility of, 56, 235; volume of, 75

The Voice, 14, 222, 238

Voice Foundation (TVF), 54

VoiceJam, 31, 187

VoiceLive, 160

voice-over work, 237

VoicePlay, 300, 302

voice production, 73

voice recognition, 306

Voices Music Publishing, 27

Voices of Liberty, 29, 220–21

volume, 142

volunteers, 298–99

vowels: exaggerated, 98; formants and, *50*, 51; harmonics and, 129; matching, 129–30, 221, 281; microphones and, 162; nationality and, 129; recording and, 238; shape of, 129; style and, 129; vocal tract and, 52; warm-ups, 129

Walken, Christopher, 262

wardrobe/costumer, 59

warm-ups, 74, 129, 133–34, 217

The War of Art (Pressfield), 313

Waurick, Tim, 239–42

wave length, 127

web design, 303–6

Weisman, Sam, 30

wellness: exercise, 69–70; hydration, 63–66; medication, 67–68; mental, 70–72; nutrition, 62–63; reflux and voice, 68–69; tea, honey, and gargling, 66–67; tips from singers, 78–80; vocal, 72–76

Well Tempered Clavier (Bach), 128

Weymouth, Tina, 96

"What You Wanted," 114

"When I'm Sixty Four," 12

Where in the World Is Carmen Sandiego?, 21–22, 104

Whiffenpoofs, 7, 26, 180, 181

the Who, 20

Williams, Vaughan, 17

Winehouse, Amy, 76

Winton Woods High School, 285

women, 7, 11; in audience, 19; larynx of, 75

Wonder, Stevie, 112

woofers, 161

WordPress, 304

work ethic, 244, 301, 317

workshops, 281, 339

work songs, 6

"Work Your Beatbox," 123

Wright State University, 31, 266, 268

Wurlitzer Sideman, 103

Yale, 181

Yaz, 14

yelling, 75

YouTube, 28–29, 254, 303; accessibility of, 222; exposure through, 214, 219; interactivity through, 310; loudness normalization and, 261; music videos and, 211; research with, 121; tutorials on, 253

"Zanzibar," 310

Zappa, Frank, 11

Zulu, 6

ABOUT THE AUTHOR

"The father of contemporary a cappella."—*Entertainment Weekly*

"A one-man a cappella revolution."—*Boston Globe*

"Deke Sharon makes a cappella cool again."—NPR

Born in San Francisco, **Deke Sharon** has been performing professionally since the age of eight and as a child toured North America and shared the stage in operas with the likes of Pavarotti. Heralded as "the "father of contemporary a cappella," he is responsible for the current sound of modern a cappella, having pioneered the modern vocal-instrumental sound in college, subsequently spreading it around the world. He produced *The Sing-Off* on NBC and worldwide (Netherlands, China, and South Africa). In addition, Deke served as arranger, on-site music director, and vocal producer for Universal's *Pitch Perfect 1, 2,* and *3,* starring Anna Kendrick and Rebel Wilson.

Deke founded the Contemporary A Cappella Society (CASA) while in college and is responsible for many seminal a cappella programs, including CARAs (Contemporary A Cappella Recording Awards), ICCA (International Championship of Collegiate A Cappella), *BOCA* (*Best of College A Cappella*) compilation, the first contemporary a cappella conferences (the A Cappella Summit), the Contemporary A Cappella League, the professional theatrical touring ensemble Vocalosity, and Camp A Cappella. He is also contemporary cappella's most prolific arranger, having arranged over two thousand songs, with many of them in print worldwide with Hal Leonard/Contemporary A Cappella Publishing. He has written five books: *A Cappella Arranging* (2012), *A Cappella* (2015), *The Heart of Vocal Harmony* (2016), *A Cappella Warmups for Pop and Jazz Choirs* (2017), and *So You Want to Sing A Cappella* (2017). He is also vocal arranger and producer for the Broadway's first a cappella musical: *In Transit* (2016).

As the founder, director, and arranger for the House Jacks for twenty-four years, the original "rock band without instruments," Deke shared the stage with countless music legends, including Ray Charles, James Brown, Crosby, Stills & Nash, Run DMC, the Temptations, LL Cool J, and the Four Tops; performed for luminaries including President Bill Clinton; and performed the "Monday Night Football Theme" with Hank Williams Jr. in 2011. He has produced dozens of award-winning a cappella albums (including *Straight No Chaser*, *Committed*, *Nota*, *Street Corner Symphony* and the *Tufts Beelzebubs*, *Pitch Perfect*, and *In Transit*); created a cappella groups for Disneyland and Disney World; and frequently tours the world teaching a variety of topics to students and professional singers. His voice can be heard in commercials and video games, including *Just Dance Kids 2*. He is one of only twenty honorary members of the Barbershop Harmony Society since 1938, as well as an honorary member of BYU Vocal Point, and received CASA's Lifetime Achievement Award in 2016 and the Tufts Barnum Award for Excellence in Entertainment in 2017. You can see him on television on Lifetime's *Pitch Slapped* (2016) and his newest show for the BBC, *Pitch Battle*.